SOCIAL SCIENCES DIVISION
CHICAGO PUBLIC LIBRARY
400 SOUTH STATE STREET
CHICAGO, IL 60605

THE SACRED LITERATURE SERIES

Edited by Kerry Brown and Sima Sharma

THAT WHICH IS

The Sacred Literature Series of the International Sacred Literature Trust in association with HarperCollins

Other titles in the series

AUSTRALIAN ABORIGINAL TRADITIONS
Warlpiri Dreamings and Histories

◆

BUDDHISM
The Words of My Perfect Teacher

◆

INDIAN TRADITIONS
In the Dark of the Heart: Hymns of Meera

◆

JUDAISM
Gates of Light

◆

TAOISM
Lao-tzu's Treatise on the Response of the Tao

Further titles are in preparation

TATTVĀRTHA SŪTRA

That Which Is

Umāsvāti/Umāsvāmī
with the combined commentaries of
Umāsvāti/Umāsvāmī, Pūjyapāda and Siddhasenagaṇi

Translated with an introduction by Nathmal Tatia

With a foreword by L. M. Singhvi and
an introduction to the Jaina faith by Padmanabh S. Jaini

THE INSTITUTE OF JAINOLOGY

HarperCollins*Publishers*

For more information about the ISLT,
please write to the ISLT at:
23 Darley Avenue, Manchester M20 8ZD
United Kingdom

HarperCollins Publishers
1160 Battery Street, San Francisco 94111
United States of America
77–85 Fulham Palace Road, London W6 8JB
Great Britain
25 Ryde Road, Pymble, NSW 2073
Australia

Designed by Caro Inglis
Copyedited by Anne Hegerty
Indexed by Annette Musker
Photoset in Linotron Sabon by Northern
Phototypsetting Company Limited,
Bolton, U. K.

Library of Congress Cataloging-in-Publication Data
Umāsvāti, ca. 135– ca. 219.
[Tattvārthādhigamasūtra. English]
That which is = Tattvārtha Sūtra / Umāsvāti/Umāsvāmi ; with the combined commentaries of Umāsvāti/Umāsvāmi, Pūjyapāda and Siddhasenagaṇi ; translated with an introduction by Nathmal Tatia ; with a foreword by L. M. Singhvi and an introduction to the Jaina faith by Padmanabh S. Janini.
p. cm. — (Sacred literature series)
Includes index.
ISBN 0-06-068985-4 (cloth)
I. Devanandī. II. Siddhasenagaṇi. III. Tatia, Nathmal. IV. Series.
BL1314.2.T382E5 1994
294.4'82—dc20 94-16468
CIP

94 95 96 97 98 RRD(H) 10 9 8 7 6 5 4 3 2 1

This edition is printed on acid-free paper that meets the American National Standards Institute Z39.48 Standard.

parasparopagraho jīvānām

Souls render service to one another
(*Tattvārtha Sūtra* 5.21)

INTERNATIONAL

SACRED

LITERATURE

TRUST

The International Sacred Literature Trust was established to promote understanding and open discussion between and within faiths and to give voice in today's world to the wisdom that speaks across time and traditions.

What resources do the sacred traditions of the world possess to respond to the great global threats of poverty, war, ecological disaster and spiritual despair?

Our starting-point is the sacred texts with their vision of a higher truth and their deep insights into the nature of humanity and the universe we inhabit. The translation programme is planned so that each faith community articulates its own teachings with the intention of enhancing its self-understanding as well as the understanding of those of other faiths and those of no faith.

The Trust particularly encourages faiths to make available texts which are needed in translation for their own communities and also texts which are little known outside the tradition but which have the power to inspire, console, enlighten and transform. These sources from the past become resources for the present and future when we make inspired use of them to guide us in shaping the contemporary world.

Our religious traditions are diverse but, as with the natural environment, we are discovering the global interdependence of human hearts and minds. The Trust invites all to participate in the modern experience of interfaith encounter and exchange which marks a new phase in the human quest to discover our full humanity.

Contents

List of Figures

Foreword

I consider it a great privilege to write the foreword to the International Sacred Literature Trust's publication of *Tattvārtha Sūtra*, an ancient magnum opus which is deeply revered and sanctified in the Jaina tradition.

The roots of our human civilization are to be found in the sacred texts of different faith traditions. An enlightened awareness of those sacred texts will enable the world of today and of tomorrow to communicate across geographical, political, ethnic and religious frontiers. The far-sighted objectives and inspiration of the International Sacred Literature Trust represent an idea whose time has now come in the long march of history. It is an idea which has been integral to the vision of seers, sages and savants in India through the ages and is central to the world-view of contemporary India. Quintessentially, that idea is rooted in the universally shared sense of the sacred which enables us, as William Blake put it in his "Auguries of Innocence": "to see a world in a grain of sand, and heaven in a wild flower/ Hold infinity in the palm of your hand, and eternity in an hour."

That idea unfolds itself in the compassionate, rational and symbiotic Jaina ethics of tolerance, interdependence and reciprocity, and in the basic pluralist postulates which preserve unity in diversity without undermining the identity of the whole or of the part. The Jaina tradition is an important tributary of this mainstream idea which found sanctuary in the heritage of India and which appears as the motif in the mosaic of Indian culture. *Tattvārtha Sūtra* vivifies that motif through its analysis of phenomena and categories of truth and in its teachings of non-violence, non-absolutism and restraint in acquisition.

Tattvārtha Sūtra is by common consent the book of books in the Jaina tradition. Acclaimed as an authentic and systematic compendium of the essence of Jainism as taught and settled by Lord Mahāvīra, and faithfully rooted in the Jaina heritage, it commands the allegiance of the different denominations within the Jaina fold and its authority is definitive and undisputed. An inspired and encyclopaedic achievement of extraordinary scholarship, it is a compact cosmic essay on cognition and conduct, a synthesis of science and ethics in the framework of philosophy. It investigates and catalogues the two basic verities of the world, soul and substance; it also draws a route map to the goal of liberation. Many of its perceptions and some of its precepts were reflected in some measure in other contemporary schools of philosophy including among others the

Vaiśesika, Nyāya, Yoga and Buddhist systems. In his work, Umāsvāti encompasses an enriching awareness of other schools of thought without disputatious pedantry or dogmatism.

It is remarkable that both the Śvetāmbara and the Digambara sects of Jainism claim and count the author as belonging to their respective branches. While Umāsvāti's date, tradition and biographical details are shrouded in obscurity and have formed the subject matter of considerable scholarly debate, there is a broad consensus on the conceptual content and the interpretation of the sutras. The leading commentaries used in the present translation, *Bhāṣya* and *Sarvārthasiddhi*, disclose certain textual variations between the two main sects, but those differences are, to my mind, minimal and marginal, of style rather than substance. These two great commentaries, together with the further two based on the *Sarvārthasiddhi*, *Rājavārtika* and *Ślokavārtika*, and the *Tattvārtha Sūtra* itself, constitute the most precious treasure of Jaina sacred literature. They illumine the constellation of Jaina concepts and precepts in the larger solar system of Indian philosophy, the soul of which is in the quest of the spirit and in the spirit of the quest.

I pay tribute to Dr Nathmal Tatia, an illustrious and eminent Jaina scholar and a living legend in the field of Jaina studies. His translation and annotation is at once simple, elegant, authentic, lucid and faithful. With the aid of Ms Kerry Brown and the scholarly advice of Professor Padmanabh Jaini, Muni Mahendrakumarji and Dr Kumarpal Desai, he has brought to this superb translation of *Tattvārtha Sūtra* a profound sense of wholesome synthesis as well as accuracy, consistency and clarity. The result is a unique contribution to the sacred literature of the world which has been happily facilitated by the indefatigable co-ordinating efforts of Mr Nemu Chandaria.

I welcome the publication of *Tattvārtha Sūtra* under the aegis of the International Sacred Literature Trust and Institute of Jainology and wish the entire interfaith enterprise of the ISLT godspeed and success. Perhaps no enterprise deserves it more or can confer greater benefit upon humanity in its quest for peace, tranquillity and equanimity.

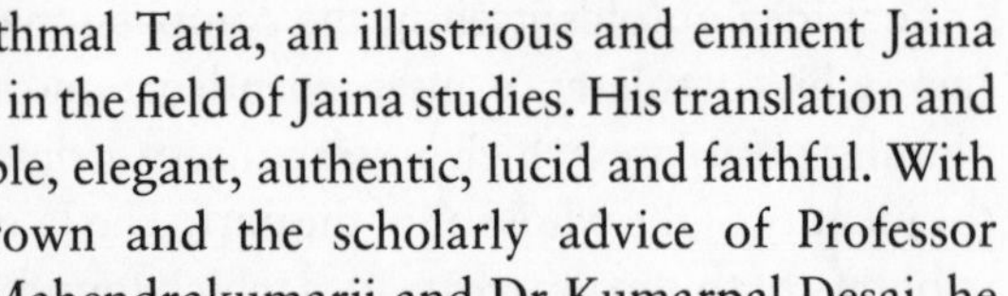

His Excellency Dr L. M. Singhvi
High Commissioner for India in the United Kingdom

Institute of Jainology's Acknowledgments

We thank the many people who have contributed to the work on this historic translation by Dr Nathmal Tatia. In particular, we acknowledge:

The Editorial Board
Professor Padmanabh S. Jaini, Munirajshri Mahendra Kumarji
Dr Kumarpal Desai, Kerry Brown

The Spiritual Leaders
Acharyashri Tulsiji, Shrutasthavira Munirajshri Jambuvijayji,
Pandit Munirajshri Mohjitvijayji, Pujyashri Atmanandji

The Benefactors
Dr Sulekh Chand and Shrimati Ravi Jain
Shrimati Saroj and Shri Babubhai Kapadia
Shri Nemchand B. Khajanchi, Khanjanchi Mohalla, Bikaner
The Khimasia family
M.A.S. Foundation
Shri Babulal Ratanshi Mehta and family
Shri Bhupatray Chatrabhuj Mehta
Dr Manibhai and Shrimati Savita Mehta
Shrimati Taraben Bhogilal Mehta
Shri Virchand Mithalal Mehta and family
Shri Ramnikbhai Ravjibhai Patel and family
Sadharmik Trust
Shrimati Shantaben Sanghrajka
Dr Surendra and Shrimati Hira Sethia
S. L. Sethia Foundation
Shri Jethalal and Hansraj Devraj Shah families
Shri Vijay Shah
In loving memory of Shrimati Amratben Amratlal Chandaria
In loving memory of Vimal Natwarlal Mithalal Mehta

The Faith Advisors
Pandit Dalsukh Malvania, Dr L. M. Singhvi, Shri Lakshmi Chandra Jain, Dr Ramanlal C. Shah, Professor Kamal Narayan Shivshankar Joshi, Dr Gopi Lal Amar, Dr Jitendra B. Shah, Shri Vinod Kapashi, Professor K. V. Mardia, Shri R. P. Chandaria, Shri Dipchand Gardi, Shri Ashok Jain, Shri Manharlal C. Shah, Shri G. C. Chandalia, Shri Shrenik Kasturbhai, Shri Ramesh Chandra Jain, Shrimati Sushila Mehta, Shri Somchand Devchand Shah, Shri Nagindas Doshi, Dr Sulekh Jain, Shri S. C. Bengani.

The Co-ordinator
Shri Nemu Chandaria

The Support Organisations
Oshwal Association of the UK
Navnat Vanik Association of the UK
Bhagwan Mahavira Memorial Samiti, India
Jain Vishva Bharati, Rajasthan, India
International Sacred Literature Trust

Translator's Acknowledgments

I would like to thank my scholarly advisors, Professor Padmanabh S. Jaini, Muni Mahendrakumarji and Dr Kumarpal Desai, for the keen interest they took in my work. Professor Jaini's valuable suggestions made the presentation more comprehensive. Muniji's advice made the exposition more precise. Dr Desai's counsel was concerned with the connotation of some ancient terms. I also thank Ms Kerry Brown whose editorial skill added conciseness and fluency to the translation.

My thanks are due to Mr Nemu Chandaria and Mr Bipin Mehta for co-ordinating the translation project; to Ms Asha W. Banthia for typing the draft translation so carefully; and to Ms Anne Hegerty for equal care in copy-editing and proofing the material.

I must not forget on this occasion to mention the Jain Vishva Bharati, my *alma mater*, which I joined in 1977 as director of its research centre, Anekant Shodh Peeth, after retiring from the directorship of Nava Nalanda Mahavihara in Nalanda. The chief projects of the centre are an encyclopaedia of Jainism and the translation into English of the Jaina canonical literature. Here I have the proud privilege of sitting at the feet of His Holiness Acharyashri Tulsi, the ninth Pontiff of the Terāpantha order, and of his successor-designate, Yuvacharyashri Mahaprajna, who are the constant source of inspiration for my work on the research projects. I have no words to express the depth of their knowledge and my gratitude to them.

Finally, I must thank Shri S. C. Bengani, President of the Jain Vishva Bharati, for providing the amenities needed for peaceful academic activity.

Nathmal Tatia

Translator's Introduction

The central themes of the *Tattvārtha Sūtra* are non-violence, non-abolutism and non-possession. Non-violence strengthens the autonomy of life of every being. Non-absolutism strengthens the autonomy of thought of every individual. Non-possession strengthens the interdependence of all existence. If you feel that every soul is autonomous you will never trample on its right to live. If you feel every person is a thinking person you will not trample on his or her thoughts. If you feel that you own nothing and no-one, you will not trample on the planet. In the second century CE, when the Jaina philosopher-monk Umāsvāti wrote the *Tattvārtha Sūtra,* these principles were the only way to global peace. Today, this is even more the case. These are the only values that can save humanity from the deadly acts of war, economic exploitation and environmental destruction.

Tattvārthādhigama Sūtra, which is the full title of Umāsvāti's work, means *A Manual for Understanding All That Is.* It encapsulates the religious, ethical and philosophical contents of the Jaina scriptures and places them in the context of the schools of logic and philosophy that flourished in India in the second century. The work was written in the ancient classical language of Sanskrit and reflects the critical and comparative approach to religious thought that characterized the age of Umāsvāti, also known as Umāsvāmī. It is a text which is accepted as authoritative by all sects of the Jainas and on which the great Jaina thinkers wrote their commentaries, and their commentaries on commentaries.

Tattvārtha Sūtra is based on the premise that the goal of human life is liberation which is defined as perfect knowledge, perfect intuition and eternal bliss. Umāsvāti begins his treatise by describing the path to liberation as enlightened world-view, enlightened knowledge and enlightened conduct (*Tattvārtha Sūtra* 1.1). Enlightened world-view is the source of enlightened knowledge and enlightened conduct. At the time, this vision of a three-fold path challenged other schools of thought which focused on one or other of the three as the means to liberation. Today, this vision challenges the supremacy we give to knowledge as absolutely true and objective and the source of all wisdom.

According to the Jaina doctrine of *anekānta*, or non-absolutism, all knowledge, except omniscience, is only partial truth from a particular viewpoint. Each individual has his or her unique perception of the world which is a mixture of truth and ignorance. All perceptions are valid, but incomplete, views of reality. To deny their validity or to see one as the total, exclusive truth leads to dogmas.

Umāsvāti presents the gateways of investigation and the philosophical standpoints (1.5–1.8) as a means for broadening one's knowledge and understanding. The "gateways" are various aspects of a phenomenon, such as its definition, cause, location, duration, etc., which provide a means of understanding it better. The "standpoints" are different perspectives from which a phenomenon can be understood. For instance, in the first standpoint, that of the "common person's view", the distinction between the remote and immediate is overlooked, and one or the other is noted as if it were the whole, depending upon the intention of the observer. So, speaking from the common person's view, we might describe an area of tropical forest as "timber" in which case we are seeing the remote, the use of the trees for building materials. On the other hand, standing two inches from a deadly snake we might describe the area as a "death trap" in which case we are describing it in terms of the immediate. Umāsvāti presents the gateways and standpoints as a means of undertaking one's own exploration of truth. They are tools against dogmatism. (For full details of the standpoints, see 1.35.)

Following the logic of non-absolutism, Umāsvāti shows that the truth or distortion of our knowledge is not determined by the grasp of practical facts but by the ethical and spiritual values which provide our viewpoint. Limited knowledge, which is all we can hope for as worldly souls, will be distorted by ignorance unless we uncover within ourselves the insight and wisdom born of an enlightened world-view.

> A person without the enlightened world-view is like an insane person who follows arbitrary whims and cannot distinguish true from false. (1.33)

The question then is: "Do I have an enlightened world-view?"

The Seven Categories of Truth

The essential concepts which a person must understand as true before they acquire an enlightened world-view are classified by Umāsvāti as the seven categories of truth:

(1) the existence of souls
(2) the existence of non-sentient entities (matter, time, space, media of movement and of rest)
(3) the inflow of karmic particles to the soul
(4) the binding of karmic particles to the soul

(5) stopping the karmic inflow
(6) the falling away of the karmic particles
(7) the liberation from worldly bondage.

These seven categories, which form the framework of the *Tattvārtha Sūtra*, recognize two fundamentals of existence. The first is the beginningless and interdependent co-existence of physical and spiritual reality. The interaction between soul and matter is the nature of worldly life. Whatever a soul possesses, whether the capacity for speech, breath or thought, is a result of its interaction with matter. But, without the soul, the organs through which these activities operate become inanimate matter. The modern world is ignoring this quintessential truth; on the one hand, scientific materialism denies or ignores the existence of the soul in its exploration of reality, while on the other, religious fervour can turn too sharply toward the spiritual verities and disregard the physical ones. This leads to an oscillating world-view in which we become unable to conceive of spiritual and material reality at once, and as a whole.

The second critical principle underlying the categories of truth is the inexorable law of cause and effect (through karma) which drives the universe. Although few people would openly deny this law which the physical sciences, history and personal experience confirm, there is nevertheless a sneaking irrational belief, seen in the behavior of individuals and nations, that we can get away with bad behaviour and that, when hardship strikes, we are victims of undeserved bad luck.

Failure to grasp these two fundamental principles of life, that of spiritual and physical symbiosis and that of cause and effect, has a profound impact. We face personality problems because of a distorted self-identity either as a purely spiritual or purely physical being. We face social disorder because individuals and nations do not see themselves as ultimately responsible for their actions. We face economic decline because we ignore the fact that it is the harmony of souls with each other and the physical world which is the source of all wealth. We face environmental problems because we do not recognize our own interdependence with the physical world, nor take responsibility for the violence we inflict upon it. The Jaina philosophy, so articulately expressed by Umāsvāti, establishes harmony between the religious and the scientific, between the spiritual and the physical, and between personal *in*dependence and social, economic and ecological *inter*dependence.

In his detailed exploration of the first category of truth, the soul,

Umāsvāti explains its function in one of the most famous sutras of the *Tattvārtha Sūtra*:

> *parasparopagraho jīvānām*
> Souls render service to one another. (5.21)

This epitomizes the Jaina view that all things are both autonomous and interdependent and spells out our joint responsibility for the common environment we create and share. The blind adherence to the Darwinian belief that the function of souls is to compete against each other was not endorsed by the author of the *Tattvārtha Sūtra*.

The interaction between the first and second categories of truth, that is, between the soul and the material world, is through the workings of very subtle material particles of karma which Jainas believe fill the universe. These karmic workings are described in the third to sixth categories of truth. The soul has always had a "karmic body" that produces its physical bodies and the vicissitudes of its many lives. The effect of the karmic body is to vibrate the soul, resulting in the activities of body, speech and mind. These actions, motivated by passion, draw more karma to the body. In this way, the karmic body is constantly being revamped as old karma falls off like ripened fruit and new karma is attracted. Evil activity attracts harmful karma, good activity attracts beneficial karma. The big question is how to break this cycle of karmic renewal that binds and blinds the soul in worldly suffering.

Umāsvāti identifies the passions, indulgences and urges as both the causes and results of karma. These are the "doors" by which karma enters and binds the soul (6.6). The four passions – anger, pride, deceit and greed – are given particular importance (8.2). These four passions dominate our world today, resulting in individual and collective violence in thought, word and deed. They are the deadliest enemies of personal and world peace.

Having identified the cause of karmic bondage, Umāsvāti then deals with its antidote. *Ahiṃsā* or non-violence is the way to unbind karma and live harmoniously. The vow to abstain from violence is the starting point and central value, the pivot on which Jainism turns. It is the vow of vows, the vow taken as the foundation of all virtues, and of the other four vows to abstain from falsehood, stealing, carnality and possessiveness. The criterion of non-violence is self-restraint.

> A creature may die or not, but it is a definite act of violence if the person has acted under the sway of non-restraint.... (7.8)

This wisdom is now apparent in a world in which the lack of self-restraint of a minority of the human race is depriving the majority of humans and other beings of adequate food and shelter, clean air and clean water.

For Umāsvāti, non-violence is unlimited, tolerance unconditional and reverence for life supreme. There is no question of a "just war". "Insistence on life" is a superior moral value to "insistence on truth" because the nature of truth varies from thinker to thinker but life is an invariable constant that is dear to all. There are never grounds for war:

> . . . angry abuse from another should be countered by looking to oneself for the cause of the anger. If the cause can be found within oneself, the other should be forgiven for his anger. Even if the fault does not lie with oneself, the other should be forgiven because his anger is due to ignorance. The ignorant should always be forgiven. If someone accuses us covertly, he should be forgiven because he did not do so overtly. If he accuses us overtly, he should be forgiven because he did not resort to physical violence. If he did resort to beating, he should be forgiven because he did not kill us. If he did attempt to kill us, he should be forgiven for not distracting us from the religious path. We should always find reason to forgive a person who harms us and should remember that whatever misfortunes confront us, they are due to our past karma. (9.6)

Cosmology

The Jaina view of the soul's beginningless karmic interaction with the material world has given rise to a philosophical tradition with an abiding interest in natural sciences. Umāsvāti's description of the infernal, middle and celestial regions, which may be read as mythical, symbolical descriptions, follow the demands of karma. Thus, we see that the infernals are not punished by an outside force; they inflict pain on one another.

Despite what would now be seen as scientific inaccuracies and myths, there is a notable degree of correct observation and astonishing insight into the natural world. The careful cataloguing of species on the basis of sensory complexity, reproductive methods and the possession of a brain (2.11–2.25, 2.32–2.36) are in tune with the logic of modern biological taxonomy. The concept of a universe teeming with submicroscopic living bodies (5.16) and of infinitesimal units of matter that make up the basic building blocks of the cosmos (5.23–5.28; appendix 5) reveal an intuitive grasp of the physical world. At the other end of the scale, the Jaina concept of a universe with concentric rings of islands and oceans (3.7–3.11), so vast they are beyond imagining except in elaborate mathematical metaphor, has echoes of planetary, solar and galactic systems. The description of the calculation of the rajju, the unit of cosmic measurement (see appendix 3), reveals that the Jaina mathematicians were struggling with concepts that were counterparts of the "light year" of modern science. The sheer scale of the Jaina vision of time and space, a vision that includes the notion of infinity (see appendices 1–3) is a tribute to the sophistication and insight of these great thinkers and mathematicians. There is also imbedded in this vision the idea of time and space as co-existents (5.38), something later identified by Einstein.

The Paradox of Existence: Impermanence and Permanence

The Jaina vision, explained by Umāsvāti, of a world that is both spiritual and physical, infinitely vast and infinitely small, is further explained as a world that is both permanent and impermanent. Here again, the broad vision of the anekānta world-view maintains that, contrary to the Shakespearean world-view, it is possible for something "to be *and* not to be". A phenomenon, or a "real" as it is called, flows through "modes" which are infinite and ever-changing. Through its constantly changing modes, a real is beginning and ending at every moment and thereby persists. Hence, we have the famous sutra that defines existence: "Origination, cessation and persistence constitute existence" (5.29). This Jaina paradox supports both the "eternalist" view and the "constant flux" view of reality, with the proviso that they each have only half the picture. A thing is neither real nor unreal, neither being nor non-being, neither one nor many, neither eternal nor non-eternal exclusively, but is both without violating the law of logic reinforced by experience.

As with many aspects of Jaina thought, this paradox finds a home in modern science and its discoveries about the very depths of material existence. At an atomic level, we discover that every apparently solid and stable object is constantly beginning and ending. Our own body, which is apparently alive and kicking at every moment of the day, is subject to the constant death and birth of cells. Even deeper, at the sub-atomic level, we find that electrons and light energy have a dual aspect; they are at once waves of probability and definite particles, despite the logical impossibility of this. Perhaps their nature is best described by the seventh proposition in the sevenfold predication of anekānta, "Existence, non-existence and inexpressibility". In other words, "It is, it is not, and it is inexpressible" (5.31).

Translating the *Tattvārtha Sūtra*

The structure of the *Tattvārtha Sūtra* is ten chapters of short, concise sutras. Each sutra has a commentary which elaborates and elucidates it. However, there is some disagreement between the two main Jaina sects, the Śvetāmbaras and Digambaras (see pp. xxxiii–xxxiv), in both the recension (version) of the sutras and their commentaries. The present translation includes these sectarian variations. To achieve this, three main versions of the *Tattvārtha Sūtra* with commentaries have been used:

1. *Svopajña Bhāṣya* (SB), believed by the Śvetāmbara sect to be the sutras and commentary of Umāsvāti himself.
2. *Svopajña Bhāṣya Ṭīkā* (SBT), a commentary by Siddhasenagaṇi of the Śvetāmbara sect on the SB (see above). The sutras are the same as for the SB.
3. *Sarvārthasiddhi* (SS), a commentary by Pūjyapāda Devanandi. The version of the sutras given by Pūjyapāda is considered by the Digambara sect to be a faithful rendering of Umāsvāti's sutras (Digambaras do not believe that the commentary of Umāsvāti is extant).

As the reader will see, a single sutra reading is given – unless there is variation between the SB/SBT tradition and the SS tradition, in which case the two variant readings are given for the same sutra. As for the commentary, this is a faithful representation of all three commentaries with their differences properly noted. At times, other commentaries and works that relate to the *Tattvārtha Sūtra* are also drawn upon, for instance the *Tattvārthavārtika* of Akalanka, a commentary based on the *Sarvārthasiddhi* commentary.

The language of *Tattvārtha Sūtra* is terse Sanskrit with technical terms that belong exclusively to Jainism. The English rendering of these terms was a difficult task, mainly because I had to find easy and simple equivalents for them without compromising their originality and depth. It was necessary to find a terminology that was unconventional but precise, simple but expressive. The task was a unique experience for me which I enjoyed very much as I had to pass through a maze of nuances of words for their proper selection.

My purpose in giving a simplified unconventional English rendering has been to promote a pleasant intimacy between the reader and the unfamiliar, sometimes strange, concepts of Jainism, in the hope that readers may draw something of value for themselves from it. The *Tattvārtha Sūtra* offers practical and ethical tools for living a restrained, tolerant and non-violent life, based on a theory of wisdom that respects the individual's power of insight, a theory of knowledge that respects the viewpoint of every thinking mind, and a theory of conduct that respects varieties of moral experience. In other words, no saint is complete, no philosophy final, there are as many philosophies as there are souls. Philosophy changes, thoughts change; to believe in a final and complete philosophy is to believe in dogmatism. And so the reader is invited to partake of this great work, not as a final statement, but as an ongoing philosophy to which they are enjoined to bring their own thoughts and experiences.

Dr Nathmal Tatia
Research Director, Jain Vishva Bharati
Ladnun, India

The Jaina Faith and its History

The image of the Jaina as a person of peace and goodwill – a committed vegetarian who believes non-violence (*ahiṃsā*) towards all beings is the foundation of all spiritual practice – is strongly imprinted on the Indian psyche. Indeed it can be said that the Jaina community has often been a morally uplifting factor in the life of Indian society as a whole. Mahatma Gandhi, perhaps the greatest champion of non-violence in our age, said he had been deeply influenced, particularly in the development of his theory of non-violence as a political instrument, by the revered Jaina layman Raychandbhai Mehta with whom he exchanged letters. "Three people have influenced me deeply, Tolstoy, Ruskin and Raychandbhai: Tolstoy through one of his books... and Raychandbhai through intimate personal contact."[1]

Jainism does not fall under the broad umbrella of the Vedic (Hindu) traditions. It is a non-theistic religion with its own sacred texts and Jinas, or "Spiritual Victors". Mahāvīra, the most recent Jina, lived in the sixth century BCE in northern India during a period in which the non-Vedic śramaṇa religions proliferated. The śramaṇa religions rejected the authority of the Hindu scriptures (Vedas) and deities, denied the efficacy of sacrifice and, most importantly, displayed pronounced antagonism to the tradition of Brahmanical (priestly) supremacy. Jainism is one of the two extant śramaṇa religions and the only one to survive in India. The other survivor, Buddhism, disappeared from India by the fourteenth century. Today there are approximately seven million followers of Jainism, the vast majority of whom live in India.

The Jinas

Jaina (also pronounced Jain) means "a follower of a Jina". The Jinas are the Spiritual Victors – human teachers who have attained infinite knowledge and preached the doctrine that there is eternal liberation (*mokṣa*) from worldly suffering when the bonds of spiritual ignorance are broken. This doctrine is not exclusive to Jainism; it is at the root of virtually all Indian philosophies and indeed, until the ninth century, "Jina" was used as a generic term in India for enlightened spiritual teachers. The Jinas are also called *Tīrthaṅkaras*, "builders of the ford (which leads across *saṃsāra*, the

[1] M. K. Gandhi, XXXII.4.

river of suffering)". Jainas believe that twenty-four Tīrthaṅkaras appear in each ascending and descending half of the time cycle, have done so from beginningless time, and will continue to do so forever. Their teachings are neither received through divine revelation nor manifested through some inherent magical power (as the Vedas are said to be). It is the individual human soul itself which, aided by the earlier teachings, comes to know the truth. Worshipping or following the teachings of a particular Jina, therefore, has no special significance as nothing new is taught, and the path remains always the same. Even so, it is natural that those teachers who most immediately precede the present age would be remembered more readily. Thus we find that the first Jina, Ṛṣabha, and the last few Jinas – Nemi, Pārśva, and especially Mahāvīra, the final teacher of the current time cycle – are taken as objects of a certain veneration. These last three Jinas are often regarded as the historical teachers and have been so placed by modern scholars. Nemi seems to have flourished in Saurashtra and to have been a contemporary of Kṛṣṇa.[2] Pārśva has been verified as a spiritual teacher who flourished in Varanasi in c. 850 BCE. Buddhist texts refer to the large number of *nirgrantha* ascetics ("unattached ones", as the Jainas were then known) who followed the fourfold restraint identified with the teachings of Pārśva.[3]

Mahāvīra

Tradition has it that Vardhamāna, later hailed as Mahāvīra or Great Hero, was born in 599 BCE in the kingdom of Vaiśāli in the Magadha region (near modern Patna). His father was a warrior chieftain and his mother was the sister of the Vaiśāli ruler.

Although the scriptures assert time and again that the Jina is a human being, born of human parents, the Jaina laity is usually raised to regard him more as a superhuman with fantastic attributes whose career is marked by a fixed and rather stylized set of supernatural occurrences. Thus, the lifestory of Mahāvīra begins with a series of dreams by his mother which indicate that she will give birth to a universal monarch or a great saint. Mahāvīra's birth is said to have been attended by numerous marvels and his saintliness is evidenced in the stories of his childhood acts of non-violence and bravery.

[2] See Renou 1953:114. See Jacobi 1884: 276–9.
[3] See Jacobi 1880.

When the Jina-to-be was thirty years old, the gods appeared miraculously and urged him to renounce the householder's life so he might awaken to his destiny, shaped by his many previous lives of great virtue. Mahāvīra renounced the world and wandered alone for twelve years engaging with resolution in severe penances. The most important of these voluntary mortifications involved complete fasting, abstaining from both food and water sometimes for as long as a week at a time. The practice has made an indelible impression upon the Jaina psyche; even today many of the Jina's followers occasionally undertake long waterless fasts as a major expression of the holy life. This emphasis upon fasting, more than any other single factor, distinguishes the religious practice of the Jaina laypeople from that of the Hindu communities which surround them. Jaina monks and nuns undergo rigorous fasts as a regular aspect of monastic life.

Mahāvīra's attainment of full enlightenment occurred exactly twelve years, six months and fifteen days after he set out upon the ascetic's path. He had attained the state of infinite knowledge from which there can be no falling away and, in so doing, became the twenty-fourth and final Jina of the descending half of the present cycle. Mahāvīra spent the next thirty years preaching the doctrine of non-violence as the path to eternal liberation from worldly suffering. His initial circle of disciples, eleven converted brahmans, is said to have grown in his lifetime to 14,000 monks, 36,000 nuns, 159,000 laymen and 318,000 laywomen.[4]

In 527 BCE, at the age of seventy-two, Mahāvīra shed his mortal body and his soul passed into nirvāṇa, ascending to the permanent resting place of all liberated souls (*Siddhas*) at the very apex of the universe. Today, over 2500 years later, his life and teachings continue to provide instruction and inspiration for Jainas in their daily lives.

The Practice

Perhaps more than any other Indian religious tradition, Jainism is imbued with an emotional commitment to self-reliance. In the soul's tormented struggle to free itself from its beginningless, and possibly endless, worldly bondage, neither Fate (*niyati*) nor the gods are at hand to assist. Even the Jinas are only able to help through their teachings. Jainas further believe

[4] *Kalpa-sūtra* (Suttāgame edition): 133–5. It is estimated that there are approximately 2500 monks and over 5000 nuns at the present time in the entire Jaina community.

that the soul has always been impure through its entanglement with the material world, just as a seam of gold has "always" been embedded in the rock where it is found. Following the logic of this analogy, absolute purification may be achieved if the proper refining method is applied. As can be seen in the *Tattvārtha Sūtra*, no other Indian school has invested so much energy in describing the precise mechanism of karmic bondage and release from that bondage nor has any other tradition conceived of the reward and retribution of karma as part of the unequivocal physical law of the universe. Karma is itself actual *matter*, rather than the sort of quasi-physical or psychological elements envisioned by other schools.

Seeking to comprehend every aspect of bondage, the philosopher-monks such as Umāsvāti produced a highly sophisticated analysis of the various types of material karmas, noteworthy not only for its coherent systemization but also for the deep psychological insight which it reveals. They correctly perceived, moreover, that no religious institution can survive without the strong involvement of the laity. Hence, they have not only played down the "inferior" nature of the lay path, but have shown their high regard for this path by producing numerous tracts on the particulars of lay conduct.[5] The earliest surviving work which includes such particulars is the *Tattvārtha Sūtra*. However, the ascetic orientation of Jainism was certainly not lost; not only does the way of the ascetic retain premier status among Jainas, but even the lay discipline is far more strict than in most other religious communities.

The degree of a person's advancement on the spiritual path, indeed the very fact of his or her commitment to the Jaina ideal, is indicated by the religious practices which are undertaken – particularly those involving various self-imposed restraints. The layperson's "minor vows" (*aṇuvratas*) of refraining from evil actions are just a modified, relatively weak version of the *real* Jaina vows, the "great vows" (*mahāvratas*) of the ascetics; they may curb evil behaviour but they cannot bring a person to liberation. In practice, however, this point has not been stressed. Jaina teachers have been realistic enough to see that most new converts will be emotionally ready only for the layperson's path.

To understand the basic restraints of Jaina lay life as well as those applied at later stages of the spiritual path, we must appreciate the Jaina preoccupation with ahiṃsā, non-violence. To abstain from violence is the

[5] Williams 1963: xxvii–xxx lists over forty such treatises, from the second to the seventeenth century CE.

foundational vow of Jainism from which follow the other vows to abstain from falsehood, theft, carnality and possessiveness. Great importance has been attached to non-violence by every Indian school, but none has carried it to the extreme of the Jainas. For them it is not simply the first among virtues, but the virtue; all others are simply elaborations of this central one. It is formalized in the ancient vow:

> I will desist from the knowing or intentional destruction of all great lives [souls with two or more senses]. As long as I live, I will neither kill nor cause others to kill. I will strive to refrain from all such activities, whether of body, speech or mind.

When one takes this first vow, a commitment is being made to a lifelong code of conduct to which one must pay meticulous attention at every moment. Even though nowadays not many Jainas formally assume the vow of ahiṃsā under the guidance of an ascetic, certain non-violent practices are so basic that they functionally define membership in the Jaina community. A Jaina must never eat meat. Fermented beverages, honey and figs are also traditionally prohibited because of the Jaina belief in *nigodas*, microscopic single-sensed beings which inhabit almost every corner of the universe and are especially prevalent in sweet or fermented substances. However, serious as it is, harm done to nigodas is considered far less grave than that done to higher life forms. The refusal to eat meat constitutes the most basic expression of the Jaina commitment to non-violence. It may well be that Jainism was the first Indian tradition to preach so strongly against the taking of life; in any case, it certainly became the primary exponent of vegetarianism in India and contributed much to the eventual triumph of vegetarianism throughout the sub-continent.

As for occupations, Jainas should not choose one involving intentional destruction, such as that of a hunter or a fisherman. Even though a farmer may destroy insects during the course of his work, such harm is done unwittingly and so does not render this means of livelihood unacceptable. Six modes of livelihood – government, writing, farming, the arts, commerce and various crafts – have been designated as "respectable" by Jaina teachers. In practice, however, followers of the Jina have been strongly encouraged to enter those professions which have the least potential for violence; hence military service and agriculture have come to be considered somewhat less desirable occupations, while a career in business is seen as the most appropriate. Even within the context of commercial activity, certain varieties of trade have been specifically prohibited for one who has entered upon the path of restraint. These include dealing in charcoal, selling timber, selling or driving oxcarts, charging fees for transport by oxcart, excavation, ploughing and quarrying, dealing in animal by-products (for example ivory), trading in lac, manufacturing or selling alcohol, trading in slaves or livestock, dealing in poisons or weapons, operating mills or oilpresses, gelding and branding animals, burning fields to encourage subsequent agricultural production, draining water so that crops can be planted, and breeding and rearing destructive animals.

Out of the various supplementary practices that support the vows of non-violence – truth, non-theft, non-carnality, and non-possessiveness – there are two of particular importance. The first is *sāmāyika*, a practice of great antiquity, wherein the layperson's religious activities are integrated with the yogic methods of the ascetic path. The meaning of sāmāyika is understood as attaining equanimity. It is a fusion with the true self through increasing detachment from all external objects. The ritual practice of sāmāyika entails a temporary renunciation of all possessions before sitting in meditation for up to one Indian hour (forty-eight minutes). The tranquillity of the mind is at first increased by forgiving, and begging forgiveness of, the entire world of beings. This is followed with the prayer:

> Friendship towards all beings,
> Delight in the qualities of virtuous ones,
> Utmost compassion for afflicted beings,
> Equanimity towards those who are not well-disposed towards me.
> May my soul have such dispositions as these forever.

The mind is then guided to a deep level of meditation on the self by inwardly repeating one of the many recitations for renouncing the passions of mind and body and feeling equanimity towards all during the meditation, with an aspiration that this state will be maintained life after life until eternal liberation is achieved. The recitations also include reminders to the self that one's eternal soul is the maker and shaper of one's fate.

Jaina lawbooks repeatedly commend this ritual as the highest form of spiritual discipline. The individuals experience a small taste of the tranquillity and bliss available to them once they overcome the gross passions which prevent them taking the vows of the ascetic. This sublime experience will sustain the aspirant even on returning to the bustle of daily life, drawing him or her again and again to the inner refuge now discovered. Thus the very austerity which makes the ascetic path initially seem so difficult tends at last to become its primary attraction. Clearly, then, the purpose of this ritual goes beyond mere temporary attainment of equanimity; it aims, finally, at leading the layperson voluntarily and irrevocably into the vows and life of an ascetic.

The second important supplementary practice is that of the *sallekhanā*, holy death through fasting and meditation. Like all Indian religions, Jainism considers the last moments of a person's life to be of the utmost importance in determining the condition of his or her subsequent incarnation. The point of sallekhanā is to meet death with all of one's faculties functioning properly, in a state of complete awareness and ability to maintain the vows one has taken. If, for example, infirmity or senility were to prevent one from maintaining one's vows, the final hours would be passed in non-restraint, adversely affecting the next birth. The total fast of sallekhanā is only performed when death is imminent due to outside causes such as calamity, famine, infirm old age or terminal illness. Only then, and only by fasting is the death "pure" because the passions are being thinned out (aspirants are warned not to undertake it with ambitions for a better re-birth or other such rewards). Any other method of terminating one's life is considered impure because the passions are thereby increased. It is a death for which the aspirant emotionally prepares him or herself over the years and which the family and community support.

Jaina Rituals and Ceremonies

If followed in full, the rules of lay conduct are severe. Indeed, even the clerics of many religions do not live so strict a life as the Jaina lay rules demand. Not surprisingly therefore, for most of the Jaina community, the lay vows and the increasingly difficult spiritual stages (see appendix 4, pp. 279–85) tend to constitute an ideal path followed only by a select few. Certainly the ethical codes which underlie these disciplines strongly influence the outlook of the community at large, but it is the rare individual who actually *vows* to accept the restraints or perform the rigorous austerities. For most Jainas, practising their faith centres upon a diverse group of daily rituals and periodic ceremonies, many of which reflect the ideal lay path, but differ in that there is no compulsion attached.

Building, consecrating and regularly venerating images of the

Tīrthaṅkaras today constitute a primary religious activity of a great many laypeople. Such images are most often, but not always, located within a temple. However, Jaina image-worship must be understood as meditational; the icon is seen merely as an ideal, a state attainable by all embodied souls. There is no "deity" actually present. Since most ancient Jaina texts seem to make no reference to Jina images (or to temples, for that matter), we must assume that the practice of erecting these icons dates from a much later time. Indeed one Jaina sect, the Sthānakavāsis (see pp. xxxxi–xxxxii), condemns image-worship altogether on the basis that it is not confirmed in the scriptures.

The absence of the Jina in a Jaina temple, in anything but a symbolic sense, renders the presence of a priest or intermediary virtually unnecessary. Hence the Jaina community has for the most part never developed a special priestly caste. Laypeople are encouraged to carry out ritual services on their own, either individually or in a group. Even in the south of India where a class of so-called "Jaina-brahmans" of the Digambara sect (see pp. xxxiii–xxxiv) has developed, they never assumed sacred status or exclusive sway over religious functions. Any Jaina was always free to perform *pūjā* (worship) in any Jaina temple even if a Jaina-brahman was "in charge" there.

Another important ritual duty of a Jaina layperson is visiting and venerating the ascetic teachers. Although charity in general is encouraged, giving alms to ascetics is the most important form of charity. An unusually close relationship has always been maintained between ascetics and householders in the Jaina tradition; monks and nuns have acted as the spiritual teachers of the layfollowers and have in turn been revered often to the point of adoration as the only "true propagators" of the Jina's message. This honoured status has carried with it the expectation of a very high standard of conduct; every layperson is well-informed on the sorts of behaviour appropriate to an ascetic, and constant vigilance by the lay community has usually enforced strict adherence to this code. The veneration of the ascetics includes a confessional aspect in which the layperson confesses transgressions of the vows and may take on more restraints.

In addition to the regular confessions there is the great annual rite of *saṃvatsarī*, which is observed on a large scale by all Jainas. During an eight to ten day period, known as *Paryūṣaṇa-parva*, the laypeople undertake to abstain from various foods, in accordance with the Jaina emphasis on fasting. Towards the end of this period they go through confession. The admissions of sins and accompanying pleas for forgiveness are directed not only to an ascetic teacher but to all one's family and friends. Letters are written to those relatives and acquaintances not in attendance, repeating the same acknowledgments of wrongdoing and solicitations of pardon. Finally, the participant in a saṃvatsarī extends his or her own forgiveness to all beings and asks that they grant the same favour:

> I ask pardon of all living creatures. May all of them pardon me. May I have a friendly relationship with all beings and unfriendly with none.

Digambaras and Śvetāmbaras

Although recent years have seen unprecedented collaborations, such as the work to produce this volume, there are two distinct and virtually irreconcilable monastic traditions within Jainism which are thought to date back over 2300 years. These two traditions are the Digambara (Sky-clad) and the Śvetāmbara (White- or Cotton-clad), designations applied to their respective layfollowers as well. The split may have originated about 300 BCE at the time of the famous Ācārya Bhadrabāhu, the last patriarch of the united ascetic community. The Śvetāmbaras believe that Bhadrabāhu was away from Pāṭaliputra (modern Patna in Bihar State) in Nepal for a long period of time engaged in yogic activities. The Digambaras maintain that, in the face of a disastrous famine, he migrated with a large group of ascetic disciples to the area of present-day Karnataka State, where they stayed for some twelve years. While there is no means of verifying either account, one thing is certain: Bhadrabāhu was absent from Pāṭaliputra during the time when a major schism took place.

The Digambara accounts state that Bhadrabāhu passed away before any return was possible, but his followers made their way back to Pāṭaliputra, only to discover that a recension of the sacred texts had been prepared in their absence. Many points of this recension were unacceptable to the recently returned monks. They declared this latest version of the canon invalid. Thus began a new ecclesiastical lineage separating the two groups. Eventually the Digambaras wrote their own canonical texts and *purāṇas* (legends) giving accounts of the Jinas' lives, particularly that of Mahāvīra, which differed considerably from those found in the texts of the Śvetāmbaras.

In the points of controversy between these two main sects, three issues seem paramount:

1. *The nature of an omniscient being*: For Digambaras, any being who

has obtained omniscience engages in no worldly activities and performs no bodily functions (eating, for example), since these are considered antithetical to omniscience. According to the Śvetāmbaras, a person who has become omniscient continues to engage in bodily functions until he or she passes from this world forever.

2. *The role of nudity in the holy life.* Digambaras, as their name implies, stress the practice of nudity as an absolute prerequisite to the ascetic's path – the only mode of conduct through which one can become truly free of shame and sexuality and thus hope to attain eternal liberation. While they recognize the fact that the Śvetāmbara monks are celibate and have renounced the household life, they nevertheless contend that by retaining their clothing they fall short of the fifth ascetic vow of non-possession (*aparigraha*). Śvetāmbaras also strongly disapprove of attachment to clothing but do not admit that the wearing of clothing is an obstacle to liberation (*mokṣa*). Their canonical texts emphasize the optional nature of the practice of ascetic nudity, but Śvetāmbaras have traditionally maintained that this practice, while available during the time of Mahāvīra, became invalid soon after his death.

3. *The position of women.* Digambaras believe that a woman lacks the adamantine body necessary to attain liberation. Therefore, she must be re-born as a man before such an attainment is possible. Śvetāmbaras reject this view, maintaining that a woman can be born with such a body and thus is capable of the same spiritual accomplishments as a man. Indeed, they claim that the nineteenth Tīrthaṅkara, Malli, was a woman. Nevertheless, it should be emphasized that neither of the Jaina traditions allows its nuns to go "sky-clad".[6]

Other differences in practice between the two traditions include details of seeking alms.

Growth and Survival of Jaina Society through the Ages

Just how has Jainism, alone among the śramaṇa traditions which arose in India around the middle of the sixth century BCE, been able to survive and prosper in India up to the present day? Most of the anti-Brahmanical sects died out soon after the passing of their respective founders; even Buddhism, with its centres of learning in ruins and the Buddha himself being described by Brahmanical writers as simply an incarnation of the

[6] For the social and doctrinal implications of this controversy, see Jaini 1991.

god Viṣṇu, faded from the sub-continent by perhaps the fourteenth century.

A cardinal feature of the śramaṇa movements was their emphasis upon the superiority of the warrior-king (*kṣatriya*) caste over the brahmans, whether in a spiritual context or a secular one. Their spiritual leaders, including Mahāvīra and the Buddha, were invariably from this caste. Hence these movements tended to find common cause with local kings who were themselves constantly battling against the claims to supremacy of the brahman (priestly) caste. While custom demanded that a king always be of kṣatriya origin, he might all too easily find himself reduced to little more than a figurehead by his brahman ministers. Furthermore, by allowing members of any caste as well as women to enter the ascetic orders, the śramaṇa groups created an entirely separate society, parallel to the Vedic one. They were able to attract large numbers of ascetics and layfollowers and thus constituted a significant force – social, political and economic as well as spiritual – within the large cities where they were concentrated.

It is not surprising, therefore, to find that Indian kings commonly formed alliances, in the form of generous patronage or even outright conversion to the faith, with one or another of these groups. The granting or withholding of royal support often determined a sect's ability to survive in a given region, not only by increasing its popularity among the common people but also by access to the court, hence to the machinery of political power. The Jaina movement was by no means an exception to this pattern; indeed, its development even during Mahāvīra's lifetime was tied to the fortunes of various ruling houses. It is in the rather remarkable ability of the Jainas to have repeatedly won kingly favour that we find the first important key to their long and relatively prosperous existence.

In the early centuries, their main rival was the śramaṇa sect of Gautama Buddha, which rose in the same region at the same time. It was the conversion of Aśoka, perhaps India's greatest ancient king, to Buddhism which probably saw the final decline of Jainism in Magadha and the beginning of the slow migration of its followers. This was intensified around 150 BCE by a Brahmanical resurgence and hard times for all non-Vedic groups in and around Magadha. The migration was along the two great caravan routes. One of these led northwest towards Delhi and Mathura, then south and west through Saurashtra and into Gujarat. The other route followed the east coast down to Kalinga (modern Orissa) and finally reached as far south as Madras and Mysore where, according to the

Digambara tradition, Bhadrabāhu had arrived so many years earlier. Thus by the fifth or sixth century the ancient centres of Jaina power were almost totally bereft of Jaina elements, and the Jaina community itself had become irrevocably divided along geographical lines, Digambaras in the south (modern Maharashtra and Karnataka) and Śvetāmbaras in the west (Gujarat, Rajasthan and Punjab). These regional concentrations prevail for the most part even today, although a certain number of Jaina communities can be found in every part of India.

One of the most striking examples of Jaina involvement with ruling houses was with the Ganga Dynasty in what is now the southern state of Karnataka. This dynasty was apparently established by a Digambara monk called Siṃhanandi, who somehow contrived to set up Mādhava Konguṇivarma as the local ruler in 265 CE. Various legends surround the circumstances of this event, some suggesting that it involved the use of great occult powers by the monk. Whatever actually transpired, it does seem that Siṃhanandi commanded sufficient political influence to function as a kingmaker. The fact that Jaina inscriptions simply report and do not condemn the monk's activities – despite their obvious unsuitability for one who has taken the vows of an ascetic – points out the moral ambivalence created by the need for royal support on the one hand and the demands of the spiritual life on the other. The subsequent Ganga dynasty provided centuries of uninterrupted pro-Jaina rule in Karnataka, but in the fourteenth century the dynasty was absorbed into a Brahmanical empire and the Jainas were forced out of their seats of power. Even so, hundreds of years of royal patronage had left them with sufficient wealth and well-endowed temples to continue their prosperous existence, albeit on the fringes rather than at the heart of the prevailing society.

Śvetāmbaras began actively to pursue royal favour around the beginning of the Christian era, although it was not until the eighth century that a Jaina ruler came to power in Western India. This was made possible when the orphan of a displaced Śaivite royal lineage in Gujarat was found and raised by the Śvetāmbara monk Śīlaguṇasūri. Upon reaching adulthood, this orphan took the name Vanarāja and established his kingdom centred in Anahilanagara.[7] During his long reign (746–806), the Jainas moved into positions of great influence as ministers and financiers. Thus they were able to establish a power base which remained relatively effective for many

[7] Account based on Hemacandra's *Kumārapālacarita*, first reported by Colonel James Tod in 1839. See Tod 1839: 149–55.

years, despite the fact that Vanarāja's successors soon reverted to Śaivism.

In the mid-twelfth century, the Śvetāmbaras even brought about a brief "golden age" of their own in the Saurashtra area. It seems that the Śaivite king died without an heir and his distant cousin, Kumārapāla, who had narrowly escaped execution by the king, was now able to seize the throne. His ascension to power was largely through the combined efforts of a Jaina minister and a great Jaina teacher (ācārya), Hemacandra. Kumārapāla's practice and patronage of the Jaina faith lasted throughout his long rule until the Muslim invasions of 1165. Although the dynasty was eventually restored, it once again became firmly Śaivite in its sympathies, and no other Jaina king ever arose. The Śvetāmbara community retained a certain measure of political and economic influence in the kingdom, but for the most part its members contented themselves with local affairs, religious activities centring on their many wealthy temples and promoting the prohibition of animal sacrifice in the Muslim kingdoms of the north.

Jainas take great pride in the degree to which they have been able to gain political support for the practice of ahiṃsā, even among non-Indian kings whose own religions were in no way opposed to the killing of animals. The most striking example of this phenomenon took place in 1582 when the Mughal potentate Akbar was persuaded by the Śvetāmbara monk Hīravijaya-Sūri to "release prisoners and caged birds and to prohibit the killing of animals on certain days. In the following year, those orders were extended and disobedience to them was made a capital offence. Akbar renounced his much-loved hunting and restricted the practice of fishing."[8]

The Jainas were by no means alone in their ability to gain royal patronage; Buddhists, in particular, often received lavish support for extended periods, perhaps to an even greater degree than did their Nirgrantha (Jaina) rivals. And yet, as we have noted, Buddhism as a social institution could not withstand the combined onslaught of Muslim invasion and Hindu devotional fervour in the twelfth century. Its development after that was in the Himalayan states, Southeast Asia and the Far East. Thus, while the support of ruling houses was extremely important, it was not in itself sufficient to ensure a sect's long-term survival. Clearly, one must look further to discover the factors that enabled Jainism to endure while its closest counterparts disappeared from the scene.

A comparative examination of the great bodies of Buddhist and Jaina

[8] Smith 1917.

literature, which initially gives a rather striking impression of similarity, reveals that for the Buddhists philosophical issues seems to have become the chief preoccupation of the learned ācāryas. Jaina teachers, on the other hand, while also deeply interested in such questions, showed equal or perhaps even greater concern with the creation of works for laypeople. The Jaina *śrāvakācāra* texts, treatises which give systematic instructions for lay conduct, are virtually without counterpart in the Indian Buddhist tradition.[9] From the earliest times the complete integration of layfollowers into religious life was thus strongly emphasized.

Whether involved in a government career, influence-gathering in the court or simply the pursuit of business or pleasure, Jainas were obliged to mingle with members of the non-Jaina community, and hence to confront systems of customs and beliefs which invariably called their own into question. It fell to the Jaina ācāryas to strike a reasonable balance between these two priorities – on the one hand, the perpetuation of orthodoxy, perhaps best achieved through enforced isolation; on the other, the need for fruitful intercourse with non-Jaina society. They appear to have handled the task with considerable skill and wisdom, striving (and usually managing) to retain the spirit of their own tradition. The Jaina attitude towards the incredible diversity of social forms which they encountered during their years of migration and colonization is well expressed by the following dictum: "All worldly practices [those not related to liberation] are valid for the Jainas, as long as there is neither loss of pure insight nor violation of the vows."[10]

As for the castes, these are depicted not as part of the cosmic order but as a system politically imposed upon the single destiny to which all human beings belong. Credit for accommodating the Hindu caste system as a worldly institution goes to the ingenuity and literary skill of the ācārya Jinasena (c. 800). Jinasena's efforts to "Jaina-ize" certain pan-Indian social norms were by no means confined to the issue of caste. He also addressed himself to rituals celebrating the important events of everyday life: birth, marriage and so forth. The work of Jinasena can perhaps be best understood as an attempt to deal with the fact that while traditionally

[9] Williams 1963 lists more than forty medieval Jaina texts on lay discipline. Theravāda Buddhists apparently produced only one such work, the *Upāsakajanālaṃkāra* of Ānanda (twelfth century); the concern of the Mahāyāna tradition with lay matters found literary expression only in a small portion of Śāntideva's *Śikṣāsamuccaya* (ninth century).
[10] *Upāsakādhyayana*, 477–80.

tolerant of *doctrinal* heterodoxy, Brahmanical society has often showed marked hostility towards deviation from accepted patterns of social behaviour. Hence, he devised a system whereby Jainas would appear to conform with Hindu practices and yet remain uniquely Jaina. It seems, moreover, that he was eminently successful in this endeavour. Whereas scholars from outside the Jaina community have often observed that Jainas are "indistinguishable from Hindus" and should not be considered an independent group at all, Jainas themselves have adamantly denied any such claim, insisting again and again that they are not and never have been Hindus in the religious sense of the term.[11]

Most fundamental to this is the fact that the Brahmanical deities which are present at religious rites are replaced by the Jinas, whose role is different. They are not gods, but noble exemplars of souls who have achieved the highest spiritual state. Nor are the priests of the Digambaras – found only in the south – seen as brahmans of the caste system whose origin is traced to a creator deity and who therefore have the exclusive privilege of performing temple rites. Jaina rites can be performed by any Jaina and are not meant to propitiate gods of creation. The offerings of fruits and milk products honour the Jinas, but are not thought to be received by the Jinas nor do the laity partake of them as *prasāda* (food blessed by the deity).

The great devotional movement (*bhakti*) which swept India around the fifth or sixth century has already been mentioned in connection with the collapse of Buddhism. While numerous mythological figures became the objects of such cult worship, two stood far above all others in terms of their power to capture the popular imagination and to generate large followings. They were, of course, Rāma and Kṛṣṇa, the great heroes whose exploits were described in the widely told stories of the *Rāmāyaṇa* and the *Mahābhārata*, respectively, and who were raised to the status of incarnations of the god Viṣṇu. Had Jaina teachers ignored the tremendous fascination which these figures held for the average layperson regardless of religious affiliation, they would have done so at the peril of their own community's disintegration. Thus we see, in Jaina literature of the period, the development of a parallel set of myths, placing Rāma and Kṛṣṇa in a Jaina context and treating their respective deeds from the standpoint of Jaina ethics. The Jaina *Rāmāyaṇas*, for example, follow the original narrative in nearly all particulars except the killing of the demon Rāvaṇa.

[11] For a collection of papers on various aspects of this issue, see Humphrey and Carrithers 1990.

Whereas in the Brahmanical version Rāma must perform this deed (being an incarnation of a god and therefore personally responsible for the destruction of evil), in the Jaina texts this murder is committed by his brother Lakṣmaṇa.[12] Thus Lakṣmaṇa must wander from birth to birth for his act of violence, but Rāma remains a true follower of the *Jina-dharma* (Sacred Law) and is shown renouncing the world and achieving eternal liberation at the end of his career.

As for Kṛṣṇa, the hero of the *Mahābhārata*, his numerous acts of violence (beginning with the killing of his uncle Kaṃsa) and his failure at the end of his life to renounce the world as Rāma did rendered it impossible to portray him as a Jaina saint. Although the Jaina authors condemned the homicidal action of Kṛṣṇa, they prophesied that after completing his karmic term in the netherworld, he was destined to be re-born as a Tīrthaṅkara.[13]

In incorporating Brahmanical figures into their mythology, Jaina writers denied any notion that these beings were manifestations of the divine. Nevertheless, they were able to portray the heroes in a popular manner that satisfied the desire of the laity for such tales, probably helping thereby to reduce the number of Jainas who actually left the faith and allied themselves with one or other of the bhakti cults (devotional theism).

The Reform Movements of the Jaina Community

Despite the wealth accumulated during their periods of great influence and the various efforts chronicled above to achieve peaceful co-existence with the Hindu majority, Jaina communities of both the north and south fell upon somewhat hard times in the twelfth and thirteenth centuries. Hindu opposition to the "atheistic" and anti-Vedic doctrines that were being propounded could not be kept down indefinitely. Thus, as the political power of the Jainas fell to a low ebb and the wave of Hindu devotionalism carried virtually everything before it, great erosions took place in Jaina society. Many people converted out of preference; others simply went along with the religious convictions of their rulers. Numerous temples were lost, either to militant Hindu sects (particularly in the Deccan) or to conversion into mosques by invading Muslims.[14]

[12] At least eighteen Jaina *Rāmāyaṇas* are known to exist. For a complete list see Kulkarni 1959–60. Compare the extent of this collection with the fact that only one such story, the Daśarathajātaka (*Jātaka:* no. 461) exists in the Buddhist tradition. See Bulche 1950: 56ff.

[13] For the Jaina version of the life of Kṛṣṇa, see Punnāṭa Jinasena's *Harivaṃśapurāṇa* (783 CE) and Hemacandra's *Triṣaṣṭiśalākāpuruṣacaritra: VII*. See Jaini 1993: 207–49.

[14] See Saletore 1938: 272–81.

Jainas have traditionally prided themselves on the austere lifestyles of their ascetics. But with the acquisition of great riches by the community, the monks fell increasingly into a temple-centred existence, living under somewhat luxurious conditions and devoting themselves more to the external trappings of religion than to the practices stressed by Mahāvīra. There even developed a special group of "administrator-clerics", who not only managed the temple and its associated holdings (schools, libraries, extensive areas of land) but also assumed control of the temple rituals that formed the core of lay practice.

It could be argued that such a situation brought with it a certain increased stability; but we must keep in mind that the solidarity of Jaina social organization had always stemmed not from the political power of the monks but from the great *moral* authority they possessed. In falling away from his proper role as a living example of the Jaina ideal (the dedicated ascetic earnestly seeking liberation), a monk forfeited this authority. Confronted by the spectacle of such moral stagnation among their "holy men", the Jaina laity could have found little or no reason to assert the superiority of the Jina's path over those set forth by the Hindu schools.

This could have led to the complete assimilation of the Jaina community into Hinduism but, fortunately, various individuals in both the Śvetāmbara and Digambara communities became aware of the gravity of the situation and strove to bring about needed reforms. Although there were earlier attempts,[15] the first truly effective rebellion against the entrenched power of the administrator-clerics and the general degeneration of the Śvetāmbara monkhood was initiated by the devout Gujarati layman, Lonkā Śāha, in 1451. A scribe by profession, he gained access to the sacred texts (at that time available in their original form only to monks) and was shocked to compare the discipline they demanded with the lax monkish behaviour which he saw around him.

It is said that Lonkā Śāha considered the institution of the temple, with its great concentration of wealth and power, to be the main source of corruption and the rituals performed there as totally irrelevant to the path set forth in scriptures. He became convinced, furthermore, that even worship of the Jina-image was against the rule of ahiṃsā, since erecting

[15] The first notable attempts at reform were by the eleventh-century ascetics of the Kharatara Gaccha and the thirteenth-century ascetics of the Tapā Gaccha. For an account of these ascetic groups, see Dundas 1992: 119–28.

such an image involved digging, quarrying, and other activities harmful to minute life forms. On the basis of such ideas Lonkā Śāha declared publicly that temple worship was a misdeed for any Jaina and that worship was not supported by the ancient texts. He also challenged the practices of the administrator-monks, with whom many were dissatisified, and so began to gain followers including a very influential minister. This new group of ascetics, which emphasized scriptural interpretation and a puritanical way of life, were known as Sthānakavāsis, "dwellers in halls" (as opposed to dwellers in buildings attached to temples). They were distinguished by practices such as retaining lay names and wearing a piece of cloth to cover their mouths (*muh-patti*) so they would not swallow minute air-borne beings.

Lonkā Śāha's movement did not flourish as his views must have appeared extreme for two reasons. Not all Jaina monks indulged in the temple-building activities that he denounced, nor did the scriptures forbid these meritorious actions for laypeople. Even so, the impact of Lonkā Śāha's reforms on the entire community was very strong. They not only curbed the excesses of laypeople, but also raised their expectations regarding ascetic conduct.[16]

Within the Sthānakavāsi ascetic community, a further reform movement took place in the eighteenth century. This was started by a monk named Bhīkhanjī in accordance with his belief in total non-interference with any living being, either to help or to hinder, except for ascetics who should still be given alms. Although Bhīkhanjī's position was probably justified for an ascetic who was free of all social obligations, to demand similar conduct of the laity must have been seen as inconsistent with the rules governing lay practices. It is said Bhīkhanjī initially had a following of only twelve disciples. The sect he founded, therefore, became known as Terāpantha, which means "the path of the thirteen". In contrast to their initial practice of "non-involvement", in recent years the Terāpantha ascetics have made important efforts to contact and influence Indian society as a whole. This tendency is most evident in their aṇuvrata movement – a call for adhering strictly to the Jaina lay practices – an attempt to purge corruption from Indian political and economic life.[17]

Digambaras also experienced an important rejuvenation as a result of a reform movement in Agra during the late sixteenth century. This was

[16] For a study of the importance given to merit-earning activities in Jainism, see Cort 1989.
[17] For a detailed account of this sect, see Dundas 1992: 218–24.

initiated by a well-known lay poet and scriptural translator, Banārasīdās, who was deeply offended by the administrator-monks' behaviour and also was convinced that the amount of ritual associated with temple worship was excessive. He maintained that emphasis should be placed upon *internal* forms of worship (meditation). He supported his arguments with the works of the great Digambara philosopher Kundakunda which he translated into Hindi. The influence of Banārasīdās and his later followers on Digambara society was profound; the crippling excesses of the temple tradition were largely eliminated and the entire community reawakened to the deep meaning of its faith.

I wish to thank the University of California Press for permission to reproduce portions from my book *The Jaina Path of Purification*, 1979.

Padmanabh S. Jaini
South and Southeast Asian Studies
University of California, Berkeley

BIBLIOGRAPHY

Texts and Translations

Harivaṃśapurāṇa of Punnāṭa Jinasena. Sanskrit text with Hindi trans. by Pannalal Jain. Bharatiya Jnanapitha, Varanasi. 1962.

Jātaka. Pali text ed. in 7 vols. by V. Fausboll. Repr., Pali Text Society, London. 1962.

Kalpa-sūtra (*Suttāgame*, II, app. I, 1–42). Ed. by Puppha Bhikkhu. Delhi. 1953.

Lives of the Jinas, List of the Sthaviras and *Rules for Yatis* (*Kalpa-sutra*). Trans. by H. Jacobi in *Jaina Sūtras*, pt. 2, 217–311. Sacred Books of the East, XLV. 1895.

Triṣaṣṭiśalākāpuruṣacaritra of Hemacandra. Ed. by Caraṇavijaya Muni. Bhavnagar (Jaina Atmananda Sabha). 1933.

Upāsakādhyayana of Somadevasūri (chaps 5–7 of the *Yaśastilaka-campū*). Sanskrit text with Hindi trans. by Kailashchandra Śāstrī. Bharatiya Jnanapitha, Varanasi. 1964.

Modern Works

Bulche, Camille. 1950. *Rāmakathā* (in Hindi). Prayag Viśvavidyālaya, Prayag. Reprinted 1971.

Cort, John C. 1989. *Liberation and Wellbeing: A Study of the Svetambar Murtipujak Jains of North Gujarat*. Harvard University PhD Dissertation.

Dundas, Paul. 1992. *The Jains*. Routledge, London.

Gandhi, Mohandas K. 1958–76. *Collected Works of Mahatma Gandhi*. Government of India: Publication Division, Delhi.

Humphrey, Carolyn and Carrithers, Michael (eds.). 1990. *The Assembly of Listeners; The Jains in Society*. Cambridge.

Jacobi, Hermann. 1880. "On Mahāvīra and His Predecessors", in *Indian Antiquary*, IX, 158–163.

Jacobi, Hermann. 1884. *Jaina Sūtras*, pt. 1. Oxford (Sacred Books of the East, XXII). Reprinted by Dover Publications, New York.

Jaini, Padmanabh S. 1991. *Gender and Salvation: Jaina Debates on the Spiritual Liberation of Women*. University of California Press.

Jaini, Padmanabh S. 1993. "Jaina Purāṇas: A Purāṇic Counter Tradition", in *Purāṇa Perennis* (ed. Wendy Doniger), State University of New York Press, 207–49.

Kulkarni, V. M. 1959–60. "The Origin and Development of the Rāma Story in Jaina Literature", in *Journal of the Oriental Institute* (of Baroda), IX, pt. 1, no. 2, 190–204; pt. 2, no. 3, 284–304.

Renou, Louis. 1953. *Religions of Ancient India*. London.

Saletore, B. A. 1938. *Medieval Jainism*. Karnatak Publishing House, Bombay.

Smith, Vincent A. 1917. "The Jain Teachers of Akbar", in *Essays Presented to Sir R. G. Bhandarkar*, Poona.

Tod, James. 1839. *Travels in Western India*. Reprinted Oriental Publishers, Delhi. 1971.

Williams, R. 1963. *Jaina Yoga: A Survey of the Mediaeval Śrāvakācāras*. Oxford University Press, Oxford.

Abbreviations

The Three Commentaries on the *Tattvārtha Sūtra* used as the Basis of the Commentary in the Present Translation

SB *Svopajña Bhāṣya* by Umāsvāti (recognised as authentic by the Śvetāmbara sect), ed. Pandit Khubchandji Siddhantashastri, Shrimad Rajchandra Jain Shastramala, Bombay, 1932.

SBT *Svopajña Bhāṣya Ṭīkā* by Siddhasenagaṇi (of the Śvetāmbara sect), 2 vols, Seth Devchand Lalbhai Jain Pustakoddhāra Fund, series nos. 67 & 76.

SS *Sarvārthasiddhi* by Pūjyapāda Devanandi (of the Digambara sect), 4th edition, Bharatiya Jnanapitha, Delhi, 1989.

Other Commentaries and Ancient Texts

JSK *Jainendra Siddhānta-Kośa*, Bharatiya Jnanapitha, Delhi.

LP *Lokaprakāśa* by Mahopādhyāya Śrī Vinayavijayagaṇi, Sresthi Devacandra Lalbhai Jaina Pustakoddhāra, series no. 65, Bombay, 1926.

ṢKHĀ *Ṣaṭkhaṇḍāgama*, Jain Samskriti Samrakṣak Sangha, Solapur (revised ed. 1985).

TV *Tattvārthavārtika* of Akalanka, 2 vols, Bharatiya Jnanapitha, Delhi, 1982.

Modern Works

DOK *The Doctrine of Karma in Jaina Philosophy*, Helmuth von Glasenapp, Bombay, 1942.

IJT *Illuminator of Jaina Tenets*, trans. Satkari Mookerjee of *Jaina-Siddhānta Dīpikā* by Acharya Tulsi, Jain Vishva Bharati, Ladnun, 1987.

JPN *The Jaina Philosophy of Non-absolutism*, Satkari Mookerjee, Calcutta, 1944.

CHAPTER ONE

The Categories of Truth

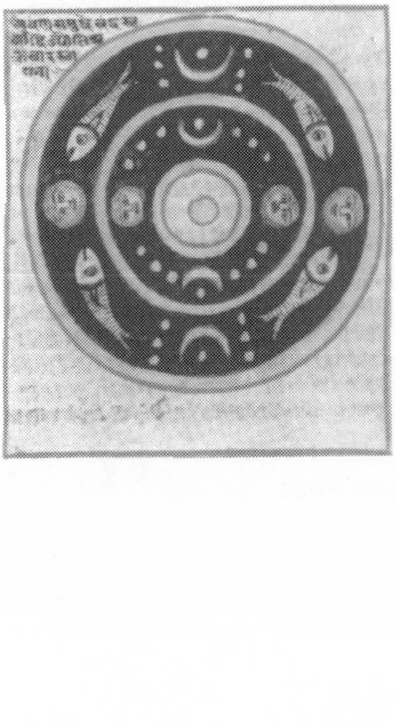

Contents

In this first chapter, Umāsvāti lays the foundation of his entire work, by introducing the three essential components of the spiritual path and the seven categories of truth which are the essential nature of reality.

samyag-darśana-jñāna-cāritrāṇi mokṣamārgaḥ

1.1 The enlightened world-view, enlightened knowledge and enlightened conduct are the path to liberation.

The world-view which sees the many and the whole is enlightened. It is true understanding, informing an individual's thoughts and actions in solving the ethical and spiritual problems of worldly bondage and of release from that bondage. It avoids dogmas which inhibit free and open thought.

Enlightened world-view begets enlightened knowledge which, in turn, begets enlightened conduct. So enlightened world-view is the cause, enlightened knowledge and conduct the effect. The spiritual path is determined by this integrated trinity.

In this first sutra and commentary, the author states his own view of the path to liberation which emphasizes his disagreement with the doctrines of other religious movements of the time. The SS commentary specifies some of these doctrines with reference to concepts of soul, liberation and the path to liberation. The Sāṅkhya-Yoga doctrine of soul as pure consciousness without particularized knowledge, the Nyāya-Vaiśeṣika concept of the liberated soul as absolutely free of thought and the Buddhist concept of the liberated soul as the burnt-out flame of the lamp are all rejected. Other concepts of the path of liberation that flourished in ancient times are similarly rejected, for instance the doctrines of knowledge alone, faith alone or conduct alone as the right path to liberation.

tattvārthaśraddhānaṃ samyagdarśanam

1.2 To possess the enlightened world-view is to believe in the categories of truth.

A view is itself neither knowledge nor intuition, but an outlook or way of seeing, a conviction backed by reason, as the SB puts it.

Belief in the categories of truth (see 1.4) means belief in categories which reason and the scriptures have established as true. The indications of enlightened belief in a person include: calmness, fear of, and distaste for, worldly life, compassion and belief in transmigration of the soul.

tan nisargād adhigamād vā

1.3 The enlightened world-view may arise spontaneously or through learning.

The worldly life of a soul has no beginning. The soul transmigrates from one birth to the next according to its karma (see 1.4), which determines its destiny. Nevertheless, each unique soul possesses the inherent knowledge and intuition which can empower it to destroy the beginningless deluded world-view tormenting it. The enlightened world-view can arise at the appropriate moment in any form of life – infernal, subhuman, human or celestial – when the painful nature of life is realized, a vision of the Jina (omniscient founders of the Jaina religion) is seen, the teachings of the Jina heard or a past life remembered. Sometimes this enlightened view breaks through spontaneously without outside assistance. Sometimes it arises through tuition or study.

jīvâ-jīvâ-srava-bandha-saṃvara-nirjarā-mokṣās tattvam

1.4 The categories of truth are:

(1) souls [sentient entities]
(2) non-sentient entities
(3) the inflow of karmic particles to the soul
(4) binding of the karmic particles to the soul
(5) stopping the inflow of karmic particles
(6) the falling away of the karmic particles
(7) liberation from worldly (karmic) bondage.

In this sutra, the categories of truth are restricted to seven, but, in some scriptures, nine are mentioned. The two additional categories are beneficial and harmful karma which the commentators include here as part of the third and/or fourth categories. The SBT considers them part of the fourth category, karmic bondage, because they are *faits accomplis* – they are the result of inflow. The SS favours including them as both karmic inflow and bondage because they are inflows in their formative state and bondages in their accomplished state.

TRANSLATOR'S NOTE

Jaina philosophers developed a unique and detailed theory of the workings of karma. The karmic particles referred to in this sutra are material clusters assimilated or "bound" by the soul as karma. These bound particles cause the soul to vibrate in association with its mind and body. The vibrations manifest as thought, speech and action and cause further karmic particles to rush into the soul from all directions, thereby perpetuating worldly bondage. As long as it is bound by karma the soul can never be liberated from worldly existence. In liberated souls there is no vibration and therefore no accumulation of karmic particles. For full discussion of the mechanics of karma and means of release from it, see chapters 6, 8 and 9.

nāma-sthāpanā-dravya-bhāvatas tannyāsaḥ

1.5 The categories of truth and the enlightened world-view etc. can be analysed by name, symbol, potentiality and actuality.

The categories of truth are explained for precision and clarity in different ways: through various gateways of investigation (see 1.7, 1.8), through the approved means of knowledge (1.6) and through philosophical standpoints (1.6, 1.34).

This sutra lists four gateways of investigation. According to these gateways, the first category of truth, the soul, can be analysed as follows:

1. Name: any substance, living or not, can be called a soul and exists as such in name at least (for example a college building can be called All Souls);
2. Symbol: an object, for instance a statue or painting, may be treated as if it were a soul though it is a soul only symbolically;
3. Potentiality: a human soul may be called a celestial soul if it occupied a celestial body in a past life or is likely to occupy such a body in a future life;
4. Actuality: a living thing may be called a soul, pointing to its actual state now.

pramāṇa-nayair-adhigamaḥ

1.6 The categories can be understood with greater accuracy through the approved means of knowledge and the philosophical standpoints.

According to some philosophers, the approved means of knowledge are twofold: immediate (innate) and mediate (acquired). In the established tradition of the ancients, they are fourfold: perception (sensation and comprehension), inference (logical deduction), analogy (comparison) and articulation (language).

The four approved means of knowledge are further classified as "for oneself" or "for others". Articulate knowledge falls into both these categories. This is because it is for the speaker/writer and also for the listener/reader. All other approved means of knowledge are for oneself only.

The approved means of knowledge are the fountainhead of the philosophical standpoints. The SS explains that general knowledge of an object provided by an approved means of knowledge is followed by a specific understanding of a particular aspect of the object through a philosophical standpoint. In other words, the philosophical standpoint gives a limited view of what is presented in its unlimited character by the approved means of knowledge.

The philosophical standpoints are twofold: related to substance and related to modes. The substance of a thing refers to its persistent existence whereas its modes are its different phases of existence. The SS explains that the standpoints related to substance take note of the name, symbol and potentialities of the past and future phases (1.5) while the standpoint related to modes explains the actuality of the present moment.

The philosophical standpoints are explained in 1.34–1.35.

nirdeśa-svāmitva-sādhanâ-dhikaraṇa-sthiti-vidhānataḥ

1.7 The categories [and their attributes] are understood in detail in terms of definition, possession, cause, location, duration and varieties.

This sutra provides a set of six gateways of investigation, in addition to that provided in 1.5. Using this set, the first category of truth, the soul, can be investigated as follows:

1. How is the soul to be defined?

   As a substance modified by various states such as the suppression, elimination, or partial suppression and partial elimination of karmic particles.

2. Who is the possessor of the enlightened world-view?
   The soul possesses the enlightened world-view as its essential attribute. (Now the investigation shifts focus from the soul to the enlightened world-view as the essential attribute of the soul.)
3. What is the cause of the enlightened world-view?
   The enlightened world-view arises spontaneously or through learning (see 1.3).
4. What is the location of the enlightened world-view?
   The enlightened world-view is located in the soul as its inalienable attribute.
5. What is the duration of the enlightened world-view in the soul?
   In some souls it is short-lived, having a beginning and an end, while in others it has a beginning, but no end. For example, the souls that progress spiritually merely by suppressing their deluded world-view have a short-lived enlightened world-view, whereas the souls that have finally eliminated their deluded world-view possess the enlightened world-view eternally.
6. What are the varieties of the enlightened world-view?
   There are three varieties of the enlightened world-view:
   (1) that which is achieved by merely suppressing the karma which covers the enlightened world-view;
   (2) that which is achieved by partially eliminating and partially suppressing the karma;
   (3) that which is achieved by completely eliminating the karma.

TRANSLATOR'S NOTE

This abridged account of the commentary is based on the SB. The SS gives a more elaborate treatment of the enlightened world-view in each of the six gateways through the fourteen-membered discipline of inquiry (see 1.8).

sat-saṃkhyā-kṣetra-sparśana-kālân-tara-bhāvâ-lpabahutvaiś ca

1.8 To explore further the categories of truth and the enlightened world-view there are the gateways of existence, numerical determination, field occupied, field touched, continuity, time-lapse, states and relative numerical strength.

Yet another set of eight gateways of investigation is prescribed. The focus in this example is the enlightened world-view, that is, the belief in the categories of truth:

1. Existence: It is accepted that the enlightened world-view is a real and constant attribute of the soul. However, the enlightened world-view will only become apparent in souls that are worthy of it. It does not surface in souls that are reprobate, their eternal transmigration being pre-destined (see 2.3). This gateway takes us through another classical set of thirteen gateways prescribed by the Jaina scripture for exploring the existence of the soul's physical, mental and ethical qualifications for the emergence of the enlightened world-view:

(1) the four transmigration realms: infernal, subhuman, human and celestial
(2) the five senses: sight, hearing, touch, taste, smell
(3) the beings with immobile and mobile bodies
(4) the activities of mind, speech, and body
(5) the passions of anger, pride, deceit and greed
(6) the three sexes: male, female and hermaphrodite
(7) the six psychic colourings: black, blue, grey, red, yellow and white
(8) the enlightened world-view
(9) the eight kinds of knowledge (1.9, 1.32)
(10) the four kinds of intuition: visual, non-visual, clairvoyant, omniscient (2.9)
(11) conduct
(12) nourishment
(13) sentience (2.8).

The SS omits gateways (11) and (13) given by the SB but adds the following three to create the fourteen-membered discipline of enquiry:

(12) self-restraint
(13) the qualities that make the soul capable or incapable of liberation
(14) rationality.

2. Numerical determination: To determine the number of souls with the enlightened world-view, it is necessary to distinguish between the souls that enjoy the enlightened world-view because the particular karma which deludes that view has been purified, and those souls that have eliminated the karma altogether. The number of the souls in the former category is only innumerable whereas the number of souls in the latter is infinite, including as it does the infinite number of liberated souls. The latter category also includes souls that have eliminated their destructive karma and are waiting for liberation.

At this point, the SBT gives a very brief classification of numbers. The number one does not lend itself to being counted (and so remains in its own classification of "one"). Two, three, four and so on, are numbers proper which are classified as numerable, innumerable and infinite. Numerable numbers are those which can be named. Innumerable are beyond naming and fall into three categories: minimum, intermediate and maximum. Beyond the innumerable are the infinite numbers which fall into the same three categories. (For further information about numbers, see appendix 1).

3. Field occupied: Only an innumerablth part of cosmic space is occupied by souls with the enlightened world-view.[1] (For the meaning of the word "innumerablth", see appendix 1.)

4. Field touched: Only an innumerablth part of cosmic space is touched by an ordinary soul with the enlightened world-view. However, the omniscient soul touches all parts of the cosmic space for the purpose of exhausting the residue of the karmic particles before attaining final liberation (see 5.16).[2]

5. Continuity: The enlightened world-view attained by partial suppression and partial elimination of karma may endure so briefly in a soul that it passes within one intra-hour[3] or it may continue for more than sixty-six ocean-measured time units (see appendix 2). However, for souls which attain the enlightened world-view by totally eliminating the relevant karma, there is a beginning but no end to their enlightened world-view. The enlightened world-view of all souls taken together has neither beginning nor end because there was no period in the past without some soul possessing the enlightened world-view, nor will there be any in the future.

6. Time-lapse: For an individual soul, the time-lapse between the end of one period of enlightened world-view and the beginning of another is less than one classical hour at the very least, and, at the very most, may be just short of half the time it takes karmic particles to undergo their complete course of binding and falling away from the soul. For the enlightened

[1] In Jaina thought, space is infinite but divided into two parts: cosmic and transcosmic. The part occupied by souls and single atoms and clusters of matter is called cosmic space. The part beyond this is called transcosmic. Cosmic space is understood to be made up of innumerable space units. There are souls in all these space units.

[2] The field touched by a soul is somewhat larger than the field occupied by it; with the former, the space units that surround the locus of the soul are also taken into account.

[3] An intra-hour is any time between two time units and forty-eight minutes less one time unit. One time unit is the smallest measurement of time; it is the time it takes for an atom to travel from one space unit (the smallest measurement of space) to another.

world-view of all souls taken together, there is no time-lapse because, among that infinite number of souls, there must always be at least some in possession of the enlightened world-view.

7. States: There are only three states in which the enlightened world-view is possible: those resulting from (1) the suppression, (2) the elimination and (3) the partial elimination and partial suppression of the karmic particles responsible for deluded world-view (see 2.1).

8. Relative numerical strength: Regarding the numbers of souls in the three states of the enlightened world-view, it is said that fewest are in the state resulting from suppression; a larger number are in the state resulting from partial elimination and partial suppression of karma; and the largest number are in the state which results from the complete elimination of karma because this is the state which accommodates the infinite number of liberated souls.

This sutra receives a further elaborate treatment in the SS, not included here, which discusses the eight gateways of investigation in the context of the fourteen stages of spiritual development (SS 9.1) and the fourteen-membered discipline of inquiry (SS 1.8).

mati-śrutâ-vadhi-manaḥparyāya-kevalāni jñānam

1.9 The varieties of knowledge are: empirical, articulate, clairvoyant, mind-reading and omniscient knowledge.

Empirical knowledge (cognition) is gained through the senses and/or the mind's ability to comprehend what is sensed.

Articulate knowledge refers to conceptualization through language.

Clairvoyance refers to the perception of things that are out of the natural range of the senses. In humans, clairvoyance is acquired through spiritual discipline whereas, for the inhabitants of heaven and hell, it is inborn (see 1.22–1.23). Clairvoyance is also possible, in moments of hardship, for beings that are not human but possess five senses and a mind (1.23/SS 1.22).

Mind-reading is the act of seeing the objects (the modes) of another's mind. This knowledge is only acquired by ascetics at a high level of spirituality.

Omniscience refers to knowledge of all substances in all their modes: past, present and future.

tat pramāṇe

1.10 These five varieties of knowledge divide into the two classes of approved means of knowledge, the mediate (acquired) and immediate (innate).

TRANSLATOR'S NOTE

The division of knowledge into two classes is an innovation of Jaina philosophers. In the established Indian tradition, the approved means of knowledge were most often divided into four classes: perception, inference, analogy and articulation/scripture. In 1.9 and 1.10, Umāsvāti follows the ancient Jaina tradition of the five varieties of knowledge and the innovative allocation of these as mediate or immediate knowledge, that is, acquired and innate knowledge.

ādye parokṣam

1.11 The first two varieties of knowledge, empirical and articulate, are acquired knowledge.

pratyakṣam anyat

1.12 The remaining three varieties of knowledge are instances of innate knowledge.

The power of knowing is innate to the soul but this power is partially, though never completely, qualified by the karmic particles.

These sutras classify the varieties of knowledge according to two classes of the approved means of knowledge, acquired (mediate) and innate (immediate). As well as including empirical and articulate knowledge, the "acquired" category includes scriptural knowledge which is articulate by the teacher. Scriptural knowledge is authentic because it derives from the pure and perfect knowledge of the Jina (omniscient teacher) who revealed it.

The remaining three varieties of knowledge, clairvoyance, mind-reading and omniscience, are considered innate because they exist independently of the senses, mind and words. Clairvoyance and mind-reading result from partial suppression and partial elimination of the relevant karma. Strictly speaking, only omniscience is perfectly innate because it alone arises out of the total elimination of knowledge-covering karma and therefore knows everything, past, present and future.

All categories of knowledge, other than omniscience, are accompanied by ignorance due to the constant rise of knowledge-covering karma. Karma exists simultaneously in three states: (1) eliminated, (2) partially eliminated and partially suppressed, and (3) rising. From the first two states comes knowledge (albeit limited). From the third state, rising karma, comes ignorance, either as absence of knowledge or misinformation.

So all categories of knowledge, other than omniscience, are a mixture of knowledge and ignorance. To have absolutely eliminated all knowledge-covering karma is to be omniscient.

matiḥ smṛtiḥ saṃjñā cintâ-bhinibodha ity anarthāntaram

1.13 Memory, recognition, reasoning and apprehension incorporate the various aspects of empirical knowledge.

In this sutra, the author uses a set of synonyms to introduce the four aspects of empirical knowledge, the first variety of knowledge.

TRANSLATOR'S NOTE

These four aspects of empirical knowledge are discussed in the various theories of knowledge in Indian philosophy. Umāsvāti's classification was accepted by all subsequent Jaina logicians who gave their own estimate of contemporary theories of knowledge in light of it.

Figure 1 provides an over-view of the classification of knowledge as given in the preceding sutras and commentaries to 1.9–1.13.

tad indriyâ-nindriyanimittam

1.14 Empirical knowledge is produced by the senses and the mind.

Empirical knowledge arises from the senses alone, the mind alone or the two acting together. There are beings without a mind such as plants, trees and some lower animals whose knowledge is necessarily through their senses alone. Plants and trees have only one sense, the tactile sense, and so their perception is produced by touch alone.

In human beings, however, empirical knowledge is sometimes produced by the joint activity of the senses and the mind and at other times by the activity of the mind alone. For instance, the empirical knowledge that "this is a table" is produced by the collaboration of the sense of sight and the mind whereas remembering what the table looks like requires only the mind to act. There is also a variety of empirical knowledge that is instinctive, such as the ability of a plant to grow towards the light or a creeper towards a support.

Table of Knowledge

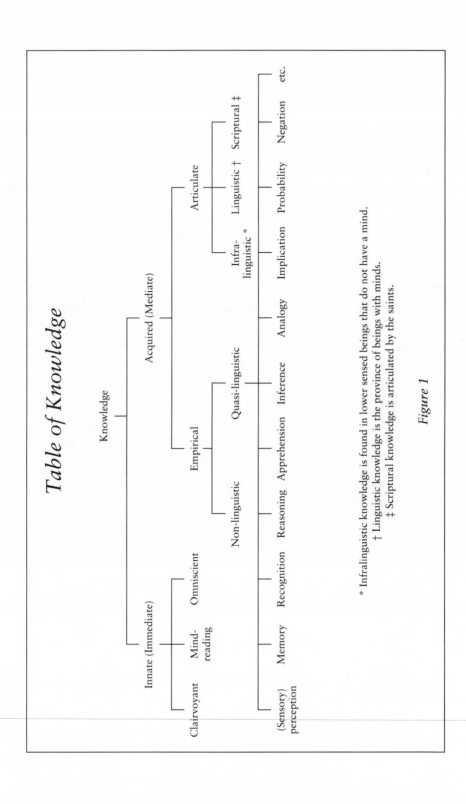

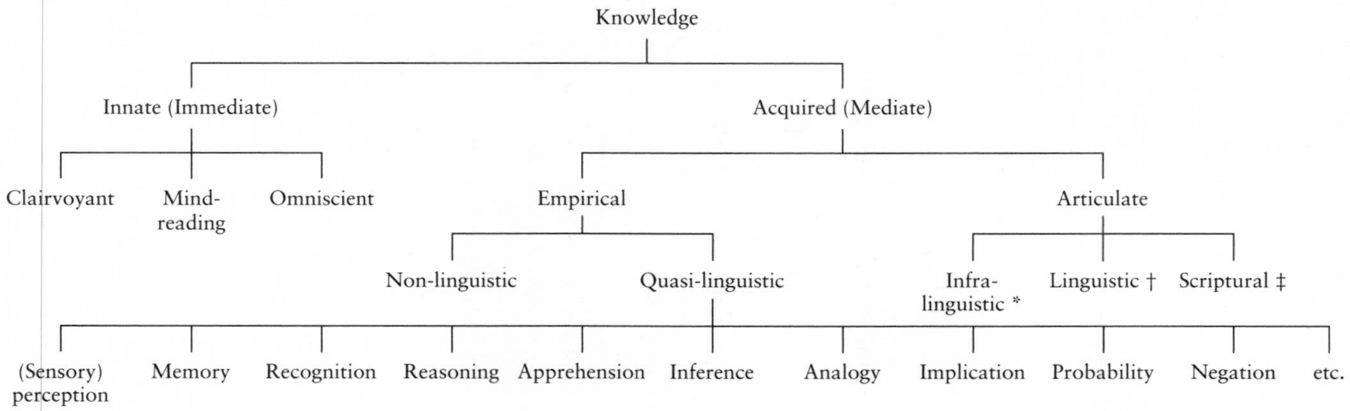

* Infralinguistic knowledge is found in lower sensed beings that do not have a mind.
† Linguistic knowledge is the province of beings with minds.
‡ Scriptural knowledge is articulated by the saints.

Figure 1

avagrahê-hâ-vāya-dhāraṇāḥ

1.15 Empirical knowledge develops through the four stages of inarticulate sensation, specific inquiry, articulate comprehension and imprint.

Inarticulate sensation is the mere sensing of objects, the grasping of their generic character (see 1.18).

Specific inquiry is the curiosity to know the whole from the part, to identify the features. It includes a process of elimination, identifying what the object does not have and what it is not. The SB equates specific inquiry with speculation, endeavour, reasoning, examination, thought, and inquisitiveness.

Articulate comprehension arises from specific inquiry. It is cognition, a definitive identification of the object, understanding both what it is and what it is not. The SB equates it with exclusion, expulsion, limitation, banishment.

Imprint is the retention of the identification of the object, creating an impression in the mind which is experienced as memory. The SB explains imprint with synonyms such as continued cognition, memory, retention and determination.

Thus the four stages constitute the formula for complete mental activity.

TRANSLATOR'S NOTE

The style of the SB is to explain philosophical ideas using the ancient device of sets of synonyms while the SS style is to explain with crisp, succinct definitions.

bahu-bahuvidha-kṣiprâ-niśritâ-sandigdha-dhruvāṇāṃ setarāṇām

1.16 (not SS) **The objects perceptible by relatively pure mental faculties are multiple and complex and the comprehension of them is quick, independent, unambiguous and constant. The objects perceptible by relatively impure mental faculties are few and simple and the comprehension of them is slow, dependent on mediation, ambiguous and inconstant.**

bahu-bahuvidha-kṣiprâ-niḥsṛtâ-nukta-dhruvāṇāṃ setarāṇām

(SS variant 1.16) The objects perceptible by relatively pure mental faculties are multiple and complex and the comprehension of them is quick, partially exposed, unspoken and constant. The objects perceptible by relatively impure mental faculties are few and simple and the

comprehension of them is slow, completely exposed, spoken and inconstant.

In this sutra, the objects of empirical knowledge and the nature of the inquiry into them are described according to the purity of the subject's mental faculties.

In the SS version of this sutra, "partially exposed" refers to empirical knowledge of an entire object, although the subject has only had access to a part of the object, whereas "completely exposed" refers to knowledge of an object which has been completely available to the subject. Similarly "unspoken" refers to empirical knowledge of an object without it being described, as opposed to "spoken" which refers to comprehending an object only when it is explicitly spoken of.

arthasya

1.17 The thing perceived continues to be the object at all four stages of empirical knowledge.

vyañjanasyâvagrahaḥ

1.18 The thing barely contacted is the object of empirical knowledge at the first stage.

Now, the objects of empirical knowledge are divided into two categories: the thing comprehended and the thing barely contacted.

Bare contact with a thing takes place at the moment it reaches the senses. This is the stage of inarticulate sensation. This contact awareness gradually proceeds towards the plane of consciousness, that is from the senses alone to the mind and the senses. (The phenomenon described here is called the "threshold level" in modern psychology, the measure of intensity at which mental or physical stimulus is perceived and produces a response.) Suppose, for example, that a man is woken by a call. The sound atoms reach the man's ears in succession and, in time, when the ears are sufficiently "saturated" with sound atoms, he wakes. (Jaina thinkers regard sound as material atoms.)

The awakening of consciousness is followed by the other three stages of empirical knowledge – specific inquiry, cognition and imprint – all of which are concerned with the object alone. The inarticulate sensation relates to both the contact with the object, and the object. In other words, there are two phases of the object, its initial appearance and its continued existence. Inarticulate sensation notes both the initial appearance and the continued existence, whereas the latter three stages recognize only the continued existence.

na cakṣur-anindriyābhyām

1.19 Inarticulate sensation of a barely contacted thing is not possible for the eye or the mind.

Inarticulate sensation of a barely contacted thing is possible only through actual physical contact and so is confined to the four senses: hearing, taste, smell and touch. The eye and the mind comprehend their object from a distance without physical contact.

TRANSLATOR'S NOTE

This sutra disputes the view of some philosophical schools that an object sends rays to the eye, i.e. there is physical contact between eye and object.

śrutaṃ matipūrvaṃ dvy-aneka-dvādaśabhedam

1.20 Articulate knowledge arises in the wake of empirical knowledge. It is of both classes of scripture, the Outer Corpus of many texts and the Inner Corpus of twelve.

The second of the five types of knowledge, articulate knowledge, is now defined.

Articulate knowledge is essentially knowledge derived from words. But, according to convention, what is referred to here is the entire Jaina sacred literature. The SB makes a clear distinction between empirical knowledge and scriptural knowledge. Empirical knowledge is concerned only with the objects that exist in the present. Scriptural knowledge relates to objects of all three phases of time – past, present and future.

The twelve texts of the Inner Corpus are the work of the Jinas and their immediate disciples. The Jinas were omniscient and their immediate disciples enjoyed a distinctive intelligence and gift for communication. The learned ascetics who followed the immediate disciples of the Jinas composed the Outer Corpus, consisting of many texts, for the benefit of their disciples whose power of understanding was inferior. The ascetics who compiled the Outer Corpus are said to have inherited complete or partial knowledge of the earlier literature.

dvividho'vadhiḥ

1.21 (not in SS) **Clairvoyance has two types.**

bhavapratyayo nāraka-devānām

1.22 (SS 1.21) **The beings of heaven and hell are born clairvoyant.**

These sutras begin the definition of the third variety of knowledge, clairvoyance, by classifying it into two types. The first is the in-born clairvoyance of the infernal and celestial beings. Ultimately, the nature of all clairvoyance is due to the kind of partial elimination and partial suppression of the clairvoyance-covering karma. But in the case of the infernal and celestial beings, it is said to be due to birth because they are born with the requisite partial elimination and partial suppression. The in-born power of clairvoyance is compared to the in-born capacity of birds to fly or fish to swim.

yathoktanimittaḥ ṣaḍvikalpaḥ śeṣāṇām

1.23 (SS 1.22) **The clairvoyance which arises from partially eliminating and partially suppressing knowledge-covering karma in a certain way is possible only in animals and humans. Such clairvoyance has six sub-types.**

The second type of clairvoyance is that of a soul which has partially eliminated and partially suppressed knowledge-covering karma in a certain way during its current lifetime. The six sub-types of clairvoyance, accessed by reducing particular karmic effects during one's lifetime, differ in the strength and constancy with which they affect the soul. The first sub-type occurs in a person in a particular place but does not continue when he or she moves to a different place. The second sub-type of clairvoyance is not restricted to any particular place but will not last a lifetime. The third is explained as clairvoyance that gradually contracts in range and the fourth as gradually expanding in range. The fifth sub-type fluctuates repeatedly, contracting and expanding in its range. The sixth, once it has arisen in a being, continues till death or into the next life and sometimes even until omniscience is achieved.

ṛju-vipulamatī manaḥparyāyaḥ

1.24 (SS 1.23) **Mind-reading has two types, simple and complex.**

viśuddhy-apratipātābhyāṃ tadviśeṣaḥ

1.25 (SS 1.24) The types of mind-reading differ in relation to their purity and infallibility.

These two sutras explain the fourth variety of knowledge, mind-reading. Simple mind-reading reads only a few general modes of the mind. However, complex mind-reading reads many different and complex modes of a mind. It is, therefore, considered purer than simple mind-reading. Moreover, it is infallible, lasting until one attains omniscience. It is wider in extent and penetrates more deeply into the minds of others. Simple mind-reading is relatively impure, fallible, limited in scope and shallow.

TRANSLATOR'S NOTE

The simple modes relate to thoughts about an object or action and the complex to the deeper motivation and beliefs that lie behind these thoughts.

According to some thinkers, only the modes of the material clusters that make up the mind are directly known in mind-reading. The thoughts expressed by these modes are not read directly, but inferred. This explanation is rejected by others. (For the concept of the physical mind, see appendix 5.)

viśuddhi-kṣetra-svāmi-viṣayebhyo'vadhimanaḥparyāyayoḥ

1.26 (SS 1.25) Clairvoyance and mind-reading differ from each other in their purity, spatial range, the species of the knowing subject and the nature of the object identified by them.

The difference between mind-reading and clairvoyance is identified through four factors.

Firstly, to be able to mind-read, a soul must be in a purer state than is necessary for clairvoyance. Mind-reading knows the thinking expressed by the modes of the material clusters which constitute the mind. Mind-reading knows the finer modes of the material clusters which are beyond the reach of clairvoyance. (See appendix 5 for further information about clusters of matter that constitute the mind.)

Secondly, clairvoyance can operate in space ranging from the innumerablth part of a finger to the entire cosmic space, whereas mind-reading is confined to the region inhabited by human beings.

Thirdly, clairvoyance is available to souls residing in any of the realms of existence whether they are fully or partially self-restrained or completely devoid of self-restraint. Mind-reading, however, is possible only in human beings with self-restraint, specified by the SB as spiritually advanced ascetics.

Fourthly, clairvoyance can identify all clusters of matter but not in all their modes. Mind-reading, however, can know the infinitesimal part of those clusters.

In short, clairvoyance is extensive but shallow, whereas mind-reading is more limited but deep.

mati-śrutayor nibandhaḥ sarvadravyeṣv-asarvaparyāyeṣu

1.27 (SS 1.26) The domain of empirical and articulate knowledge extends to all substances, although not in all their modes.

The description of the domain of the five varieties of knowledge begins with empirical and articulate knowledge.

There are six substances in the cosmos: the medium of motion, the medium of rest, space, matter, souls and time (see 5.1, 5.2, 5.38). All these, in a limited range of modes, constitute the domain of empirical and articulate knowledge. Only the omniscient soul fully knows the infinite modes of all six substances.

rūpiṣv avadheḥ

1.28 (SS 1.27) The domain of clairvoyance extends to all matter, though not in all its modes.

tadanantabhāge manaḥparyāyasya

1.29 (SS 1.28) The domain of mind-reading extends only to an infinitesimal part of the domain of clairvoyance.

These sutras describe the domain of the next two varieties of knowledge, clairvoyance and mind-reading.

The domain of mind-reading is narrower than that of clairvoyance because mind-reading can only identify the modes of the material clusters that constitute the mind, while clairvoyance can identify all kinds of material clusters in cosmic space. However, clairvoyance cannot read the mind, that is, it cannot identify the modes of the mind's material clusters, because these are too subtle. (For further points of difference between mind-reading and clairvoyance see 1.26.)

sarvadravya-paryāyeṣu kevalasya

1.30 (SS 1.29) The domain of omniscience extends to all substances in all their modes.

Here, the domain of the final variety of knowledge is described. Omniscience is autonomous, perfect, whole, incomparable, independent, pure and all-encompassing. No substance or mode lies beyond its range.

ekādīni bhājyāni yugapad ekasminn ācaturbhyaḥ

1.31 (SS 1.30) Up to four of the five varieties of knowledge may be simultaneously available in a soul.

The availability of the varieties of knowledge to a particular soul are now discussed.

In the soul, empirical knowledge can be available on its own. The combination of empirical knowledge with articulate knowledge is also possible, as is a triple combination such as empirical, articulate and clairvoyant knowledge or empirical, articulate and mind-reading knowledge. Sometimes empirical, articulate, clairvoyant and mind-reading knowledge occur together.

According to the scriptures, empirical and articulate knowledge are always available in all living beings including one-sensed organisms and plants. The articulate knowledge of souls without a mind is "infralinguistic" in nature, that is, the conceptualization is very feeble (see figure 1).

The first four varieties of knowledge, all of which are due to the partial-elimination and partial suppression of knowledge-covering karma, cannot exist with omniscience which occurs when knowledge-covering karma is completely eliminated. The SB notes that, according to some thinkers, the other four varieties of knowledge do, in fact, co-exist with omniscience but, being overshadowed by it, they become, as do the senses, effectively defunct in its presence. In this view, omniscience is like the appearance of the bright sun in the cloudless sky; it so outshines the other luminous bodies that it deprives them of their luminosity.

The SB maintains that knowledge as well as intuition, both of which are pure and perfect, are simultaneously present in the Jinas. The SBT objects to this view on the grounds that it is not stated in the scripture.

mati-śrutâ-vadhayo viparyayaś ca

1.32 (SS 1.31) Empirical, articulate and clairvoyant knowledge may be enlightened as well as deluded.

This introduces the double nature of the first three varieties of knowledge as either enlightened or deluded. The criterion for the enlightened or deluded character of these varieties of knowledge is the enlightened or deluded world-view of the respective subject. The last two varieties of knowledge, mind-reading and omniscience, are inherently enlightened.

Deluded empirical, articulate and clairvoyant knowledge added to the five pure varieties of knowledge enumerated in 1.9 make a total of eight varieties of knowledge.

sadasator aviśeṣād yadṛcchopalabdher unmattavat

1.33 (SS 1.32) A person with a deluded world-view is like an insane person who follows arbitrary whims and cannot distinguish true from false.

The empirical, articulate and clairvoyant knowledge of a person with a deluded world-view are bound to be deluded because the world-view is the foundation of one's knowledge and conditions all speculations. The true or deluded nature of knowledge is not determined by the grasp of practical facts but by the ethical or spiritual value which provides the viewpoint. The deluded world-view misleads thinking and conduct, overpowering them with delusion.

naigama-saṃgraha-vyavahāra-ṛjusūtra-śabdā nayāḥ

1.34 (not SS) The philosophical standpoints are: the common person's view, generic view, practical view, linear view and literal view.

naigama-saṃgraha-vyavahāra-ṛjusūtra-śabda-samabhirū-ḍhai-vambhū-tā nayāḥ

(SS variant 1.33) The philosophical standpoints are: the common person's view, generic view, practical view, linear view, literal view, etymological view and actuality view.

ādya-śabdau dvi-tri-bhedau

1.35 (not SS) The common person's view has two sub-types and the literal view has three.

The doctrine of philosophical standpoints mentioned in 1.6 is introduced for detailed explanation. The philosophical standpoints allow for different estimates of reality using different frames of reference.

The first standpoint, the common person's view, overlooks the distinction between the remote and immediate, noting one or the other as if it were the whole, depending upon the intention of the observer.

The second standpoint, the generic view, combines the part with the whole. A general term is used for a specific. The emphasis on general rather than specific has led to the absolutist systems of philosophy.

The third standpoint, the practical view, concentrates on the function of a thing or being. It is analytic in approach and often uses metaphors to explain the nature of things.

The fourth standpoint, the linear view, considers as real only those modes which exist at the moment. The past and future modes of a thing are not real as they have served or will serve their purpose and do not exist at the moment.

The fifth standpoint, the literal view, uses words at their exact face value to signify the real nature of things. Each word has a very particular meaning. In the literal view, even changing the gender, number, word-ending or tense of a word is thought to change its meaning and, therefore, to change the object to which it refers. So it is not appropriate to use words in different genders, number etc. to refer to the same object or event.

The three sub-types of the literal view are: (1) the view of the immediately present, (2) the etymological view, (3) the actuality view. The view of the immediately present restricts the meaning of the word to the actual state of the thing to which it refers. The other two sub-types are classified by the SS (1.33) as standpoints in their own right (see below).

The sixth standpoint in the SS tradition, the etymological view (classified by the SB as a sub-type of the fifth standpoint), discards the conventional use of a word in favour of the meaning derived from its root. The etymological view asserts that, because the roots of synonyms are different, they are not actually "synonyms" in the sense of words that mean the same as each other.

The seventh standpoint in the SS tradition, the actuality view (classified in the SB as a sub-type of the fifth standpoint), recognizes only the action implied by the root-meaning of a word. To be real, the object must satisfy the activity meant by the word.

(For examples of each of the philosophical standpoints, see translator's note, below.)

According to the SS, a philosophical standpoint is a proposition established by logic. The propositions are of two kinds: (1) those related to substance, that is, to the essential features of a thing, and (2) those related to modes, that is, to the different phases of a thing's existence (see 1.6).

The SB describes the philosophical standpoints as guides, ushers, agents, proofs, determiners, revealers, finders and indicators, which represent the concept from different perspectives. They are insights into the different facets of reality. They are complementary rather than mutually exclusive, helping to place all varieties of knowledge in their proper perspective.

The first three philosophical standpoints (common person's, generic and practical) recognize all eight varieties of knowledge, of which two, mind-reading and omniscience, are always true (as they are always accompanied by the enlightened world-view) and three, empirical, articulate and clairvoyant knowledge, are true when accompanied by the enlightened world-view and deluded when accompanied by a deluded world-view (1.32). Even the three deluded varieties are considered valid in practical life because each involves awareness of the object albeit within a limited capacity.

The fourth philosophical standpoint, the linear view, does not recognize the validity of empirical knowledge whether enlightened or deluded because both tend to be indeterminate and indecisive in their identification of objects. Instead, the linear view recognizes scriptural knowledge as authentic because it knows its objects in all their modes and characteristics.

The fifth philosophical standpoint, the literal view, accepts scriptural knowledge and omniscience as the most valuable varieties of knowledge. The literal view does not accept the validity of empirical knowledge, clairvoyance and mind-reading because they are subordinate to scriptural knowledge and as such have no essential functions of their own. Nor does the literal view recognize the importance of the deluded varieties of empirical, scriptural (articulate) and clairvoyant knowledge because, according to this view, all souls have the power of knowledge and this cannot be damaged.

The philosophical standpoints solve many philosophical disputes by clarifying the perspective of the disputants. The first four standpoints (common person's, generic, practical and linear) analyse the logical implications of the conflicting doctrines, whereas the last three focus on the linguistic nuances.

TRANSLATOR'S NOTE

Speaking from the first standpoint, the common person's view, we might describe an area of tropical forest as "timber" in which case we are seeing the remote, the use of the trees for building materials. On the other hand, standing two inches from a deadly snake we might describe the area as a "death trap" in which case we are describing it in terms of the immediate.

From the second standpoint, the generic view, we might describe the jungle as "lots of trees" or "woods" thus generalizing from one particular lifeform on that area of land.

From the third standpoint, the practical view, we might say, "This is a treasure trove," referring metaphorically to the financial benefit from cutting and selling the trees. We might as easily say, "These are the lungs of the earth," referring to the function of the trees in releasing oxygen, or, "This is the gene pool" of the earth, referring to the millions of diverse species living there which provide the basis for new life.

From the fourth standpoint, the linear view, we would recognize the area in question as a breathing organ for the planet and as a rich collection of species but would not perceive the area as timber or as the money derived from this, as these latter would be potential modes, not present ones.

In the fifth standpoint, the literal view, we would say that most of the lifeforms in this area of land were not in fact trees, and even those that were called "trees", such as banana plants, were not trees as they did not have wooded trunks. We would also seek to describe the area of land by the most appropriate term: wood, forest, wilderness, jungle. This would lead to the etymological and actuality view (sub-types of the fifth standpoint, according to the SB, but the sixth and seventh standpoints, according to the SS).

In the etymological view, we would say that this was not a "jungle" as the root of this is *jaṅgala*, the Sanskrit for dry/desert. If we called them "woods" we would name the *wud* of the trees, but would not be including the large amount of herbaceous, fungal and animal life. "Forest" from the latin *foris* meaning "outdoors" would be so general as to also include gardens, plantations and so on. "Wilderness" is from *wild(d)eor* ("wild deer") and so is inaccurate. "The wild" meaning simply untamed nature might perhaps be the most accurate.

From the seventh standpoint, the actuality view, we would reject jungle and wilderness but accept "woods", "forest" and "the wild" as all describing some actual reality in that area which does support the activities of being wood, being outdoors and being wild.

The SB clearly accepts the inherent purity of the soul at all times. This is in accord with the great Jaina philosopher Kundakunda who argued that the transcendental perspective is superior to the empirical one in assessing the essence of Jaina philosophy. However, the SB does not specifically distinguish between the transcendental and empirical viewpoints as did Kundakunda.

An important outcome of the SB recognizing the inherent capacity of all souls to know the truth is that all the traditional approved means of knowledge, perception, inference, analogy and scripture, are seen as valid.

The classification of the philosophical standpoints in sutras 1.34 and 1.35 and their exposition by the SB are endorsed in the ancient Ṣaṭkhaṇḍāgama and Kaṣāyapāhuḍa of the Digambara scripture. This points to the antiquity of the sutras and the SB.

CHAPTER TWO

The Nature of the Soul

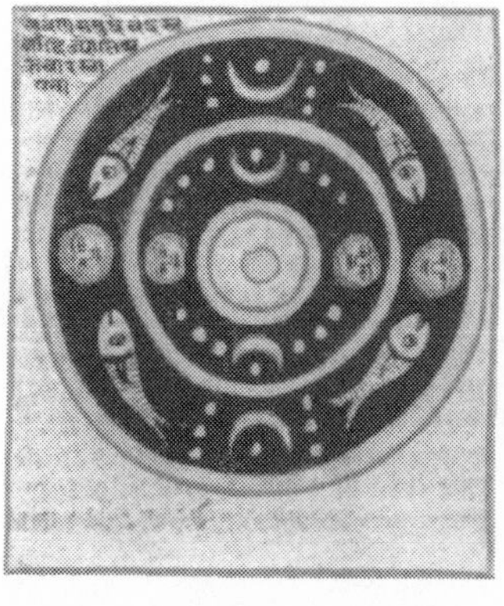

Contents

The first chapter explained the categories of truth that constitute reality. Now the author turns his attention to the first category, the soul.

aupaśamikar-kṣāyikau bhāvau miśraś ca jīvasya svatattvam audayika-pāriṇāmikau ca

2.1 The states that distinguish the soul from other substances are those that:

(1) **are due to the suppression of the deluding karma**
(2) **are due to the elimination of the eight types of karma**
(3) **are mixed because of the partial elimination and partial suppression of the four destructive karmas**
(4) **are due to the rising of the eight types of karma**
(5) **constitute the innate nature of the soul**

Now the nature of the soul, the first among the seven categories of truth (see 1.4), is explained in terms of the states that distinguish it from other substances. This sutra groups these states into five classes according to karmic processes. The states in the first four classes are produced as a result of the soul's interaction with karma. Directed by the various processes of karma, the soul passes through these different states which generate changes in its nature and which constitute its worldly career.

There are eight types of karma:

1. knowledge-covering
2. intuition-covering
3. sensation-producing
4. deluding
5. lifespan-determining
6. body-making
7. status-determining
8. obstructive

Of these eight karmas, (1), (2), (4) and (8) are called destructive because they cover or distort the intrinsic qualities of the soul. The remaining four are non-destructive.

The mixing of karma with the soul is due to karmic inflow (see 6.1–6.2). The binding of the particles of karma to the soul is called bondage (8.1). However, this binding is not permanent. The soul has an inherent capacity which can affect how the bondage is ended, thereby affecting its own fate. It can exert power to suppress the karmas so that they remain as inactive "sediment" in the soul. This suppression causes the first distinguishing class of states. But if the soul goes further and actually succeeds in eliminating the karma, this brings about the second class of states. It is also possible for the soul to partially eliminate and partially suppress its karma so that the soul becomes like clean water mixed with mud. This generates the third class of states. However, karmic particles that have not been eliminated cannot be suppressed forever; they must eventually mature and rise up like disturbed sediment to produce their effect. This active arising of karma generates the fourth class of states.

The states of the fifth class are integral to the soul and, therefore, distinct from its karmic alliance. These innate states will be explained in 2.7.

The SBT draws attention to a sixth, "combined" state, a mixture of two or more of the above states, which it says is also mentioned in the scriptures.

Although it has size and shape, determined by karma, the soul does not possess the material qualities of touch, taste, smell and colour.

dvi-navâ-ṣṭādaśai-kaviṃśati-tribhedā yathākramam

2.2 The five classes of states cause two, nine, eighteen, twenty-one and three states, respectively.

samyaktva-cāritre

2.3 The enlightened world-view and enlightened conduct.

The description of the five classes of states of the soul begins with the first class, those caused by suppressing the deluding karmas. Of the eight types of karma, only deluding karma can be suppressed.

This karma has two varieties, view-deluding and conduct-deluding.

The enlightened world-view referred to in this sutra is due to the suppression of conduct-deluding karma in the form of the four tenacious passions of anger, pride, deceit and greed, and of the three sub-types of view-deluding karma which cause, respectively, deluded world-view, near-perfect enlightened world-view and a mixture of enlightened and deluded world-view (see 8.10). Enlightened conduct is due to the suppression of conduct-deluding karma, specifically the four passions. However, both the enlightened world-view and enlightened conduct are very short-lived in this case because they are achieved by temporary suppression and not the elimination of karma.

Furthermore, the enlightened world-view will not come to all. There is no beginning to the transmigration of souls from birth to birth and for some there is no end. Not all will attain liberation. Those who are destined to attain liberation are capable of achieving the prerequisite enlightened world-view through suppressing, eliminating or partially suppressing and partially eliminating the view-deluding karma. Once they do this, they have a set period of time left before attaining liberation. The maximum span of this period is equal to half the time it takes for a soul to bind and release all the karmic particles scattered in the cosmos (something it has done an infinite number of times in its beginningless career).

There is a second essential condition for the initial attainment of the enlightened world-view – that the karmas being bound by the soul are of intermediate duration, that is, the time it takes for them to bind and be released by the soul is between one intra-hour (just less than forty-eight minutes) and 10^{14} ocean-measured periods (o.m.p.) minus one time unit. Furthermore, these intermediate karmas must be stabilized by the spiritual purity of the soul at a duration of 10^{14} o.m.p. minus numerable thousands of o.m.p. (See appendices 1 and 2 for information about Jaina measurement of numbers and time.)

The third condition, given in the SS, for attaining the enlightened world-view is that the soul must be inherently worthy of liberation (2.7). It should, moreover, have five fully developed senses (2.15), a mind (2.11), all the maturations (8.12) and complete purity. Humans, gods, infernal beings or subhumans (animals and plants) that fulfil these conditions are capable of attaining the enlightened world-view. There are many other factors, including memory of past lives, which are instrumental in achieving the enlightened world-view.

jñana-darśana-dāna-lābha-bhogô-pabhoga-vīryāṇi ca

2.4 The enlightened world-view and enlightened conduct, together with knowledge, intuition, beneficence, gain, satisfaction, comfort and power.

Now the states in the second of the five distinguishing classes of states are described. In this class, there are nine states which are generated by the total elimination of the four types of destructive karma. The four destructive karmas generate nine states because of their sub-types, that is the two varieties of deluding karma, (1) view-deluding and (2) conduct-deluding karma; as well as (3) knowledge-covering and (4) intuition-covering karma, and the five sub-types of obstructing karma, (5) beneficence-obstructing, (6) gain-obstructing, (7) satisfaction-obstructing, (8) comfort-obstructing and (9) power-obstructing karma.

When these nine varieties of karma are eliminated, the positive states underlying these karmas become attainable. These are respectively: (1) the enlightened world-view, (2) enlightened conduct, (3) omniscience, (4) pure and perfect intuition, and the abilities to (5) inspire fearlessness, (6) meet one's nutritional needs, (7) create divine surroundings (call up the gods, generate celestial light, create beautiful gardens, etc.), (8) produce divine paraphernalia (canopies, thrones, etc.) and (9) achieve omnipotence.

The above interpretation is only in the SS. However, there is no controversy among the commentators about the soul attaining the first four states after it has eliminated the destructive karmas. The other five states can be identified with the unimpeded bliss of omniscience. The physical pain and pleasure caused by the arising of sensation-producing karma have no effect on the spiritual bliss of the omniscient soul.

TRANSLATOR'S NOTE

In 2.1, the states of the second class are described as those which arise due to the total elimination of the eight types of karma, yet here the elimination of only the four destructive karmas is mentioned. The reason for this apparent inconsistency is that the state of worldly souls is being considered, for whom only the elimination of the four destructive karmas is possible. The elimination of all eight types of karmas occurs only on liberation from worldly life.

jñānâ-jñāna-darśana-dānādilabdhayaś catus-tri-tri-pañcabhedā yathākramaṃ samyaktva-cāritra-saṃyamâsaṃyamāś ca

2.5 Four kinds of knowledge, three kinds of deluded knowledge [knowledge held by a deluded person], three kinds of intuition, five kinds of potential, the enlightened world-view, enlightened conduct, "partial restraint and partial non-restraint".

These are the states in the third distinguishing class, those due to partial elimination and partial suppression of the destructive karma. The four kinds of knowledge are: empirical, articulate, clairvoyant and mind-reading (see 1.9). The three kinds of deluded knowledge are: deluded empirical, deluded articulate and deluded clairvoyant (1.32). The three kinds of intuition are: visual, non-visual and clairvoyant. The five kinds of potential are for beneficence, gain, satisfaction, comfort and power. The enlightened world-view and enlightened conduct have been explained in 1.1. "Partial restraint and partial non-restraint" is limited self-restraint according to one's capacity.

The karmic particles that are eliminated and suppressed are those which are capable of covering totally the properties of the soul such as knowledge, intuition, the enlightened world-view, enlightened conduct, and the potentials (beneficence, etc.). In the partially eliminated and partially suppressed state, the actively arising karmic particles are only able to cover partially the properties of the soul and must leave a part of them exposed. They are the common property of all souls, even the most undeveloped ones.

Non-destructive karma (sensation-producing, body-making, status-determining, lifespan-determining) is not subject to partial elimination or partial suppression.

gati-kaṣāya-liṅga-mithyādarśanâ-jñanâ-saṃyatâ-siddhatva-leśyāś catuś-catus-trye-kai-ke-kai-ka-ṣaḍbhedāḥ

2.6 Transmigration in the four realms, four passions, three genders, the deluded world-view, ignorance, non-restraint, the unliberated state and the six colourings.

Here, the fourth class of the states of the soul, those that are due to the rising of the eight types of karma, is described. The four transmigration realms are the respective habitats of infernal beings, subhumans (plants and animals), men and gods. The four passions are anger, pride, deceit and greed. The three genders are female, male and hermaphrodite. The deluded world-view is a perverted understanding of the categories of truth. Ignorance is the state following the active arising of the most intense karma that covers knowledge, intuition and the enlightened world-view. Non-restraint is total absence of self-control. The unliberated state is caused by the active arising of the four non-destructive karmas. The six colourings are black, blue, grey, red, yellow and white. There are many other states and sub-types of these states, but these twenty-one are representative of all the others.

The following table indicates the types of karma which cause the different states:

STATES	KARMA
Transmigration in the four realms	body-making (see 8.12)
Four passions	conduct-deluding (8.10)
Three genders	conduct-deluding (sexual disposition) (8.10) body-making (sexual organs) (8.12)
Deluded world-view	view-deluding (8.10)
Ignorance	knowledge-covering (8.7) intuition-covering (8.8) view-deluding (8.10)
Non-restraint	conduct-deluding (8.10)
Unliberated state	four non-destructive (8.9, 8.11–8.13) (sensation-producing, body-making, lifespan-determining, status-determining)
Six colourings	conduct-deluding (passions) (8.10) body-making (8.12)

jīva-bhavyâ-bhavyatvādīni ca

2.7 Being a soul, being worthy of liberation, being unworthy of liberation and so on constitute the innate nature of the soul.

Here, the fifth and final class of the states of the soul is described. These states are innate and do not result from karmic processes. They may be with or without a beginning (see 5.42, 5.44). This sutra lists those that are beginningless.

According to the SB, the phrase "and so on" in the sutra refers to attributes such as existence, otherness from the body, capacity to act, capacity to enjoy, the possession of qualities, non-ubiquity, non-materiality, etc. Of these properties, some are common to all substances and some are exclusive to either sentient substances (souls) or non-sentient ones (media of motion and rest, space and matter). The three attributes explicitly mentioned are exclusive to the soul.

upayogo lakṣaṇam

2.8 Sentience is the defining characteristic of the soul.

Having described the various states of the soul generated by karma, the author now defines soul with regard to its essential quality.

Sentience is awareness or consciousness. It is twofold: knowledge and intuition. The soul is never bereft of sentience, however feeble and indistinct this may be in undeveloped organisms.

sa dvividho'ṣṭa-caturbhedaḥ

2.9 Sentience is of two kinds: the first has eight varieties and the second has four.

The two kinds of sentience are determined and undetermined. Determined sentience is knowledge and undetermined sentience is intuition.

Sentience as knowledge has eight varieties: empirical, articulate, clairvoyant, mind-reading, omniscient, deluded empirical, deluded articulate and deluded clairvoyant (see 1.9, 1.32).

Sentience as intuition has four varieties: visual, non-visual, clairvoyant and omniscient. Non-visual intuition uses senses other than sight. According to some thinkers, however, it occurs independently of the senses.

The SS mentions the fact (as does the SB in 1.31) that, although knowledge and intuition cannot occur simultaneously in souls that are not omniscient, they can in those that are.

TRANSLATOR'S NOTE

Jaina thinkers accept unanimously that knowledge and intuition cannot occur simultaneously in souls that are not omniscient. However, there is a divergence of view as to whether or not they occur simultaneously in omniscient souls.

saṃsāriṇo muktāś ca

2.10 Souls are divided into two broad classes: worldly beings and liberated souls.

This sutra begins the classification of souls. Worldy beings transmigrate from one birth to another. The transmigration has no beginning but it ends if the soul is liberated.

The transmigration of worldly beings is explained in the SS with respect to five types of change, namely, changes in the clusters of matter, space units, time units, realms of birth, and states.

The change of the clusters of matter is the soul's absorption and subsequent release of all material particles in cosmic space an infinite number of times.

The change of the space units refers to the soul's occupation of each space unit in cosmic space at some time in its various lives. A soul's occupation sometimes spreads over a limited number of space units and sometimes over the entire cosmic space as in the case of an omniscient soul enjoying the effect of sensation-producing karma in the short time before liberation (see 5.16).

The change of the time units refers to the soul's succession of births and deaths in each time unit in each ascending and descending aeon in the recurring cycles of time (3.27).

The change of the realms of birth refers to the soul's frequent transmigration from one realm of birth to another, from the lowest hell up to the "neck-dwelling" heavens (mid-heavens), due to its deluded world-view (4.20).

The change of the states of the soul is defined by the type, duration, intensity and quality of effect and material mass of the soul's karma due to its deluded world-view (8.4).

samanaskâ-manaskāḥ

2.11 The worldly souls fall into two groups, souls that possess a mind and souls that do not.

Only souls that possess a mind have the power of thought. Souls which are said to have a mind are those with both a psychic and physical mind. Those with a psychic mind but no physical mind are said to be without a mind.

In the SBT, the psychic mind is attributed to the partial elimination and partial suppression of the karma which obscures articulate knowledge. According to the SS, it is the result of the partial elimination and partial suppression of both the mind-covering (knowledge-covering) karma and energy-obstructing karma. The psychic mind finds expression as consciousness, awareness, sensation, attention and so on.

The SS explains the physical mind as the result of actively arising karma. The physical mind is made of material particles and has a size and location. The physical mind is the essential aid to the psychic mind's potential for thought. Memory is only possible for souls with a physical mind. (For a further description of the mind, see 5.19.)

TRANSLATOR'S NOTE

In modern parlance, the physical mind is the brain and the psychic mind is the capacity and activity of the brain. However, in the Jaina view it is the psychic mind that creates the physical mind, not vice versa. Furthermore, the physical mind is made of very subtle matter. According to the SBT, it pervades the whole body of a being. In another view (*TV*, V.19), the location of the mind changes with the location of attention. In yet another view (*JSK*, III. 270), the heart is the seat of the mind which has the shape of a tiny eight-petalled lotus.

saṃsāriṇas trasa-sthāvarāḥ

2.12 The worldly souls are further classified as mobile and immobile beings.

Mobile beings can move from one place to another. Immobile beings cannot move themselves from one place to another and are all one-sensed organisms (see 2.23).

pṛthivy-ambu-vanaspatayaḥ sthāvarāḥ

2.13 (not SS) The earth-bodied, water-bodied and plant-bodied souls are immobile beings.

pṛthivy-ap-tejo-vāyu-vanaspatayaḥ sthāvarāḥ

(SS variant 2.13) The earth-bodied, water-bodied, fire-bodied, air-bodied and plant-bodied souls are immobile beings.

There are many varieties of earth-bodied, water-bodied and plant-bodied souls. For instance, raw soil or a clod of earth, particles of dust, sand, raw minerals are earth-bodied beings. Snow, ice, rain and so on are water-bodied beings. (For further details on the immobile bodies, see 2.14.)

The classification of beings as mobile and immobile is only formal and in reference to body-making karma. The automatic movement for the maintenance of life does not qualify a being as "mobile". This term refers to those that are capable of voluntary movement. For this reason, the SS variant of this sutra includes the fire-bodied and air-bodied as immobile beings.

TRANSLATOR'S NOTE

When souls are born with bodies made of material clusters of earth (soil, stone, copper, salt, etc), they are called "earth-bodied", when their bodies are made of water clusters, they are called "water-bodied" and so on. When these elements are abandoned by their resident souls and assume an inanimate state they are called "earth-bodies" etc. Another variety, called "earth-soul" etc., is defined as a soul that is destined to occupy a body made of earth, etc.

tejo-vāyū dvīndriyādayaś ca trasāḥ

2.14 (not SS) Fire and air, as well as those with two or more senses, are mobile beings.

dvīndriyādayas trasāḥ

(SS variant 2.14) Those with two or more senses are mobile beings.

Only beings with at least two senses are genuinely mobile creatures. The SBT explains that the fire-bodied and air-bodied do not move of their own accord and as such, truly speaking, do not belong to the class of mobile creatures.

In the SS, the element of vitality is added to explain the nature of all beings, however many senses they have. There are ten vitalities in all:

1. sense of touch
2. body
3. respiration
4. lifespan
5. sense of taste
6. faculty of speech
7. sense of smell
8. sense of sight
9. sense of hearing
10. rationality

The table below gives the number of vitalities for life-forms classed according to the number of senses they possess.

BEINGS	VITALITIES
One-sensed	(1) – (4)
Two-sensed	(1) – (6)
Three-sensed	(1) – (7)
Four-sensed	(1) – (8)
Five-sensed non-rational	(1) – (9)
Five-sensed rational	(1) – (10)

pancendriyāṇi

2.15 There are five senses.

This sutra begins the description of the senses and their sphere of operation. The five senses are: touch (skin), taste (tongue), smell (nose), seeing (eye) and hearing (ear).

dvividhāni

2.16 There are two kinds of senses.

The senses can be viewed in two ways, senses as clusters of matter and senses as modes of the soul.

nirvṛtty-upakaraṇe dravyendriyam

2.17 The senses as clusters of matter have a dual nature: as the physical organs themselves and as the capacity of those organs to perceive.

labdhy-upayogau bhāvendriyam

2.18 The senses as modes of the soul are also dual in nature: sentient potential and sentient application.

Sentient potential is the capacity of the soul to apply the physical senses. The SB explains that sentient potential is released by the active arising of the body-making karma and also the partial elimination and partial suppression of the knowledge-covering karma. The SS affirms this latter cause but does not mention the former. It identifies sentient application with the striving of the soul to produce the physical senses.

upayogaḥ sparśādiṣu

2.19 (not in SS) Touch and the like are the objects of sentient application.

Sentient application relates to empirical knowledge (cognition), that is, the perception of touch, taste, smell, colour, and sound by the senses. It does not relate to articulate knowledge because this is not possible by the senses alone. Nor does it relate to clairvoyance, mind-reading or omniscience because they do not use the senses at all. The SB describes sentient application as attention, specific mental activity, the continuing identity and transformation of the soul. The SBT describes it as both the perception of external objects and the experience of one's own pleasures and pains.

The SB explains that a sense, as (1), a physical organ, is the necessary condition of a sense as (2), the capacity to perceive, and as (3), sentient application. However, a sense as (4), sentient potential, lies at the root of the other three varieties of sense. All four varieties of sense, the first two related to substance and the latter two related to modes, are necessary for perception to occur.

The senses as (3) sentient application are not senses in the true meaning of the word. The term is used figuratively. There is no substantial difference between sentient application and perception, which is the result of the four varieties of the senses.

sparśana-rasana-ghrāṇa-cakṣuḥ-śrotrāṇi

2.20 (SS 2.19) The five senses are skin, tongue, nose, eye and ear.

sparśa-rasa-gandha-varṇa-śabdās teṣām arthāḥ

2.21 (SS 2.20) The objects of the five senses are, respectively, touch, taste, smell, colour and sound.

śrutam anindriyasya

2.22 (SS 2.21) Articulate knowledge [the scriptural lore] is the domain of the internal organ.

Having defined the domain of the senses, the domain of mind is now defined. Articulate knowledge, here understood as the Inner and Outer Corpus of the scriptures (see 1.20), is the subject matter of the internal organ, that is, the mind.

The SBT gives an alternative explanation in which articulate knowledge is said to be empirical knowledge (cognition) beginning with the stage of specific inquiry (1.15). This empirical knowledge is by the mind and not by any sense organ such as the ear or eye. It is a mental perception that understands the scripture.

vāyvantānām ekam

2.23 (not SS) **The classes of beings, up to the air-bodied ones, have only the sense of touch.**

vanaspatyantānām ekam

(**SS variant 2.22**) **The classes of beings, up to the plant-bodied ones, have only the sense of touch.**

Now having described the nine classes of beings, earth, water, fire, air, plant, two-sensed, three-sensed, four-sensed, and five-sensed, and also having mentioned the five kinds of senses (see 2.12–2.15), the author distributes the senses according to the classes of beings.

There are variants in the wording of this sutra, because of the variations in sutras 2.13–2.14 in the listed order of the first five classes of beings. However, all the commentators are saying the same thing, that these five classes – earth-, water-, plant-, fire- and air-bodied beings – have only the sense of touch.

kṛmi-pipīlikā-bhramara-manuṣyādīnām ekaikavṛddhāni

2.24 (SS 2.23) **Worms and the like, ants and the like, bees and the like and humans and the like, have an additional sense progressively [they have two, three, four and five senses, respectively].**

The following table shows the varieties of elemental bodies, plants, animals, humans, infernals and gods, and the number of senses they possess.

NUMBER OF SENSES	BEINGS
One sense (touch)	earth-, water-, fire-, air- and plant-bodied
Two senses (touch and taste)	worms, leeches, *mollusca* (oysters, mussels, snails etc.), *curculionidae*, *vermes*

Three senses (touch, taste, smell)	some minibeasts such as ants, fleas, plant-lice, cotton-seed insects, termites, centipedes
Four senses (touch, taste, smell and sight)	some minibeasts such as wasps, flies, gnats, mosquitoes, butterflies, moths, scorpions, etc.
Five senses, (touch, taste, smell, sight and hearing)	larger animals such as fish, birds, and quadrupeds, humans, infernals and gods

In 2.11, souls were classified as those that have a (physical) mind and those that do not. All beings with less than five senses are born through agglutination (material particles joining together) and as such are devoid of a (physical) mind. Among those possessed of five senses, again, there are two categories, those that are born through agglutination, and as such are devoid of a mind, and those that are born of the womb and have a mind.

TRANSLATOR'S NOTE

As noted in 2.11, beings without a physical mind are said to be without a mind although all beings have a psychic mind, that is, an awareness, an experience of sensation. This differs from the pure consciousness of the soul because the physical mind has an element of matter in it.

saṃjñinaḥ samanaskāḥ

2.25 (SS 2.24) Those that have a mind are intelligent beings.

This sutra explains the unique quality of those who have a physical mind. Intelligence or rationality means the capacity to remember the past and ponder the future. Only the five-sensed beings who have a mind have this capacity. So, human beings and animals born of the womb, the gods and the infernals, are rational beings. This excludes humans and five-sensed animals born by agglutination (asexual reproduction through material particles coalescing).

The SB differentiates between intelligence as thoughtful knowledge and intelligence as subconsciously motivated behaviour. Intelligence as thoughtful knowledge is engaged in judging objects and situations that arise in the wake of specific enquiry. Intelligence as subconsciously motivated behaviour is the survival instinct concerned with acquiring food, resorting to fight or flight, sexual activity and provision for the future (possessiveness).

vigrahagatau karmayogaḥ

2.26 (SS 2.25) **If the soul makes one or more turns when it is in transit after death, the only activity is that of its karmic body.**

Having dealt with the senses and mind of the soul, we now turn to its worldly career transmigrating from one life to the next. The SBT distinguishes two varieties of transit: transit from one place to another and transit which is transformation in one place. The second variety takes place when the soul is reborn in the same body after death. (Death is defined as the exhaustion of the lifespan karma and active arising of new lifespan karma. Rebirth in the same body may occur in single-celled organisms co-habited by many souls.) Both varieties of transit entail effort on the part of the soul. Here our main concern is transit from one place to another.

According to the SB, when the soul is in transit from one birth to another, it has neither a gross body (physical mass), speech organs or a mind and so, naturally, the activities of the body, speech and mind are absent. The motion of the soul in transit, however, may be straight or with one or more turns. When the soul goes in a straight line to the place of rebirth, the impetus is provided by the previous body at the time of death. But if the soul has to make a turn during its transit, to maintain momentum, it needs a fresh impetus from the subtle karmic body that always accompanies it. On reaching the place of birth the soul creates a new gross body through the power of its past karma.

The SS interprets the sutra in a different way. During a transit to another body, the karmic body of the soul absorbs clusters of karmic matter but cannot absorb those clusters needed for speech, mind, gross bodies etc.

anuśreṇir gatiḥ

2.27 (SS 2.26) **Motion is in a straight line along the rows of the space units.**

This sutra describes the motion of the soul in transit after death and of material particles and clusters. The rows of space units run in straight lines from east to west, north to south and also up and down.

The SS says that the transit of the worldly souls is always in a straight line, upwards or downwards to a different realm or horizontally to another place in the same realm. The transit of the liberated souls is always in a straight line. The motion of the material particles and clusters towards the border of the cosmos is also in a straight line. Any deviations from this law are due to the influence of external factors; never the "traveller's" own effort.

The rotation of the luminous bodies such as the sun and moon is not governed by this law.

avigrahā jīvasya

2.28 (SS 2.27) **The liberated soul always moves in a straight line without any turn.**

This describes the motion of the disembodied liberated soul from the place of liberation to the horizontal plane at the top of cosmic space where liberated souls dwell. This plane is parallel to the horizontal plane in the middle of the cosmos where humans dwell. As only humans can be liberated, the human soul goes up from the human plane to the plane of liberation, without any turn, to arrive and occupy space units that exactly parallel the space units of the soul's place of departure. (The journey is illustrated in figure 2 on p. 49.)

vigrahavatī ca saṃsāriṇaḥ prāk caturbhyaḥ

2.29 (SS 2.28) **In transit, the worldly soul may make up to three turns.**

The path of a transmigrating worldly soul may be a straight line without any turn or a path with one, two or three turns. These four alternatives are illustrated by figures 3–6 on p. 49. The polygonal outline of these figures represents the shape of cosmic space, beyond which lies transcosmic space. This cosmic shape often necessitates turns as the soul cannot travel through transcosmic space which has no medium of motion, the substance necessary for all movement (see 5.17).

Transit without turning: When the space units of departure after death and the space units of arrival for new birth are situated in the same vertical row, the path of transit is a straight line without turn (figure 3).

Transit with one turn: when the space units of departure are situated on the vertical border of the lower region of the cosmos and the soul has to reach a point in the middle or upper region, it has first to travel horizon-

Transits of Souls

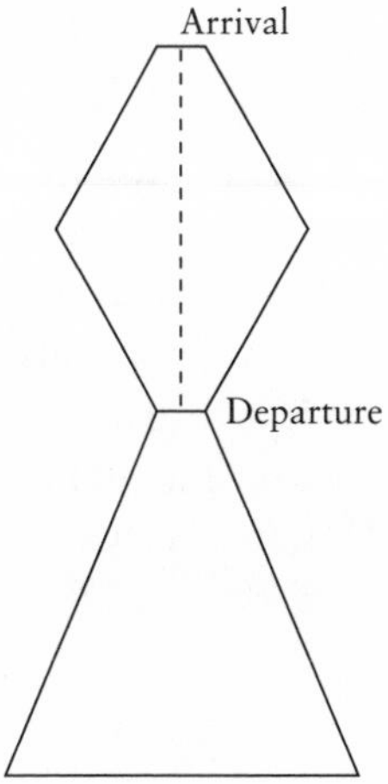

Figure 2

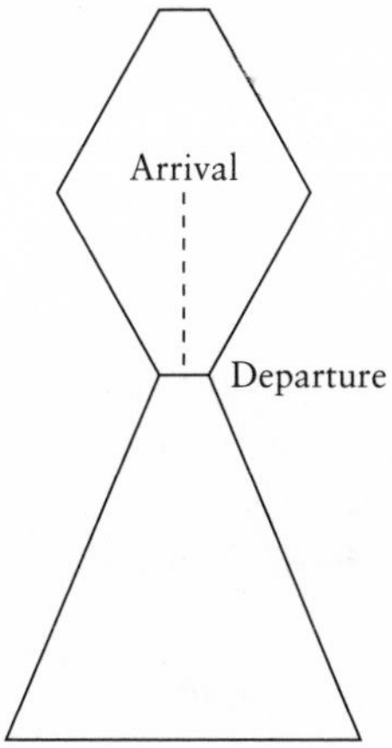

Figure 3

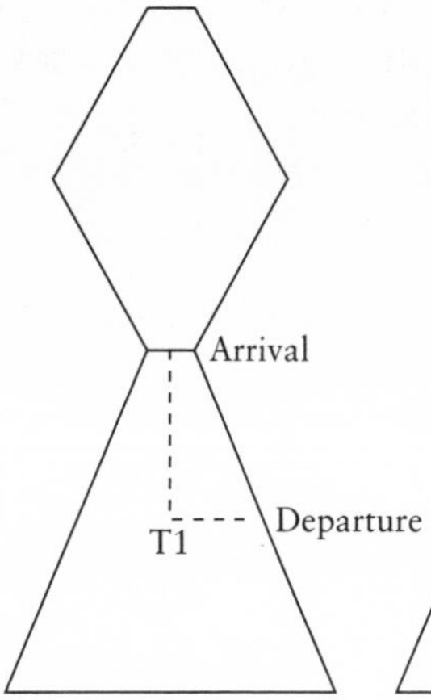

Figure 4

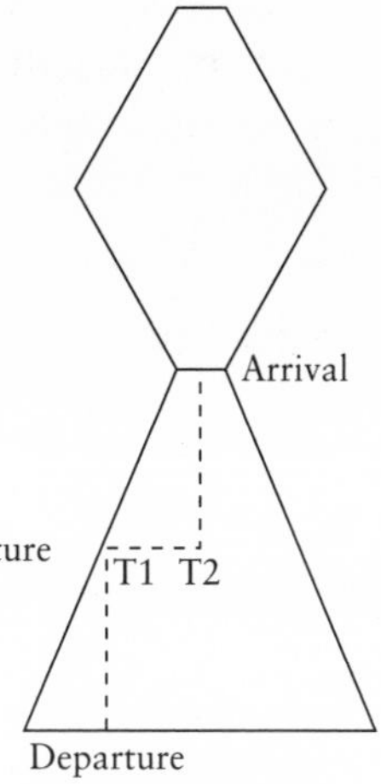

Figure 5

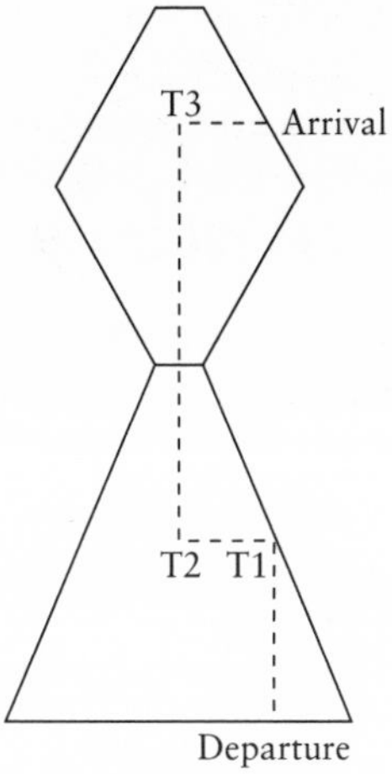

Figure 6

tally to reach the place directly below the new space units and then make one turn before travelling straight up to its destination (figure 4).

Transit with two turns: when the space units of departure are off-centre in the lower region of the cosmos and the soul is travelling to a destination near the centre of the middle region, the shape of the cosmos dictates that it must travel vertically till it touches the vertical border of the lower region, turn and travel horizontally till it is directly below the space units of its destination, turn and travel straight up to its destination (figure 5).

Transit with three turns: when the space units of departure are off-centre in the lower region of the cosmos and the destination is in the higher heavens, the soul travels up till it meets the vertical border of the cosmos, turns and travels horizontally until it is able to turn and continue its journey upwards, then turns again when it is on the plane of the higher region and travels horizontally to the space units directly above its space units of departure (figure 6).

ekasamayo 'vigrahaḥ

2.30 (SS 2.29) The duration of a transit without any turns is one time unit.

One time unit is the smallest indivisible unit of time (see 5.39). A transit without turns, even to the edge of cosmic space, is possible in a single time unit. Transits with one turn take two time units, with two turns take three time units and with three turns take four time units.

ekaṃ dvau vâ-nāhārakaḥ

2.31 The soul in transit remains without nourishment for one or two time units.

ekaṃ dvau trīn vâ-nāhārakaḥ

(SS variant 2.30) The soul in transit remains without nourishment for up to and including three time units.

The soul in transit for one time unit receives nourishment before it leaves and so there is no time unit when it is not nourished. Similarly, when the soul transits for two time units, it receives nourishment in the first time unit before it leaves and in the second time unit when it arrives. However, when the soul transits for three time units (taking two turns), it receives nourishment in the first and third time units in the manner explained above, but there is no nourishment in the second time unit. Similarly, when the soul is in transit for four time units, the second and third time units pass without nourishment.

In the tradition of SS, the maximum number of time units without nourishment is three, because the last time unit in the journey is also without nourishment.

As regards the types of nourishment, according to one tradition, there are three varieties: (1) sap of the parents drawn by the karmic body of the soul while in the womb,[1] (2) nutrients, such as air and water, absorbed through the pores of the skin of the gross (physical) body, and (3) alimental food taken through the mouth of the gross body as solid food and drink.

In the other tradition, six varieties of nourishment are identified as: (1) nourishment from the karmic body, (2) nourishment from material bodies other than the karmic, (3) alimental food, (4) nourishment through pores of the skin, (5) sap drawn in the womb from the parents, (6) nourishment from the mind (*JSK*, I. 285).

In the SS, nourishment is defined as the absorption of clusters of matter suitable for making the gross, protean and conveyance bodies (see 2.37) and the six maturations (the development of the capacity to ingest nourishment, the body, senses, respiration, speech and mind; see SS 8.11).

sammūrchana-garbhô-papātā janma

2.32 (SS 2.31) There are three types of birth: by agglutination of material particles, by the womb and by descent.

Now that the transit from the place of death to the place of the next birth has been explained, this sutra explains the types of birth.

1. The agglutination of material particles is how all beings with one, two, three or four senses are born. Some five-sensed animals and humans are also born this way (see 2.36). As well as this form of asexual reproduction, there is also reproduction in which the sperm and ovum meet outside the parent bodies. Beings born of this method are invertebrate (without a backbone), hermaphrodite (they have both female and male sexual organs) and without a physical mind (without the power of thought). All

[1] This only applies to mammals. In the case of others, the equivalent nourishment is drawn from the material clusters that serve as the birthplace (see 2.33).

insects, worms and animals not born of the womb belong to this class. In this first type of birth, the soul absorbs the material particles that lie at the spot of its birth and uses the power of its karma to convert them into an agglutinated body.

2. Birth in the womb is dependent on a sexual relationship. The soul absorbs the zygote formed by the semen and blood (or ovum) in the womb of the mother and builds it into a gross (physical) body – the foetus.

3. Birth by descent is without parents and with a fully developed body. Infernal beings and gods are born this way, building their bodies out of protean material particles which can change form. The soul of the would-be god goes to a site in heaven covered with a celestial robe which is, in turn, covered with a celestial wrapper. It builds its protean body with the material particles available there. The soul of the would-be infernal being goes to a vessel-like place with a narrow opening in the infernal lands and builds its protean body with the material particles lying there.

The SS explains that the nature of a worldly soul's birth is determined by the fruition of the karma bound to that soul because of its good and bad propensities.

sacitta-śīta-saṃvṛtāḥ setarā miśrāś caikaśas tadyonayaḥ

2.33 (SS 2.32) **The nine main varieties of birth places are: occupied by living things only, cold, covered, occupied by non-living things only, hot, uncovered, occupied by living and non-living things, both hot and cold in part, and both covered and uncovered in part.**

The place of birth is the site the soul reaches after its transit to a new birth. The varieties of birth places listed above describe the three aspects of any birth place: the nature of the substances that occupy it, its temperature, and whether or not it is covered (e.g. in a womb, dwelling or open air). For each aspect there is a choice of opposites or a combination of the two.

According to the SB tradition, the birth places of gods are: occupied by non-living things, both hot and cold in part, covered. The SS differs on the second aspect, saying that the temperature of the gods' birth places is either cold or hot.

The SB tradition describes the birth places of infernal beings as occupied by non-living things, cold or hot or both, covered. Again the SS differs regarding temperatures, saying it is either cold or hot.

The SB tradition describes the birth places of beings born in the womb as occupied by living and non-living things, hot and cold in part, covered and uncovered in part. The SS explains that the birth place is occupied by living and non-living things because the semen and ovum are inanimate while the mother is a living thing.

The birth places of beings with two, three, and four senses and of five-sensed humans and animals not born of the womb are occupied by living things or by non-living things or by both, cold or hot or both in part, uncovered.

The birth places of the fire-bodied variety of immobile beings are occupied by living things or by non-living things or by both, hot, covered.

The birth places of the other four varieties of one-sensed immobile beings, that is the earth-, water-, air- and plant-bodied beings, are occupied by living things or by non-living things or by both, cold or hot or both in part, covered.

The different places of birth described in this sutra are distinguished from the different types of birth. A place of birth is the base, whereas the birth is the act of the soul entering the base. The varieties of places of birth are said to be 8,400,000, distributed, according to the varieties of living things, as follows:

VARIETIES OF LIVING THINGS	NUMBER OF VARIETIES OF PLACES OF BIRTH
1. Beings destined to be sub-microscopic vegetation eternally	700,000
2. Beings destined to be sub-microscopic vegetation temporarily	700,000
3. Earth-bodied beings	700,000
4. Water-bodied beings	700,000
5. Fire-bodied beings	700,000
6. Air-bodied beings	700,000
7. Vegetation	1,000,000
8. Beings with two senses	200,000
Beings with three senses	200,000
Beings with four senses	200,000
9. Celestial beings	400,000
10. Infernal beings	400,000
11. Animals with five senses	400,000
12. Humans	1,400,000
Total	**8,400,000**

However, the basic varieties in (1)–(6) are 350, in (7) they are 500, in (8) they are 300, in (9)–(11) they are 200, and in (12) they are 700. The varieties of 700,000 etc. are arrived at by multiplying the basic varieties in each case by 2000. This figure is the total number of permutations of five colours, two smells, five tastes, eight touches and five shapes, i.e. $5 \times 2 \times 5 \times 8 \times 5 = 2000$. (For the types of colours, etc., see 5.23–5.24.)

jarāyv-aṇḍa-potajānāṃ garbhaḥ

2.34 (SS 2.33) Viviparous and oviparous animals and vertebrates without placenta are born in the womb.

nāraka-devānām upapātaḥ

2.35 (SS 2.34) Infernal beings and gods are born by descent.

The three types of birth mentioned in 2.32 are now related to the species which they govern. These two sutras describe the second and third types.

Viviparous animals, that is vertebrates born with placenta, include humans, cows, buffaloes, goats, etc. The oviparous, or hatched, beings include snakes, lizards, chameleons, tortoises, birds, etc. The vertebrates without placenta include porcupines, elephants, hares, ichneumon, etc.

śeṣāṇāṃ sammūrchanam

2.36 (SS 2.35) All other beings are born by agglutination.

This first type of birth includes the immobile, one-sensed beings (earth-, fire-, water-, air- and plant-bodied), beings with two, three and four senses and the humans and five-sensed animals not born of the womb. The humans born of agglutination originate in human excreta such as faeces, urine, sputum, mucus, vomit, bile, pus, blood, semen, etc. Their lifespan is very short (the tiniest lifespan is 2^8 āvalikās, see appendix 2). The animals of this category are born outside the cosmic region inhabited by humans.

audārika-vaikriyâ-hāraka-taijasa-kārmaṇāni śarīrāṇi

2.37 (SS 2.36) The five types of bodies are gross, protean, conveyance, fiery and karmic.

The description of the soul's birth complete, we now begin the description of the bodies which the soul makes for its life. The five bodies given above are made for different purposes.

1. The gross body is described by the SBT as the visible bulky body made from the suitable class of material clusters (for the eight classes of material clusters, see appendix 5).

2. The protean body is made of clusters of matter with various supernatural powers. The SS describes the supernatural forms the protean body can assume as subtle, huge, light, heavy, able to reach any distance, walk at will, exert lordship, subdue, etc.

3. The conveyance body is made from clusters of matter that are auspicious, white and pure. The SS gives the two purposes of this body as seeking knowledge on subtle problems from the distant omniscient one and avoiding injury, while in transit, to subtle living beings. Such a body is used by an ascetic who is endowed with self-restraint but is not yet free from laxity. To actually acquire such a body, the ascetic must have reached the spiritual stage which is free of laxity.

4. The fiery body is made of fiery particles.[2] It is a permanent possession of the worldly soul. The ordinary function of the fiery body is to digest food for the nourishment of the gross body. But, through certain austerities, it can become capable of transmitting hot rays to burn or cold rays to cool an object at a distance.

5. The karmic body is made from suitable clusters of matter (see appendix 5). It is a sub-type of the body-making karma but at the same time it is the "basket" that holds all the karmic particles of the soul. It is the seed from which all bodies are grown by the soul.

(For further information about the five bodies, see 2.38–2.49.)

paraṃ paraṃ sūkṣmam

2.38 (SS 2.37) The five bodies are progressively finer.

The gross body is composed of thinly assembled clusters of matter (see appendix 5). The protean body contains denser and more numerous clusters of matter. This increase in number and density continues progressively with the conveyance, fiery and karmic bodies. However, the volume of these bodies does not increase.

[2] "Fiery" is the literal rendering of the Sanskrit *taijasa*. The more appropriate rendering, however, would be "electrical" because it can emit cold rays as well as hot.

pradeśato 'saṃkhyeyaguṇaṃ prāk taijasāt

2.39 (SS 2.38) The protean body contains innumerable times the clusters of matter in the gross body and the conveyance body contains innumerable times those in the protean body.

anantaguṇe pare

2.40 (SS 2.39) The karmic body contains infinite times the infinite number of material clusters in the fiery body.

These two sutras explain the increasing density of the five bodies. The number of material clusters in the fiery body is infinite times the number in the conveyance body.

The SS likens the dense and less dense bodies to the difference between a ball of iron and bundle of cotton.

apratighāte

2.41 (SS 2.40) The last two types of body travel unobstructed.

This sutra begins the explanation of the distinguishing characteristics of the fiery and karmic bodies. When two gross bodies meet there is collision but when two subtle bodies meet or when a subtle body meets a gross body, it is like fire meeting an iron ball; there is no collision. Since both the fiery and the karmic bodies are subtle, there is nothing to prevent them co-existing in the same soul. The movement of subtle bodies is obstructed only when they reach the border of the cosmos because beyond the border there is neither the medium of motion nor the medium of rest (see 5.1, 5.17).

anādisambandhe ca

2.42 (SS 2.41) And they have been associated with the soul since beginningless time.

The association of the fiery and karmic bodies with the soul has no beginning in the sense that they are never absent from the soul during its worldly existence. However, the fiery and karmic bodies are changing from moment to moment and so do have a beginning in the sense that they are constantly becoming something new. Each continues to exist in a sequence of mutual cause and effect, just as tree follows seed and seed follows tree in an ongoing cycle.

Unlike fiery and karmic bodies, the gross, protean and conveyance bodies are only occasional and not continual properties of the soul.

sarvasya

2.43 (SS 2.42) **All worldly souls have these two types of body.**

There is some controversy about the beginningless association of these two bodies with the soul. It is noted in the SB that some teachers held that only the karmic body is associated with the soul since beginningless time. According to them, the acquisition of the fiery body depended on the practice of specific austerities. Successful practitioners acquired the power to emit cooling and burning rays as a form, respectively, of favour and curse. However, later authors were generally agreed about the beginningless co-existence of karmic and fiery bodies.

The double role of the fiery body to digest food and, following the practice of appropriate austerities, to emit burning and cooling rays across a distance, has led scholars to interpret the fiery body and the fiery power as two independent entities, though, in fact, the latter is only an attribute of the former.

tadādīni bhājyāni yugapad ekasyācaturbhyaḥ

2.44 (SS 2.43) **Including the fiery and karmic bodies, which are necessarily co-existent with the soul, up to four bodies can be simultaneously available to a worldly soul.**

According to those who affirm the necessary co-existence of the karmic and fiery bodies, five combinations can be present simultaneously in the worldly soul:

1. fiery and karmic
2. fiery, karmic and gross
3. fiery, karmic and protean
4. fiery, karmic, gross and protean
5. fiery, karmic, gross and conveyance

According to those who accept that only the karmic body is associated with the soul from beginningless time, the possible combinations are eight:

1. karmic body alone
2. karmic and fiery (this is rejected by SBT)
3. karmic and gross
4. karmic and protean

5. karmic, gross and protean
6. karmic, gross and conveyance
7. karmic, fiery, gross and protean
8. karmic, fiery and gross (variant reading adds conveyance)

The combination of all the five bodies is not possible because the protean and the conveyance cannot co-exist; these two bodies are acquired through the practice of two different kinds of austerities by ascetics possessing specific qualifications. The bodies can be acquired in succession, but they cannot be activated at the same time.

nirupabhogam antyam

2.45 (SS 2.44) The last type of body, the karmic, cannot serve the purpose of pleasure or pain.

The purposes served by each body, touched upon in 2.37, are now explained further.

The karmic body cannot produce pleasure or pain on its own. These must be experienced through the operation of the senses and/or the mind. Moreover, the karmic body cannot bind fresh karma or eliminate or suppress past karma. These services are provided by all the other bodies with the exception of the fiery body. Although the karmic body cannot serve any of these purposes or those listed below, it is the underlying cause for all the instruments of suffering and enjoyment.

The fiery body is, like the karmic body, unable to bind, suppress or eliminate karma but, unlike the karmic body, it is unable to set up any activity in the soul. (It provides "the fire", that is, the energy for the activity of the other bodies.)

The gross body of a human or subhuman (animals and plants, etc.) experiences pleasure and pain through the physical mind and/or senses. (For gods and infernals, who do not have a gross body, the protean body serves this purpose.)

The conveyance body helps the soul reach the Jina (omniscient religious founder) when it is seeking information.

The protean body enables gods, infernals, some animals and also ascetics, to assume different shapes. For the gods and infernals, it is also the medium through which they experience pleasure and pain.

garbha-sammūrchanajam ādyam

2.46 (SS 2.45) The first body, the gross body, is formed in the womb or by agglutination.

vaikriyam aupapātikam

2.47 (SS 2.46) The protean body is formed at birth by descent.

labdhipratyayaṃ ca

2.48 (SS 2.47) The protean body can also be created by the power potential acquired through practising special austerities.

These sutras begin the explanation of the origins and nature of the five types of body.

The protean body, produced through the power potential of humans and animals born of the womb who have undergone the necessary austerities, is superior to the protean body of the infernals and gods produced as their body of birth. Air-bodied beings also have the power potential needed for a protean body but this is not acquired by austerities; their gross body has this power potential in-born.

TRANSLATOR'S NOTE

Power potential is the capacity for action, from the mundane doings of daily life to supernatural acts such as hurling fire, emanating rays and creating protean bodies.

taijasam api

(SS only 2.48) The fiery body is also produced by the power potential.

The commentators all agree that the karmic body is a permanent possession of the soul until its liberation whereas the gross, protean and conveyance bodies are generated by the power potential of the soul. However, there is uncertainty over whether or not the fiery body is permanent (see 2.44). The SS says that there are two permanent bodies, the karmic and the fiery, but there is a second fiery body that can be produced by power potential. The SBT says that both karmic and fiery bodies are permanent but the power of the latter is activated by power potential. The SB does not consider the fiery body permanent in the way the karmic body is. It explains that the fiery body in all living things results from specific austerities. In 2.49, it affirms this sutra to the extent that the fiery body may be due to the power potential.

śubhaṃ viśuddham avyāghāti cāhārakaṃ caturdaśa-pūrvadhara eva

2.49 (not SS) **The conveyance body is made of auspicious, pure, non-obstructive and non-obstructed matter. It can be created only by a learned ascetic conversant with the fourteen books of the early literature.**

śubhaṃ viśuddham avyāghāti cāhārakaṃ pramattasaṃyatasyaiva

(**SS variant 2.49**) **The conveyance body is made of auspicious, pure, non-obstructive and non-obstructed matter. Only an ascetic who is self-restrained but prone to laxity uses this body.**

The conveyance body is used by a learned ascetic to enable him to approach the Jina to shed light on difficult scriptural questions. However, the description of the ascetic in the SS variant as "prone to laxity" suggests that the desire to use the conveyance body is a sort of greed which is detrimental to spirituality. An ascetic enjoying freedom from such greed would not use this body.

Unlike other bodies, the conveyance body is very short-lived. When the ascetic has any doubt in his mind about the meaning of a very difficult and obscure issue of the doctrine, he uses the conveyance body, expands his soul into this subtle body, reaches the distant Jina instantly and withdraws to the gross body within an intra-hour (less than forty-eight minutes). The conveyance body is abandoned as soon as the mission is completed.

The expression "auspicious matter" in the sutra means that the clusters of matter that constitute the conveyance body are pleasant in colour, odour, touch and taste and that they produce merit. "Pure matter" implies that the clusters are transparent, shiny and conducive to harmless conduct. "Unobstructive and unobstructed matter" signifies that these clusters have free unimpeded movement to the destination.

The SB also introduces a discussion of the origin of various bodies. The fiery body, like the conveyance body, can also be created as a power potential. The karmic body is its own cause and also the cause of all other bodies in the same way that the sun illuminates both itself and also all other objects.

The SB details the ability of the protean body to take different shapes. It can become one and many; it can be as small as the innumerablth[3] part of a

[3] For a brief explanation of the Jaina numerical system, see 1.8, and for further details, see appendix 1.

finger and as big as a mountain; it can be visible and invisible; it can be terrestrial and aerial; it can be resistant and non-resistant; it can create all forms and shapes simultaneously.

Regarding size, the gross body can somewhat exceed 1000 yojanas in length, the protean body can somewhat exceed 100,000 yojanas, the conveyance is one cubit, the fiery and karmic can be as big as cosmic space.

Regarding duration, the gross body lasts at least one intra-hour, and up to three pit-measured units of time (see appendix 2). The conveyance body lasts an intra-hour. The fiery and karmic bodies are eternal possessions of the worldly soul.

nāraka-sammūrcchino napuṃsakāni

2.50 The infernals and beings born by agglutination are necessarily hermaphroditic.

na devāḥ

2.51 The gods are never hermaphroditic.

śeṣās trivedāḥ

(SS only 2.52) The other varieties of living beings have one of the three genders.

Having described the five possible types of body of worldly beings, the author now begins the description of the possible genders.

Two aspects of gender need to be distinguished: physical sex and sexual disposition. Whereas the physical sex refers to the sexual organ, the sexual disposition refers to an emotional attitude irrespective of the anatomy. There are three kinds of physical sex and of sexual disposition: female, male and hermaphroditic (see 2.6, 8.10). The physical sex and sexual disposition may not be correlate.

According to the doctrine of karma, the body-making karma determines the physical sex, while the rise of the quasi-passions of the conduct-deluding karma determines the sexual disposition. The hermaphroditic sexual organ is caused by the inauspicious body-making karma and the male and female sexual organs by the auspicious body-making karma.

The infernal beings and all those born by agglutination, that is, the one-sensed beings (earth-, fire-, water-, air- and plant-bodied), those with two, three and four senses, and "humans and animals not born of the womb", are all hermaphroditic. All worldly souls up to the ninth stage of spiritual development are of male, female or hermaphroditic sexual disposition. In the tenth to fourteenth stages of spiritual development, there is no disposition (for the fourteen stages of spiritual development, see appendix 4).

The vertebrates born with placenta (viviparous) or without placenta and the beings which hatch from an egg (oviparous) may be female, male or hermaphroditic.

Each of the four classes of gods are either female or male. According to the SBT, the mansion, sylvan and luminous gods and the empyrean gods dwelling in Saudharma and Aiśāna, the first and second heavens (see 4.1, 4.20), are of either female or male disposition. Higher gods than these are always of male disposition. As the levels of celestial life become higher because of greater spiritual attainment in previous lives, there is a gradual sublimation of sexual disposition.

aupapātika-caramadehô-ttamapuruṣâ-saṃkhyeyavarṣāyuṣo 'napavartyāyuṣaḥ

2.52 (not SS) **The lifespans of beings who are born by descent, destined to attain liberation in their current life, very noble, or destined to live for innumerable years, cannot be ended prematurely.**

aupapādika-caramottamadehâ-saṃkhyeyavarṣāyuṣo 'napavartyāyuṣaḥ

(SS variant 2.53) **The lifespans of beings who are born by descent, destined to attain liberation in their current noble life, or destined to live for innumerable years, cannot be ended prematurely.**[4]

Now the lifespan of worldly beings is addressed, with specific reference to those whose allotted lifespan cannot be prematurely curtailed. The beings born by descent are the infernals and gods. There are sixty-three very noble beings: twenty-four spiritual ford-makers, twelve supreme lords, nine lords, nine brothers of the lords and nine rivals of the lords. Beings destined to live for innumerable years are found among the human and animal populations.

[4] The SS gives this reading that integrates the second and third clauses of the sutra but it also recognizes the SB reading as an ancient variant

The lifespan of other beings can be ended prematurely by poison or contact with poisonous objects, weapons, emotional impulses, distress, accident, and suffocation. The SB explains that the fulfilment of the lifespan-determining karma is merely hastened in the cases of premature death by poison, weapons, etc. Although made to produce its effect early, the power of the karma remains intact.

The SB introduces the idea that the lifespan karma for a soul's current life is bound to the soul at particular moments in its previous life. Karma that was loosely bound is vulnerable to premature termination; karma that was closely bound is invulnerable to premature termination. The SB compares the closely bound karma of an invulnerable lifespan to the closely pressed bale of dry hay that, when ignited, burns slowly and gradually part by part. The loosely bound karma of the vulnerable lifespan is like a loosely bound bundle that burns quickly, fanned by the wind.

A soul involuntarily reduces its lifespan through agony and fear of death. The soul's angst instigates a process in which it expands its own space units beyond the gross body, thereby reducing the length of the lifespan-determining karma. This accelerates its experience of the full fruits of its past good and bad karma. The illustration given is of the soul being like a wet cloth which, when fully spread out and exposed to the elements of sun and wind, dries more quickly than a tightly folded cloth kept in a shaded place.

Even lifespans that are not vulnerable to premature termination may be vulnerable to trouble and pain, though not fatally so. Others are invulnerable to such things.

CHAPTER THREE

The Lower and Middle Regions

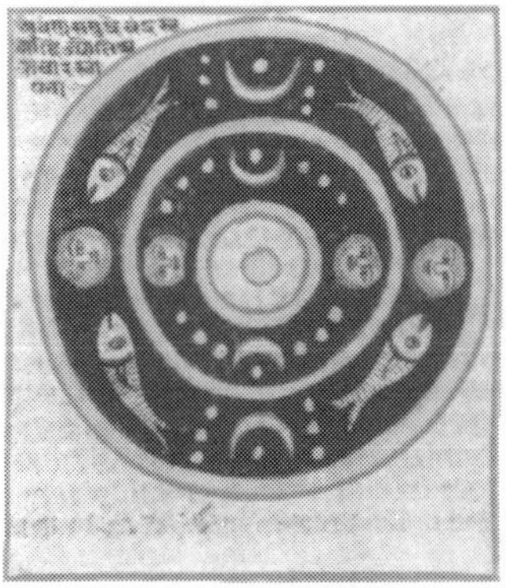

Contents

The Cosmic Dimension and the Seven Hells

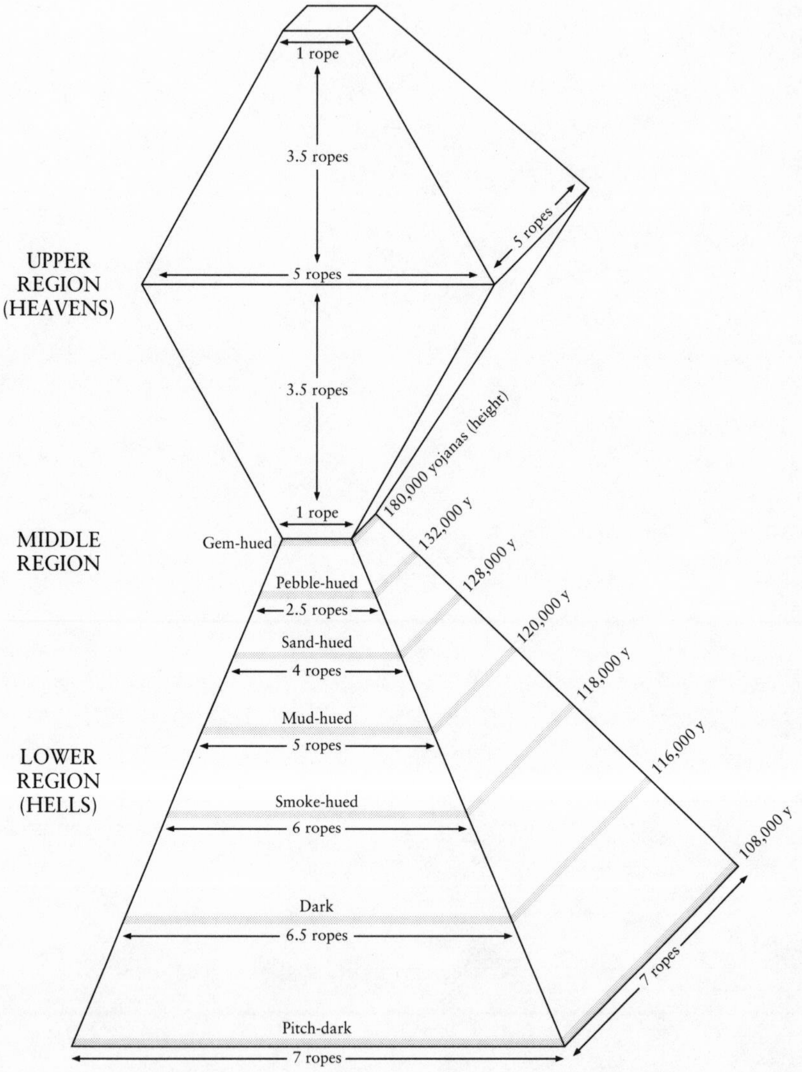

Figure 7

Having described the essential nature of the soul in the previous chapter, the author now explains the various births the soul can take in the lower and middle regions of the cosmos.

ratna-śarkarā-vālukā-paṅka-dhūma-tamo-mahātamaḥprabhā bhūmayo ghanāmbu-vātâ-kāśa-pratiṣṭśhāḥ saptâdhodhaḥ (pṛthutarāḥ)

3.1 The infernal beings live in seven lands which are one below the other (with each lower land having a wider base than the one above).[1] From top to bottom, these lands are the gem-hued, pebble-hued, sand-hued, mud-hued, smoke-hued, dark and pitch-dark lands. Each land floats on a dense ocean which floats on a layer of dense air which floats on a layer of thin air which floats on self-supporting space.

We begin with the description of the infernal lands in the lower half of the cosmos.

The cosmos is shaped like a human standing with legs apart and palms resting on his waist (see figure 7, p. 68) and is therefore known as "the cosmic person". It is also compared to three vases stacked on top of each other with the bottom and top vases turned upside-down. The cosmos is four-sided with a base that is 7 × 7 = 49 square *rajjus* or ropes (an astrophysical unit of measurement, see appendix 3). Gods reside in the upper section, or "vase", of the cosmos, humans and animals in the middle section and infernal beings in the seven lands of the lower section. Each infernal land is named after the dominant colouring of its environment: precious gems, pebbles, sand, mud, smoke, darkness and intense darkness (see figure 7, p. 68).

According to the SBT, the respective width of each infernal land from the highest to the lowest is 1, 2.5, 4, 5, 6, 6.5 and 7 ropes. The respective

[1] In the SS tradition, this sutra does not include *pṛthutarāḥ*, translated as "with each lower land having a wider base than the one above".

depths of the infernal lands from the highest to the lowest are 180,000, 132,000, 128,000, 120,000, 118,000, 116,000, 108,000 yojanas. (A yojana is a unit of terrestrial measurement equal to 9.09 miles, see appendix 3.) In the SS tradition, these depths are 180,000, 32,000, 28,000, 24,000, 20,000, 16,000, 8,000 yojanas, respectively.

The lands are divided by huge gaps occupied by layers of dense ocean, dense air, thin air and space. The dense ocean between each land is 20,000 yojanas deep, but the layers of dense and thin air and of space increase, the further down the cosmos they are, so that the deepest layers are above the seventh infernal land. None of the air and space layers are less than innumerable yojanas deep. (For the concept of numbers, see appendix 1.) In the SS tradition, the layers of dense ocean, dense air and thin air are each 20,000 yojanas deep.

The SBT, following the scriptures, explains the ocean floating on air with an example of a balloon which can be (1) inflated with air and tied at its neck, (2) tied tightly with a cord in the middle, (3) untied at the neck so the upper portion is emptied of air and then (4) filled with water, (5) retied at the neck and (6) untied in the middle. At the end of this process, the water in the balloon will be floating on the air in it.

tāsu narakāḥ

3.2 The dwelling places of the infernal beings are within those lands.

Infernal beings inhabit all of the infernal lands except for the top 1000 yojanas and the bottom 1000 yojanas of each. According to the SB, the number of strata and the dwelling places in the infernal lands are as follows:

INFERNAL LAND	NUMBER OF STRATA	NUMBER OF DWELLING PLACES
Gem-hued	13	3,000,000
Pebble-hued	11	2,500,000
Sand-hued	9	1,500,000
Mud-hued	7	1,000,000
Smoke-hued	5	300,000
Dark	3	99,995
Pitch-dark	1	5

nityâ-śubhatara-leśyā-pariṇāma-deha-vedanā-vikriyāḥ

3.3 The infernal beings in those lands are constantly subject to

increasingly inauspicious colouring, poor metabolism, ugly bodies, horrible experiences and awful shapes, all of which multiply their miseries.

The miserable lives of the infernal beings are now described.

There are two types of colouring. Physical colouring is a type of body-making karma (that is, it affects the body) and is a product of the soul's mental, vocal and physical activity and its passions in past lives. Physical colouring is assumed at birth and continues till death. The second colouring, psychic colouring, is a transformation of the soul itself and is due to its current passions and activities. Psychic colouring changes all the time. It is the colour index of the soul and is revealed in its aura (colouring of the space around the body).

There are six colourings. The first three, black, blue and grey, are inauspicious; the second three, fiery (red), filament-coloured (yellow) and white, are auspicious. The infernal beings always feature inauspicious colourings: black, blue or grey. This is determined by the land of their birth which also determines their species. From the first infernal land at the top to the seventh at the bottom, the respective colourings of the inhabitants are pure grey, greyish, grey and blue, pure blue, blue and black, pure black, blackish. Throughout its long life in hell, an infernal being is never without such colouring. Generally, no worldly soul is ever bereft of colouring, auspicious or inauspicious.

The physical make-up of the infernals – their gait, shape, colour, smell, taste, touch and sound – is perpetually disagreeable. They have a cruel, pitiable and fearful appearance and become increasingly ugly and hefty in the succeeding hells. They are in darkness at all times and surrounded by streams of bad humours like mucus, urine, faeces, blood, flesh, fat and pus. The infernal lands resemble cemeteries strewn with the rotten flesh, hair, bone, skin, teeth and nails of corpses. There is the foul smell of dead bodies of dogs, jackals, cats, mongooses, snakes, mice, elephants, horses, cows and humans. There is constant weeping and wailing from all the miserable creatures seeking relief from their sufferings. They use their protean bodies to assume different shapes in the hope of escaping their suffering, but they multiply it instead.

The sufferings become increasingly horrible in the succeeding hells. The gruelling heat increases gradually from the first to its maximum in the third hell. In the fourth hell, there is extreme cold in one small area with the rest at the maximum temperature. In the fifth hell, the reverse applies, intense heat in a small area and the rest intensely cold. In the sixth hell it is extremely cold and in the seventh colder still.

The SS has a slightly different version: heat continues up to the fourth hell. In the fifth, there is heat in a large part of the upper region and cold in the small part of the lower region. In the sixth and seventh hell, there is cold only.

parasparodīrita-duḥkhāḥ

3.4 They inflict pain on one another.

The sources of the infernal beings' suffering are twofold: their conspicuous enmity towards each other and their nightmarish physical surroundings. In the extreme cold and heat, they all suffer from insatiable hunger and thirst. They wish to devour everything and drink the oceans dry but their environment prevents any satisfaction of their desires.

The infernals possess the power of clairvoyance, but this clairvoyance is deluded by their perverse outlook that perceives objects and events topsy-turvy. They can perceive remote objects but only those that frighten and cause pain. They harbour mutual hostilities like that between the crow and the owl or the snake and the mongoose. They assume frightful shapes and will fight with any lethal weapon that they create *ad hoc* out of earth – sharp nail, rock, sword, mace, hatchet, axe, spear, pike, javelin, crow-bar and also with their bare hands, feet and teeth. They fight constantly, shouting and inflicting unbearable pain on one another, creating an environment resembling a slaughterhouse.

saṃkliṣṭâ-surodīritaduḥkhāś ca prāk caturthyāḥ

3.5 The inhabitants of the first three infernal lands are tortured by the mansion-dwelling gods of evil thoughts and deeds.

Because of their past evil deeds, the infernal beings are born to a life of damnation. They suffer three types of agony: the ghastly environs, the vengeance which they inflict upon one another, and the gods of evil thoughts and deeds who revel in inciting the infernal beings to torture one another. According to the SBT, these three agonies prevail up to the third hell. The lower hells have only the first two agonies as the gods have no access to these hells.

There are fifteen classes of the demonic gods, who are born among the mansion-dwelling deities (see 4.1) because of their deluded world-view and predilection for wicked acts in past lives which led them to perform misguided austerities and to unwittingly expel beneficial karma. These demonic gods do not know the misfortune that awaits them but take pride in their status, considering themselves the luckiest of all creatures. By nature, they are sadists who find pleasure in devising torments for the infernal beings. They force them to drink molten iron, embrace red-hot iron pillars, climb up and down thorny trees. They strike them with hammers, attack them with hatchets and knives, sprinkle boiling oil on them, fry them in pans, bake them in ovens, drown them in the hellish streams, crush them in grinders. Since the lifespans of the infernal beings cannot be shortened, their agonies are unremitting.

The SB compares these gods to humans overwhelmed with lust and hate who delight in heinous crimes such as instigating fatal fights between cows, bulls, buffaloes, pigs, sheep, cocks and boxers. They squandered good karma in former lifetimes which offered them opportunity for better, more wholesome pastimes. They undertook austerities motivated by impious and immoral ambitions. Because the austerities were performed in a state of deceit, greed for karmic rewards, deluded world-view (8.1), strong passion and denial of their evil motives, they generated karma which was apparently beneficial but had a sting in the tail.

TRANSLATOR'S NOTE

Austerities differ from religion to religion. It is not the nature of the austerity so much as the nature of its motivation that determines its benefits. Austerities are misguided when they are motivated by passion rather than faith.

teṣv eka-tri-sapta-daśa-saptadaśa-dvāviṃśati-trayastriṃśat-sāgaropamāḥ sattvānāṃ parā sthitiḥ

3.6 The maximum lifespans of the beings in the seven infernal lands are respectively one, three, seven, ten, seventeen, twenty-two and thirty-three ocean-measured periods.

The lifespans of infernal beings, like those of gods, cannot be counted in ordinary numerical figures; they are calculated in ocean-measured periods (see appendix 2).

Souls are born in hells according to their karma and the nature of the species to which they belonged in the immediately previous life, as shown below:

SPECIES	HELLS OF BIRTH	
1. all non-rational five-sensed animals	1st	(gem-hued)
2. reptiles with legs (rational, five-sensed)	1st–2nd	(down to pebble-hued)
3. birds (rational, five-sensed)	1st–3rd	(down to sand-hued)
4. rational, five-sensed land animals (e.g. lions)	1st–4th	(down to mud-hued)
5. legless reptiles (rational, five-sensed)	1st–5th	(down to smoke-hued)
6. female humans	1st–6th	(down to dark)
7. male humans and five-sensed, rational aquatic animals (fish, crocodiles)	1st-7th	(down to pitch-dark)

The gods and infernal beings cannot be immediately re-born in hells because they are not capable of the virulent aggression and excessive possessiveness which cause birth in infernal regions (see below, translator's note). Nor can the infernal beings be re-born in heavens; they are not capable of the self-restraint, austerity, etc. which cause birth in the heavens (see 6.20). After completing their lives in the infernal lands, souls are born either as subhumans (animals, plants etc.) or human beings. In this next life, those from all seven hells are capable of attaining the enlightened world-view; those from the first six hells are capable of partial restraint (as householders); those from the first five hells are capable of self-restraint (as monks/nuns); those from the first four hells are capable of attaining liberation; and those from the first three hells who are re-born as humans can attain the status of a Jina (religious founder).

As regards flora and fauna and inhabitants of the hells, there are islands, oceans, mountains, rivers, lakes, villages, towns, sea ports, plants, trees, grass, animals, men and gods in the upper part of the first hell which is in the middle region of the cosmos. But these do not actually belong to hell. A soul can be born as a god in this part of the first hell but in no other part of hell. Such a soul can travel only down as far as the third hell. It is a resident of hell, but not a native. However, there are some exceptions to entering the lower hells; the most demonic gods (3.5) may sometimes go there and when an omniscient soul expands all its space units, it permeates all the hells. Moreover, people from the middle region, who have the power to create a protean body, can also enter all the hells to visit a friend from a previous life.

The SB explains that the two substances, the medium of motion and the medium of rest (5.13, 5.17), sustain the stability of the cosmos. It is they which give it its particular shape resembling a pyramid at the bottom, a cymbal in the middle and a drum placed at the top (3.1).[1]

TRANSLATOR'S NOTE

Jaina philosophy says that the human, and particularly the male human's, capacity for good and bad is more extreme than with any other being. A demon or god is not capable of such a wide range of behaviour. The sexuality of women limits them more than men.

jambūdvīpa-lavaṇādayaḥ śubhanāmāno dvīpa-samudrāḥ

3.7 There are islands and oceans that bear propitious names such as Jambū Island, Lavaṅa Ocean and so on.

dvirdvirviṣkambhāḥ pūrva-pūrva-parikṣepiṇo valayākṛtayaḥ

3.8 The islands and oceans are concentric rings, the succeeding ring being double the preceding one in breadth.

tanmadhye merunābhir vṛtto yojanśatasahasra-viṣkambho jambūdvīpaḥ

3.9 At the centre of these island and oceans is the round island of Jambū with a diameter of 100,000 yojanas and Mount Meru at its navel.

Having described the lands of the lower region, the author now describes the lands of the middle region.

Jambū is an island, as perfectly round as a potter's wheel, at the centre of the middle region of the cosmos. The diameter of the island is 100,000 yojanas (909,000 miles). Mount Meru, in the middle of the island, is 100,000 yojanas high with 1000 of these yojanas below the surface of the earth. From its position in the dead centre of the cosmos, the base of Mount Meru touches the top of the first infernal land and its peak touches the bottom of the celestial region above.

Jambū is ringed by the Lavaṇa Ocean (Salt Ocean) which is twice as wide as Jambū. The Lavaṇa Ocean is ringed by Dhātakīkhaṇḍa Island which is twice as wide as the Lavaṇa (see figure 8, p. 76). Dhātakīkhaṇḍa is ringed by the Kāla Ocean which is twice as wide as Dhātakīkhaṇḍa. This pattern continues with Puṣkara Island, the Puṣkara Ocean, Varuṇavara

[2] The reference to the cymbal has caused some speculation that the various regions may be circular rather than square.

The Islands and Oceans of the Middle Region

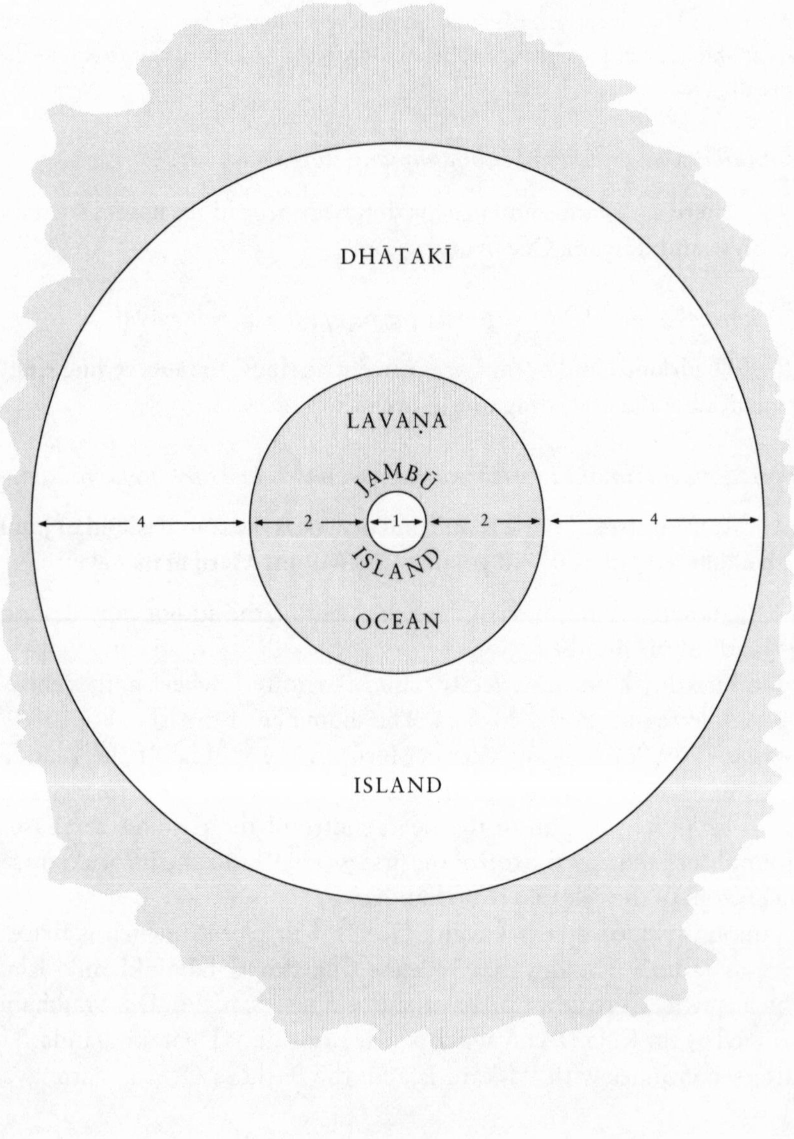

Figure 8

Island, the Varuṇa Ocean, Kṣīra Island, the Kṣīra Ocean, etc. up to the Svayambhūramaṇa Ocean which rings the last island of the same name. There are innumerable islands and oceans.

tatra bharata-haimavata-hari-videha-ramyaka-hairaṇyavatai-rāvatavarṣāḥ kṣetrāṇi

3.10 There are seven continents on Jambū Island: Bharata, Haimavata, Hari, Videha, Ramyaka, Hairaṇyavata and Airāvata.

We begin the description of Jambū with its seven continents. Bharata is the southernmost continent of Jambū. The continent of Haimavata is to the north with Hari further north and so on to Airāvata which is northernmost (see figure 9, p. 78).

Although Mount Meru is in the centre, it is to the north of all the continents. This apparent anomaly has been explained in the SBT by pointing out that what is to the east for the inhabitants of Bharata continent is to the west for the inhabitants of the eastern part of the fourth continent, Videha. It follows from this that according to ancient Jaina geographers, Jambū is not a flat circular plate but a sphere.

The SB also mentions a rectangular space, consituted by eight space units in the centre of cosmic space, that determines geographical directions independently of the sun.

tadvibhājinaḥ pūrvāparāyatā himavan-mahāhimavan-niṣadha-nīla-rukmi-śikhariṇo varṣadharaparvatāḥ

3.11 The six mountains that extend from east to west and divide the seven continents are Himavan, Mahāhimavan, Niṣadha, Nīla, Rukmin and Śikharin.

The SB details the locations and dimensions of the seven continents of Jambū and the six mountains which divide them. (For these details, see SS 3.32.)

hemâ-rjuna-tapanīya-vaiḍūrya-rajata-hemamayāḥ

(SS 3.12) The mountains are, respectively, as golden as Chinese silk, as white as the Arjuna tree, as crimson as the rising sun, as blue as sapphire, as white as silver, as golden as Chinese silk.

This sutra begins the twenty-one additional sutras in the SS which describe

The Continents and Mountains of Jambū

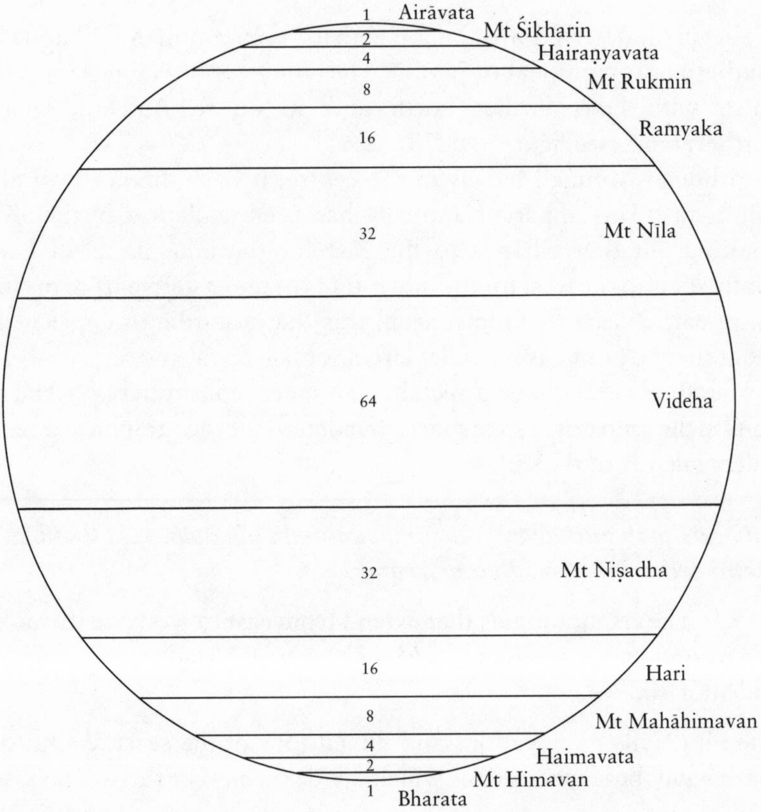

Figure 9

the colours of the mountains and their mineral wealth, as also the lakes, rivers, gardens, and so on with their locations and dimensions. These sutras also include an account of the inhabitants of these areas and the concept of time cycles.

maṇvicitrapārśvā upari mūle ca tulyavistārāḥ

(SS 3.13) **The sides of these mountains are spotted with variegated jewels and their peaks are of equal dimensions, as are their middles and bases.**

padma-mahāpadma-tigiñcha-kesarī-mahāpuṇḍarīkā-puṇḍarikā hradās teṣām upari

(SS 3.14) **On the mountaintops are the lakes Padma, Mahāpadma, Tigiñcha, Kesarī, Mahāpuṇḍarīka and Puṇḍarīka.**

prathamo yojanasahasrāyāmas tadardhaviṣkambho hradaḥ

(SS 3.15) **The first lake is 1000 yojanas east to west and 500 yojanas north to south.**

daśayojanāvagāhaḥ

(SS 3.16) **It is ten yojanas deep.**

tanmadhye yojanaṃ puṣkaram

(SS 3.17) **In the middle of this lake, there is a lotus with a spread of one yojana.**

taddviguṇadviguṇā hradāḥ puṣkarāṇi ca

(SS 3.18) **The length, width and depth of the lakes and the size of the lotuses in the other mountains are progressively double.**

tannivāsinyo devyaḥ śrī-hrī-dhṛti-kīrti-buddhi-lakṣmyaḥ palyopamasthitayaḥ sasāmānika-pāriṣatkāḥ

(SS 3.19) **The nymphs residing in palaces on the lotuses are Śrī (Fortune), Hrī (Modesty), Dhṛti (Patience), Kīrti (Fame), Buddhi (Wisdom) and Lakṣmī (Wealth). Their lifespan is measured in**

pit-measured periods. Their companions are the co-chief and counsellor gods.

gaṃgā-sindhu-rohid-rohitāsyā-harid-harikāntā-sītā-sītodā-nārī-narakāntā-suvarṇa-rūpyakūlā-raktā-raktodāḥ saritas tanmadhyagāḥ

(SS 3.20) **The rivers flowing across the continents are Gaṃgā, Sindhu, Rohit, Rohitāsyā, Harit, Harikāntā, Sītā' Sītodā, Nārī, Narakāntā, Suvarṇakūlā, Rūpyakūlā, Raktā and Raktodā.**

dvayor dvayoḥ pūrvāḥ pūrvagāḥ

(SS 3.21) **Of these fourteen rivers, every odd-numbered one flows to the eastern ocean.**

śeṣās tv aparagāḥ

(SS 3.22) **The others flow to the western ocean.**

Of the rivers mentioned above, the Gaṃgā (Ganges) rises from Lake Padma and passes through the eastern archway. The Sindhu (Indus) passes through the western archway. The Rohitāsyā passes through the northern archway. The Rohit rises from Lake Mahāpadma and passes through the southern archway. The Harikāntā passes through the northern archway. The Harit rises from Lake Tigiñcha and passes through the sourthern archway. The Sītodā passes through the northern archway. The Sītā rises from Lake Kesarī and passes through the southern archway. The Narakāntā passes through the northern archway. The Nārī rises from Lake Mahāpuṇḍarīka and passes through the southern archway. The Rūpyakūlā passes through the northern archway. The Suvarṇakūlā rises from Lake Puṇḍarīka and passes through the southern archway. The Raktā passes through the eastern archway. The Raktodā passes through the western archway.

caturdaśa-nadīsahasra-parivṛtā gaṃgā-sindhvâ dayo nadyaḥ

(SS 3.23) **The Gaṃgā, Sindhu and other rivers are joined by 14,000 tributaries.**

There are 14,000 tributaries of each of the rivers Gaṃgā and Sindhu in the continent of Bharata. For these rivers in the other continents, the number of tributaries doubles progressively up to the continent of Videha and then reduces by half regressively till the last continent.

bharataḥ ṣaḍviñśa-paṃcayojanaśata-vistāraḥ ṣaṭ caikonaviṃśatibhāgā yojanasya

(SS 3.24) **The continent of Bharata is 526 6/19 yojanas wide.**

taddviguṇa-dviguṇa-vistārā varṣadharavarṣā videhāntāḥ

(SS 3.25) **The mountains and continents double in width progressively up to the continent of Videha.**

uttarā dakṣiṇatulyāḥ

(SS 3.26) **The continents and mountains in the north beginning from the continent of Airāvata up to Mount Nīla are like the southern ones beginning from the continent of Bharata.**

bharatai-rāvatayor vṛddhi-hrāsau ṣaṭsamayābhyām utsarpiṇy-avasarpiṇībhyām

(SS 3.27) **During their time cycles of six ascending and six descending aeons, the continents of Bharata and Airāvata experience periods of prosperity and decline.**

Having completed its description of the geographical dimensions and conditions of the seven continents of Jambū, the SS now begins a description of the temporal dimensions and conditions.

The cycles of prosperity and suffering peculiar to Bharata and Airāvata affect the lifespan, height (number of spinal joints), pleasures and pains, morality, spirituality, and so on, of the human inhabitants of these continents. In the descending half of the cycle, a state of supreme plenty gradually dwindles to a state of extreme privation through the six aeons of:

1. supreme plenty
2. plenty
3. plenty-with-privation
4. privation-with-plenty
5. privation
6. extreme privation.

In the ascending half of the cycle, these aeons reverse as the state of extreme privation is gradually replaced by supreme plenty.

The ascending and descending semi-cycles are each 10^{15} ocean-measured periods. Together they constitute a kalpa or full time cycle. The aeon of supreme plenty is 400×10^{12} ocean-measured periods. At the start of this aeon, the humans in the two continents of Bharata and Airāvata enjoy unlimited luxury on a par with that enjoyed by the humans in the land of North Kuru in the continent of Videha. By the start of the aeon of plenty, which lasts for 300×10^{12} ocean-measured periods (for time units, see appendix 2), they are enjoying the state that prevails in the continent of Harivarṣa. By the start of the aeon of plenty-with-privation, which lasts for 200×10^{12} ocean-measured periods, their pleasures are equal to those of the continent of Haimavata. By the start of the aeon of privation-with-plenty, which lasts for 100×10^{12} ocean-measured periods less 42,000 years, they enjoy the state that prevails in the continent of Videha. The last two aeons of privation and of extreme privation are each 21,000 years, and are then immediately repeated in the subsequent aeons of extreme privation and of privation which begin the ascending semi-cycle.

The aeon in which we live is the fifth in the descending semi-cycle, the aeon of privation. This started three years and eight months after the liberation of Mahāvīra (over 2500 years ago) and runs for 21,000 years.

tābhyām aparā bhūmayo'vasthitāḥ

(SS 3.28) The conditions in the other continents are constant.

Only Bharata and Airāvata are affected by time cycles. The people in the other continents experience stable conditions. Videha inhabitants have privation-with-plenty, except for those in the land of North Kuru where they enjoy supreme plenty. The people in the continents of Haimavata and of Hairaṇyavata enjoy plenty-with-privation and the people in Hari and Ramyaka enjoy plenty.

eka-dvi-tri-palyopamasthitayo haimavataka-hārivarṣaka-daivakuravakāḥ

(SS 3.29) The inhabitants of Haimavata, Hari and Deva Kuru have lifespans of one, two and three pit-measured periods, respectively.

In the islands inhabited by humans (SS 3.35), there are five continents called Haimavata, five continents called Hari and five lands called Deva

Kuru (in the five continents of Videha). (This will be explained further in SS 3.33–3.35.)

In the five continents called Haimavata where plenty-with-privation always prevails, the people have a lifespan of one pit-measured period. They are 2000 bows high (one bow = six feet), take only one meal every two days and are the colour of blue lotus. (For measurements of time and space, see appendices 2 and 3.)

In the five continents called Hari where plenty always prevails, people have a lifespan of two pit-measured periods. They are 4000 bows high, eat a meal every three days and are the colour of a conch.

In the five lands called Deva Kuru, where supreme plenty always prevails, people live for three pit-measured periods, are 6000 bows high, eat a meal every four days and are the colour of gold.

tathottarāḥ

(SS 3.30) **The conditions of the inhabitants of the northern continents are just like those of their southern counterparts.**

The conditions and the inhabitants of the continent of Hairaṇyavata are the same as Haimavata. Those in Ramyaka are like those in Hari. Those in the land of North Kuru are like those of the land of Deva Kuru.

videheṣu saṃkhyeyakālāḥ

(SS 3.31) **The humans of Videha live for numerable years.**

In the five continents of Videha where plenty-with-privation prevails, the people are 500 bows high, take their meals daily and live at least one intra-hour and at most one pūrvakoṭi. (1 pūrva = $8{,}400{,}000^2$ and 1 koṭi = 10^7, so 1 pūrvakoṭi = $8{,}400{,}000^2 \times 10^7$. See appendix 2 for further details.)

bharatasya viṣkambho jambūdvīpasya navatiśatabhāgaḥ

(SS 3.32) **The width of Bharata is $1/190$ of the diameter of Jambū Island.**

Jambū Island has seven continents and six mountains (see figure 9, p. 78). The continent of Bharata is succeeded by Mount Himavan which is twice as wide as Bharata. Similarly, the width of the next continent, Haimavata, is twice that of Himavan and so on for Mount Mahāhimavan, the continent Hari, Mount Niṣadha and the continent Videha. After this, the sizes begin to diminish. The continent Videha is succeeded by Mount Nīla which is half the width of Videha. Simiarly Ramyaka is half the width of Nīla and so on for Mount Rukmin, the continent Hairaṇyavata, Mount Śikharin and the continent Airāvata.

So, if the width of the continent Bharata is given as the standard measurement, that is, as one unit, the widths of the mountains and continents going from one side of Jambū to the other, beginning with Bharata, will be: 1, 2, 4, 8, 16, 32, 64, 32, 16, 8, 4, 2, 1 units, respectively, giving a total of 190 units for the diameter of Jambū Island. Now, as the diameter of Jambū Island is 100,000 when measured in yojanas, the value of one unit = 100,000/190 = 526 6/19. Therefore Bharata is 526 6/19 yojanas wide (as given in SS 3.24).

The table below gives the widths of the continents and mountains.

CONTINENTS AND MOUNTAINS	UNITS		YOJANAS
Continent of Bharata	1 unit	=	526 6/19
Mount Himavan	2 units	=	1,052 12/19
Continent of Haimavata	4 units	=	2,105 5/19
Mount Mahāhimavan	8 units	=	4,210 10/19
Continent of Hari	16 units	=	8,421 1/19
Mount Niṣadha	32 units	=	16,842 2/19
Continent of Videha	64 units	=	33,684 4/19
Mount Nīla	32 units	=	16,842 2/19
Continent of Ramyaka	16 units	=	8,421 1/19
Mount Rukmin	8 units	=	4,210 10/19
Continent of Hairaṇyavata	4 units	=	2,105 5/19
Mount Śikharin	2 units	=	1,052 12/19
Continent of Airāvata	1 unit	=	526 6/19

dvir dhātakīkhaṇḍe

3.12 (SS 3.33) **There are twice as many continents and mountains on Dhātakīkhaṇḍa Island as there are on Jambū Island.**

In this sutra, which begins the descriptions of the islands beyond Jambū inhabited by humans, the SB, SBT and SS traditions converge once more.

Dhātakīkhaṇḍa Island is divided into two parts by two mountains spreading north to south. There are also two Mount Merus, one in the east and one in the west. Around each of the two Merus, there are seven continents and six mountains, each named exactly as on Jambū Island. So, there are two Bharatas, two Mount Himavans, etc., on Dhātakīkhaṇḍa Island. The island is surrounded by Kāla Ocean which is surrounded by the Puṣkara Island.

puṣkarārdhe ca

3.13 (SS 3.34) **Half of Puṣkara Island has as many continents as all of Dhātakīkhaṇḍa Island.**

prāṅ mānuṣottarān manuṣyāḥ

3.14 (SS 3.35) **The human species exists up to Mount Mānuṣottara.**

Now we consider the human species and the area of the middle region which they inhabit.

Puṣkara Island is four times as wide as Jambū Island. Therefore, there should be four Bharatas, etc., but here the description is of only half of Puṣkara Island. On this island, the mountain range called Mānuṣottara (literally "furthest limit of human habitation") runs around the middle of the island ring, dividing it into two rings. The inner ring is inhabited by humans. Beyond this, there are only animals.

In the inner ring of Puṣkara, there are two sets of seven continents and six mountains of the same names as on the islands of Jambū and Dhātakīkhaṇḍa. So, altogether on the first two islands and half of the third island, there are five Bharatas, five Haimavatas and so on. Therefore, there are 7 × 5 = 35 continents in total that are inhabited by humans.

āryā mlecchāś ca

3.15 (SS 3.36) **Human beings fall into two classes: Āryas and Mlecchas.**

In this broad classification of the human race, the commentators differ on the details, but generally the Āryas are better born, better behaved, better spoken and more highly developed, both physically and spiritually, than the Mlecchas. Some of the Mlecchas are said to have the faces of animals such as the ram, horse, elephant, lion and tiger.

The SB classifies the Āryas as those who qualify as such by race, family, profession, expertise or language. The SS attributes supernatural powers to some Āryas and divides those without such powers into those who are Āryas by country of birth, race, profession, conduct or because of their enlightened world-view.

In general, Mlecchas are said to be born in islands between the main islands and on "teeth" or peninsulas extending into the Lavaṇa Ocean. The SS also allows that some Mlecchas are born in the fifteen lands where spiritual effort is possible (see 3.16 below).

TRANSLATOR'S NOTE

The very detailed descriptions of the Āryas and Mlecchas, not given in full here, include lists of particular dynasties and geographical regions of India. They are a mixture of myth, history and politics. The term Ārya commonly refers to peoples north of the Ganges, descendants of the tribes who swept down into the Indian sub-continent in the second millenium BCE. The term Mlecchas, as described by the commentators, embraces the more ancient peoples of India south of the Ganges, including great emperors, and also Greek and Ionian invaders of the past.

bharatai-rāvata-videhāḥ karmabhūmayo 'nyatra devakurū-ttarakurubhyaḥ

3.16 (SS 3.37) Spiritual effort is possible in the continents of Bharata, Airāvata and Videha, excepting Deva Kuru and Uttara Kuru.

There are fifteen lands where spiritual effort is possible: the five Bharatas, five Airāvatas and five Videhas. One of each is on Jambū Island and two of each are on Dhātakīkhaṇḍa and Puṣkaravara Islands, respectively. There are thirty-two sub-continents in each of the five Videhas, making 32 × 5 = 160 provinces of spiritual conquest, known simply as "conquests".

The Jinas and people capable of attaining liberation because of their experience of suffering, essential to spiritual effort, are born in the fifteen lands. In the five Videhas, there are at least twenty Jinas – four in each Videha – available at any time. There may be as many as 160 Jinas – one in each of the 160 conquests – available at any one time. In each of the Bharatas and Airāvatas, there are twenty-four successive Jinas who are only born during the third and fourth aeons of the descending semi-cycle of time and the second, third and fourth aeons of the ascending semi-cycle (see SS 3.27). The highest number of Jinas that can possibly be in the world at the same time is 170: 160 in the five Videhas and one in each of the five Bharatas and five Airāvatas.

The Deva Kurus and Uttara Kurus in the Videha continents are not lands where spiritual effort is possible. Unlike the rest of the Videhas in which the state of plenty-with-privation prevails, these regions enjoy supreme plenty which is detrimental to spiritual effort. The people are born in pairs and have their needs satisfied by desire-giving trees.

nṛsthitī parāpare tripalyopamâ-ntarmuhūrte

3.17 (SS 3.38) Humans live for at least one intra-hour and at most three pit-measured periods.

tiryag-yonīnāṃ ca

3.18 (SS 3.39) The lifespans of animals are similar to those of humans.

The lifespans of humans and animals are of two kinds: time spent in the same body and time spent as the same species.

The SB gives a detailed description of these two kinds of durations for the different species. The maximum lifespan of a pure earth-bodied being is 12,000 years; of the hard earth-bodied being, 22,000 years; of the water-bodied, 7000 years; of the air-bodied, 3000 years; of the fire-bodied, three days and nights; and of the vegetation-bodied, 10,000 years. The time spent in the same type of body can, in the case of the earth-, water-, air – and fire-bodied beings, be innumerable descending and ascending time cycles (see SS 3.27). For vegetation-bodied beings, the time spent can be infinite descending and ascending cycles.

Two-sensed beings have a maximum lifespan of twelve years, three-sensed beings have forty-nine days, four-sensed have six months. All of these beings spend numerable thousands of years being reborn into the same type of body.

Five-sensed animals are divided into aquatics, legless reptiles, legged reptiles, aerials and terrestrials. Each of these groupings has two classes, those born by sexual reproduction and those born by agglutination of material particles (see 2.32, 2.36). The former are rational beings, the latter non-rational (2.24). The maximum lifespan of these creatures is as follows:

TYPE	MAXIMUM LIFESPAN
Aquatics (e.g. fish)	
rational	one pūrvakoṭi
non-rational	one pūrvakoṭi
Legless reptiles (e.g. snakes)	
rational	one pūrvakoṭi
non-rational	53,000 years

Reptiles with legs (e.g. lizards)	
rational	one pūrvakoṭi
non-rational	42,000 years
Aerials (e.g. birds)	
rational	innumerable years equal to one innumerablth part of one pit-measured period
non-rational	72,000 years
Terrestrials (quadrupeds, e.g. lions)	
rational	three pit-measured periods
non-rational	84,000 years

The number of repeated births of these animals in the same species is seven or eight. The minimum duration of human and animal births is one intra-hour (just less than forty-eight minutes). (For an explanation of the time units, see appendix 2.)

CHAPTER FOUR

The Gods

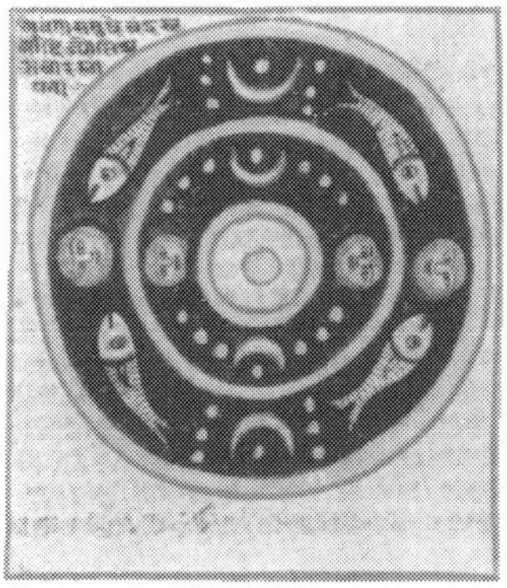

SB/SBT TRADITION
The Cosmos

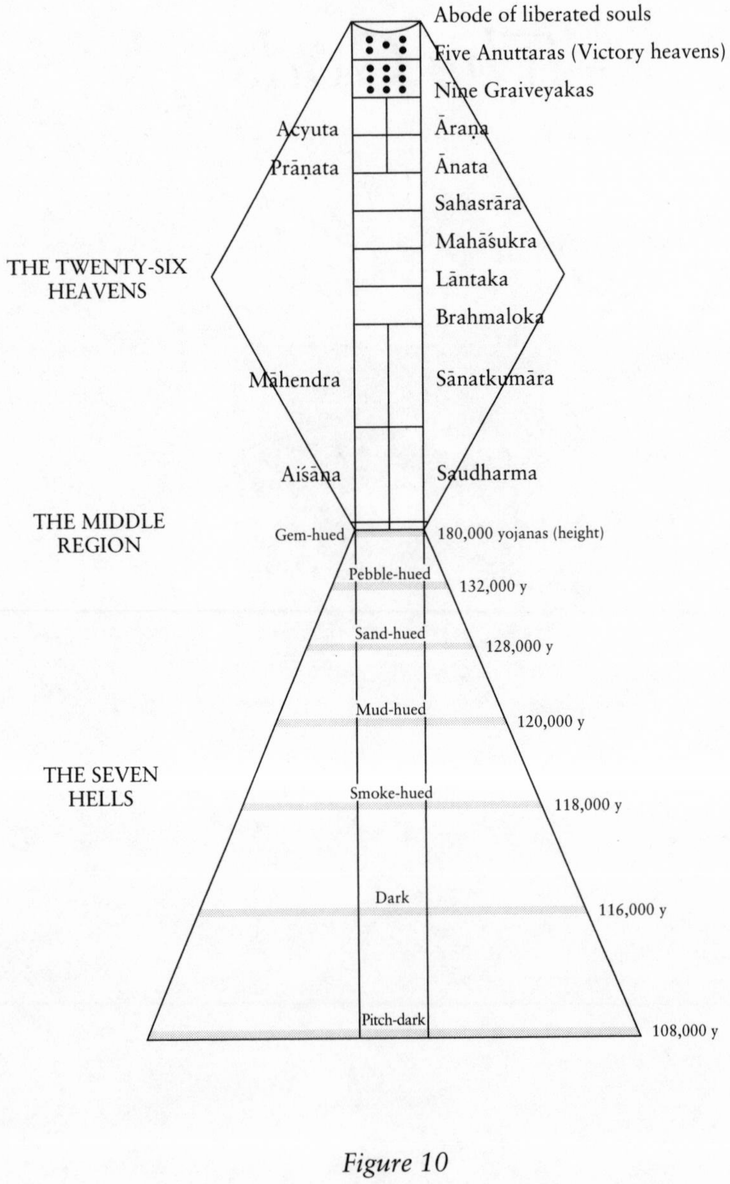
Abode of liberated souls
Five Anuttaras (Victory heavens)
Nine Graiveyakas
Acyuta
Āraṇa
Prāṇata
Ānata
Sahasrāra
Mahāśukra
THE TWENTY-SIX HEAVENS
Lāntaka
Brahmaloka
Māhendra
Sānatkumāra
Aiśāna
Saudharma
THE MIDDLE REGION
Gem-hued
180,000 yojanas (height)
Pebble-hued
132,000 y
Sand-hued
128,000 y
Mud-hued
120,000 y
THE SEVEN HELLS
Smoke-hued
118,000 y
Dark
116,000 y
Pitch-dark
108,000 y

Figure 10

SS TRADITION
The Cosmos

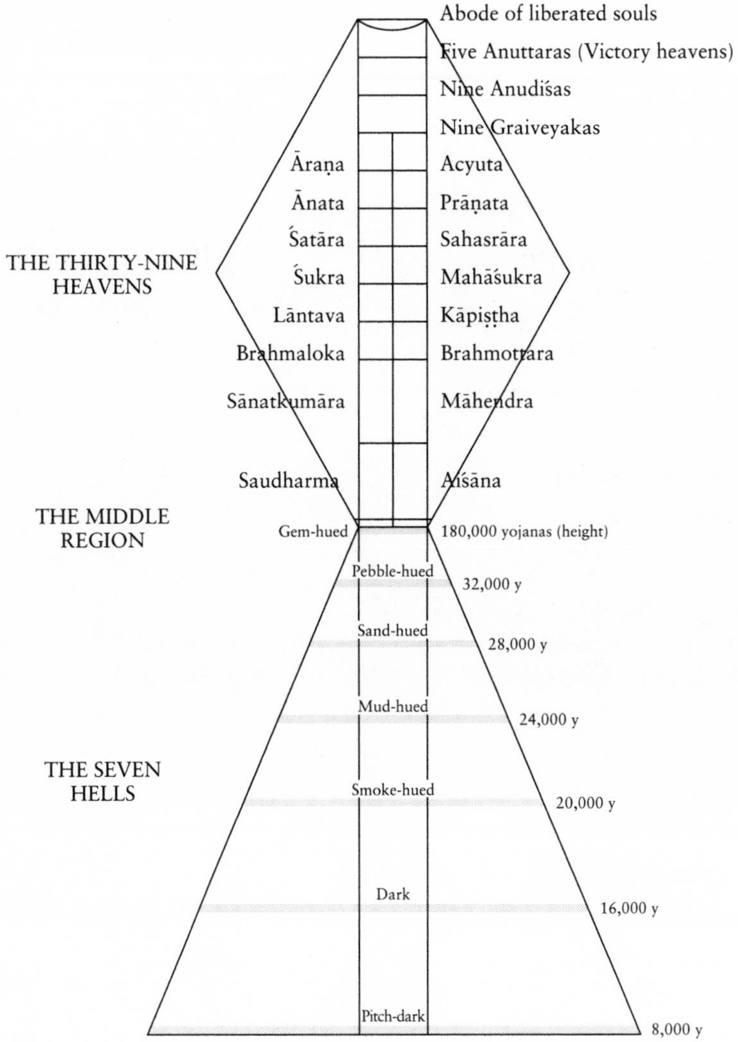

Abode of liberated souls
Five Anuttaras (Victory heavens)
Nine Anudiśas
Nine Graiveyakas
Āraṇa
Acyuta
Ānata
Prāṇata
Śatāra
Sahasrāra
THE THIRTY-NINE HEAVENS
Śukra
Mahāśukra
Lāntava
Kāpiṣṭha
Brahmaloka
Brahmottara
Sānatkumāra
Māhendra
Saudharma
Aiśāna
THE MIDDLE REGION
Gem-hued
180,000 yojanas (height)
Pebble-hued
32,000 y
Sand-hued
28,000 y
Mud-hued
24,000 y
THE SEVEN HELLS
Smoke-hued
20,000 y
Dark
16,000 y
Pitch-dark
8,000 y

Figure 11

Contents

The description of the different births a soul can take continues now with specific reference to birth as a god.

devāś caturnikāyāḥ

4.1 The gods fall into four classes.

The four classes of gods are: mansion-dwelling, forest, luminous and empyrean.

tṛtīyaḥ pītaleśyaḥ

4.2 (not SS) The gods belonging to the third class, that is the luminous gods, have red [fiery] colouring.

āditas triṣu pītāntaleśyāḥ

(SS variant 4.2) The first three classes of gods, that is the mansion-dwelling, forest and luminous, have the first four colourings: black, blue, grey and red [fiery].

According to the SB tradition, the mansion and forest gods have any one of the first four colourings, the luminous gods are only ever red, the first two varieties of empyrean gods (see 4.20) are red (fiery), the next three varieties are yellow (filament) and the rest are white.

The SS concurs with the colourings for empyrean gods, but says that all three classes of gods except the empyrean can be born with any one of the four colours, although in maturity they are necessarily red (fiery).

The SBT clarifies that it is only the physical colour that is defined with respect to different classes of gods; their psychic colour may be any one of the six colours – black, blue, grey, red, yellow or white.

daśâ-ṣṭa-pañca-dvādaśa-vikalpāḥ kalpopapannaparyantāḥ

4.3 Within the classes of gods, there are ten types of mansion, eight of forest, five of luminous and twelve of graded empyrean gods.[1]

Of the four classes of gods, the mansion gods inhabit the upper part of the first hell and also parts of the Videha continents and Mount Mānuṣottara in the middle region of the cosmos (SS 3.35). The forest gods also live in part of the highest hell realm (4.12) and the middle region. The luminous gods inhabit the skies of the middle region and the empyrean gods are in the upper (heavenly) region.

The gods are, by nature, playful. They live a happy extravagant life. Because of their austerities in past lives, they have powerful bodies capable of unimpeded movement through any part of the cosmos.

(For full details of the types of gods, see 4.11–4.13, 4.18–4.20.)

indra-sāmānika-trāyastriṃśa-pāriṣadyâ-tmarakṣa-lokapālâ-nīka-prakīrṇakâ-bhiyogya-kilviṣikāś caikaśaḥ

4.4 There are chiefs, co-chiefs, ministers, counsellors, sentinels, custodians, army chiefs, citizens, attendants, and menials in each of the four classes of gods.

trāyastriṃśa-lokapālavarjyā vyantara-jyotiṣkāḥ

4.5 The forest and luminous gods are, however, devoid of ministers and custodians.

pūrvayor dvīndrāḥ

4.6 There are two chiefs for each type of mansion and forest god.

The two chiefs for each type of mansion god are as follows.

	CHIEFS	TYPE
1.	*Camara, Bala* (*Vairocana* in SS) Deer-tail, Vigorous (Shining in SS)	*Asurakumāra* Fiendish youths

[1] Above these are the non-graded empyrean gods (4.18).

2.	*Dharaṇa, Bhūtānanda* Protector, Joy of Beings	*Nāgakumāra* Serpentine youths
3.	*Hari, Harisaha* (*Harisiṃha, Harikānta* in SS) Tawny, Tawny-tolerant (Tawny Lion, Tawny Glaze in SS)	*Vidyutkumāra* Lightning youths
4.	*Veṇudeva, Veṇudhārī* Flute Devotee, Flautist	*Suparṇakumāra* Vulturine youths
5.	*Agniśikha, Agnimāṇava* Fire-flame, Man of Fire	*Agnikumāra* Fiery youths
6.	*Velamba, Prabhañjana* (*Vailamba*) Trembling, Hurricane (Furious in SS)	*Vātakumāra* Stormy youths
7.	*Sughoṣa, Mahāghoṣa* Sonorous, Loud	*Stanitakumāra* Thundering youths
8.	*Jalakānta, Jalaprabha* Loved by Water, Colour of Water	*Udadhikumāra* Oceanic youths
9.	*Pūrṇa, Vasiṣṭha* Fully-fledged, Most Excellent	*Dvīpakumāra* Island youths
10.	*Amitagati, Amitavāhana* Infinite Speed, Infinitely Fast Chariot	*Dikkumāra* Guardians of the cardinal (compass) points

The two chiefs for each type of forest god are as follows:

	CHIEFS	TYPE
1.	*Kinnara, Kiṃpuruṣa* Deformed Human, Deformed Person	*Kinnara* Deformed human
2.	*Satpuruṣa, Mahāpuruṣa* Good Person, Great Person	*Kiṃpuruṣa* Deformed person
3.	*Atikāya, Mahākāya* Giant, Big-bodied	*Mahoraga* Great serpent
4.	*Gītarati, Gītayaśas* Music Devotee, Music Celebrity	*Gandharva* Musician

5.	*Pūrṇabhadra, Maṇibhadra* Fully Auspicious, Auspicious Gem	*Yakṣa* Treasure keeper
6.	*Bhīma, Mahābhīma* Dreadful, Terrible	*Rākṣasa* Demon
7.	*Pratirūpa, Atirūpa* (*Apratirūpa* in SS) Devilish, Giant Devil (Supreme Devil in SS)	*Bhūta* Devil
8.	*Kāla, Mahākāla* Death, Great Death	*Piśāca* Goblin

The SB names the chiefs of the luminous gods as the suns and moons.

pītānta-leśyāḥ

4.7 (not in SS)　The colouring of these gods [mansion and forest] are black, blue, grey and red [fiery].

kāyapravīcārā ā aiśānāt

4.8 (SS 4.7)　The gods up to the Aiśāna in the second heaven enjoy sexual pleasure through copulation.

With respect to their sexual propensities, the gods are divided into three groups: (1) those with goddesses and sexual appetites, (2) those without goddesses but with sexual appetites, (3) those without goddesses and without sexual appetites.

All the mansion, forest and luminous gods in the upper part of the infernal region and in the middle region, as well as the first two types of empyrean gods, Saudharma and Aiśāna, in the heavenly region, are of the first group; they have goddesses and indulge in sexual copulation. These gods are as intense in their passion for sex as human beings.

śeṣāḥ sparśa-rūpa-śabda-manaḥ-pravīcārā dvayor dvayoḥ

4.9 (SS 4.8)　The rest of the empyrean gods, taken successively in groups of two, satisfy their sexual appetite through touch, sight, sound and thought, respectively.

The empyrean gods of Sānatkumāra in the third heaven and Māhendra in the fourth heaven are satisfied simply by touching the goddesses who appear before them to gratify their desires. The desires of the gods in

Brahmaloka and Lāntaka, the fifth and sixth heavens, are fulfilled simply by gazing at the goddesses dressed in beautiful garments in response to their desires. The gods of Mahāśukra and Sahasrāra, the seventh and eighth heavens, are satiated by the sweet song and music from the goddesses who appear to gratify them. The gods of Ānata, Prāṇata, Āraṇa and Acyuta, the ninth to twelfth heavens, feel satisfied through sexual fantasy.

Each of these sexual appetites is a refinement of the passions of the previous one and, as a result, the pleasure increases successively to incomparable excellence in the case of sexual fantasy.

pare 'pravīcārāḥ

4.10 (SS 4.9) **The other gods are devoid of sexual indulgence.**

Now the gods who are without goddesses and sexual needs are described. These are the empyrean gods without rank. They live in a state of joy which is far superior to the sensual gratification that arises from copulation, touch, sight, sound or sexual fantasy.

bhavanavāsino 'sura-nāga-vidyut-suparṇâ-gni-vāta-stanito-dadhi-dvīpa-dikkumārāḥ

4.11 (SS 4.10) **The mansion gods are of ten types: fiendish youths, serpentine youths, lightning youths, vulturine youths, fiery youths, stormy youths, thundering youths, oceanic youths, island youths and youths who rule the cardinal points.**

Having dealt with the sexual propensities of the gods, the types of gods in each class are now detailed beginning with the lowest class, the mansion-dwelling gods.

With the exception of the first type, all the mansion gods are named according to the natural phenomenon to which they are akin. The SB gives a vivid description of the appearance, demeanour and symbol of each type:

1. Fiendish youths are huge, black and handsome with a serene but severe demeanour. They wear a crown with a crest jewel.
2. Serpentine youths are bluish black with an exceedingly graceful head and face. They have a soft, delightful gait and the hood of a snake on their head.
3. Lightning youths are white, mild-mannered and resplendent with a thunderbolt as their emblem.

4. Vulturine youths are bluish white with an exceedingly graceful neck and chest. They have a powerful, soaring flight and the garuḍa bird (vulture) as their emblem.
5. Fiery youths are curvaceous, white and radiant. The jar of plenty is their symbol.
6. Stormy youths are white with a round solid body but a slim belly. They are swift and agile and have the horse as their emblem.
7. Thundering youths are light black with a mild look and a soft, deep, sonorous voice which can be heard at great distances. They wear the insignia of prosperity.
8. Oceanic youths are bluish black with graceful thighs and waist. They have an unyielding manner and their emblem is the crocodile.
9. Island youths are bluish white with exceedingly graceful chest, shoulders, arms and palms. They are brave and ferocious and their symbol is the lion.
10. Guardians of the cardinal points are bluish with exceedingly graceful legs and feet. They are regal and their symbol is the elephant.

vyantarāḥ kinnara-kimpuruṣa-mahoraga-gandharva-yakṣa-rākṣasa-bhūta-piśācāḥ

4.12 (SS 4.11) There are eight types of forest gods: deformed human, deformed person, great serpent, musician, treasure keeper, demon, devil and goblin.

The forest gods reside freely in many regions of the cosmos, especially the vacant places, up to the top of Mount Meru and the areas of the first hell also occupied by the mansion gods. They live in mountains, caves and forests and some attend on humans. Their bodies are black, red or white and they are fond of colourful dresses, garlands and ornaments. Some have beautiful faces, radiant bodies and melodious voices. Others have a fearful appearance. They carry emblems of various trees.

In the SS, these gods are said to live on innumerable islands far remote from Jambū Island.

jyotiṣkāḥ sūryāś candramaso graha-nakṣatra-prakīrṇatārakāś ca

4.13 (SS 4.12) There are five types of luminous gods: suns, moons,

planets, constellations and scattered stars.

The luminous gods live in the area of the middle region which begins at a height of 790 yojanas above the plateau of Mount Meru and extends up another 110 yojanas with a spread across innumerable islands and oceans. Eight hundred yojanas above the plateau of Mount Meru, that is, ten yojanas into the region of luminous gods, there are flying vehicles of the suns. Eighty yojanas above these are the vehicles of the moons. In the next twenty yojanas, there are the planets, constellations and scattered stars. Scattered stars have no fixed path of motion, so they are sometimes above the suns and moons and sometimes below them.

The constellations are four yojanas above the moons with the planet group Budha (Mercury) three or four yojanas higher. Above this, in succession, are the planet groups Śukra (Venus), Guru or Bṛhaspati (Jupiter), Aṅgāraka or Mangala (Mars) and Sanaiścara (Saturn), each three yojanas higher than the one before.

merupradakṣiṇā nityagatayo nṛloke

4.14 (SS 4.13) **Above the region inhabited by humans, the luminous gods are always moving in their space vehicles around Mount Meru.**

The region inhabited by humans (see SS 3.35) is 45×10^5 yojanas across. There are two suns above Jambū Island, four over Lavaṇa Ocean and twelve over Dhātakīkhaṇḍa Island.

Beyond Dhātakīkhaṇḍa Island, the number of suns over any island or ocean is calculated by multiplying the number of suns in the previous island or ocean by three and then adding the suns in all the regions preceding that. Therefore, Kālodadhi Ocean which follows Dhātakīkhaṇḍa has $(12 \times 3) + 4 + 2 = 42$ suns. In Puṣkara Island, the number of suns is calculated as $(42 \times 3) + 12 + 4 + 2 = 144$. Therefore, in the half of Puṣkara Island inhabited by humans there are 72 suns. The number of suns in the entire region inhabited by humans is $2+4+12+42+72=132$.

The number of moons in the region inhabited by humans is the same as that of suns and the above formula applies in their calculation. Each moon has an entourage of 28 constellations, 88 planets and $66{,}975 \times 10^{14}$ stars.

The suns, moons, planets and constellations are in the middle region. The other luminous bodies (some of the scattered stars) are in the upper, heavenly region.

The vehicles of the sun gods are $48\frac{1}{60}$ yojanas long and $24\frac{1}{60}$ yojanas wide. They are semi-circular. The sun gods are each seated on a vehicle with four principal goddesses. The vehicle is drawn by 16,000 gods: 4000 lion gods on the eastern side, 4000 elephant gods on the southern side, 4000 bull gods on the northern side and 4000 horse gods on the western side.

The vehicles of the moon gods are $56\frac{1}{60}$ yojanas long and $28\frac{1}{60}$ yojanas wide. The other descriptions are as for the sun vehicle.

tatkṛtaḥ kālavibhāgaḥ

4.15 (SS 4.14) Time is measured by the movements of the vehicles of the luminous gods.

The smallest unit of time is simply called a "time unit" and is the time it takes for the very subtle movement of an atom from one space unit to another. The length of a time unit is too small to be measurable in the ordinary sense. An innumerable number of time units make one āvalikā which is the smallest unit of countable time. The largest is the śīrṣaprahelikā, beyond which time is so vast as to be again "unmeasurable". Time is then expressed metaphorically as pit-measured and ocean-measured periods. (See appendix 2 for details of time units.)

bahir avasthitāḥ

4.16 (SS 4.15) The space vehicles of luminous gods are stationary above the regions which are outside human habitation.

The physical colouring and lustre of these stationary gods is also constant. They radiate cool and warm rays, both of which are pleasing and agreeable.

vaimānikāḥ

4.17 (SS 4.16) The empyrean gods are the fourth class of gods.

kalpopapannāḥ kalpātītāś ca

4.18 (SS 4.17) There are graded and non-graded ones [empyrean gods].

The empyrean gods live in space vehicles. The graded ones have various ranks such as chiefs, co-chiefs, etc (see 4.4). There are no such ranks among the non-graded ones.

uparyupari

4.19 (SS 4.18) The empyrean heavens are situated one above the other.

saudharmai-śāna-sānatkumāra-māhendra-brahmaloka-lāntaka-mahāś-ukra-sahasrāreṣv ānata-prāṇatayor āraṇâ-cyutayor navasu graiveyakeṣu vijaya-vaijayanta-jayantâ-parājiteṣu sarvārthasiddhe ca

4.20 (SS 4.19) The heavens are: Saudharma, Aiśāna, Sānatkumāra, Māhendra, Brahmaloka, Lāntaka, Mahāśukra, Sahasrāra, Ānata, Prāṇata, Āraṇa, Acyuta, the nine Graiveyakas, Vijaya, Vaijayanta, Jayanta, Aparājita and Sarvārthasiddha.[2]

The gods of the first twelve heavens, below the nine Graiveyakas, have ranks and chiefs. These gods are graded and the heavens are named after the chiefs who reign there.

The chief of each heaven of graded empyrean gods is given as:

	CHIEF	HEAVEN
1.	*Śakra* (*Saudharma* in SS)	*Saudharma*
	Mighty (Righteous in SS)	Abode of the Righteous
2.	*Īśāna*	*Aiśāna*
	Great Lord	Abode of the Great Lord
3.	*Sanatkumāra*	*Sānatkumāra*
	Perpetual Youth	Abode of the Perpetual Youth
4.	*Mahendra*	*Māhendra*
	Supreme Lord	Abode of the Supreme Lord
5.	*Brahmā*	*Brahmaloka* (*Brahmaloka* and *Brahmottara* in SS)
	Big Lord	Abode of the Big Lord (Abode of the Big Lord and Abode of the Super Lord in SS)

[2] There are some additional variations in this sutra between the SS and SB/SBT traditions. These are noted in the list of heavens in the commentary.

6.	*Lāntaka* (*Lāntava* in SS) Mystic (Mysterious in SS)	*Lāntaka* (*Lāntava* and *Kāpiṣṭha* in SS) Abode of the Mystic (Abode of the Mysterious/of the Banyan in SS)
7.	*Mahāśukra* (*Śukra* in SS) Supremely Radiant (Radiant in SS)	*Mahāśukra* (*Śukra*/*Mahāśukra* in SS) Abode of the Supremely Radiant (Abode of the Radiant/Supremely Radiant in SS)
8.	*Sahasrāra* (*Śatāra* in SS) Thousand-faceted (Hundred-faceted in SS)	*Sahasrāra* (*Śatāra*/*Sahasrāra* in SS) Abode of the Thousand-faceted (Abode of the Hundred-faceted/Thousand-faceted in SS)
9.	*Prāṇata* (*Ānata* in SS) Prostrated (Bent in SS)	*Ānata* Abode of the Bent
10.	*Prāṇata* Prostrated	*Prāṇata* Abode of the Prostrated
11.	*Acyuta* (*Āraṇa* in SS) Unswerving (Deep in SS)	*Āraṇa* Abode of the Deep
12.	*Acyuta* Unswerving	*Acyuta* Abode of the Unswerving

In both the SS and SB/SBT traditions, the first four chiefs have one heaven each. The second four have two heavens each according to the SS but only one each according to the SB. The next four chiefs have one heaven each in the SS tradition, but in the SB tradition, there are only two chiefs in the last four heavens. Accordingly, there are ten chiefs and twelve heavens in the SB tradition, whereas there are twelve chiefs and sixteen heavens in the SS tradition.

The gods of the remaining heavens above these first twelve are non-graded. The first of these are the gods of the nine Graiveyaka or "Neck-dwelling" heavens on the neck (grīvā) of the cosmic person (the human-shaped area that is cosmic space). The nine Graiveyaka heavens are: Sudarśana (Handsome), Amogha (Efficacious), Suprabuddha (Highly Awakened), Yaśodhara (Glorious), Subhadra (Fortunate), Viśāla (Illustrious), Sumanas (Gracious), Saumanas (Cheerful) and Prītinkara

(Agreeable). There is some variation in these names between the different traditions and the SS has nine additional heavens above the Graiveyakas called "subdirectional heavens" (see figures 10 and 11, pp. 92–3).

The last five heavens are located in the highest area of the cosmos inhabited by gods. Vijaya (Victory), Vaijayanta (Victorious) and Jayanta (Conquering) are so called because the gods who reside there have achieved victory over their karma and are destined to attain liberation soon. Aparājita (Unvanquished) is so called because the gods there are not liable to defeat in their spiritual struggle and Sarvārthasiddha (Fully Accomplished) refers to the fact that those who live there have achieved all goals.

sthiti-prabhāva-sukha-dyuti-leśyāviśuddhî-ndriyâ-vadhiviṣayato 'dhikāḥ

4.21 (SS 4.20) **Each succeeding type of empyrean god is superior to the preceding one in lifespan, sovereignty, blessedness, lustre, purity of colour [aura], cognitive faculties and clairvoyance.**

The qualifications listed above successively increase in both quantity and quality for the empyrean gods in higher heavens. The gods of the first two heavens, Saudharma and Aiśāna, can see below as far as the first (gem-coloured) hell, horizontally to innumerable islands and oceans and above to the pinnacle of their own heaven. The gods of the next two heavens, Sānatkumāra and Māhendra, can see down to the second (pebble-coloured) hell, horizontally to many more innumerable islands and oceans and above to the pinnacle of their own heaven. Similarly, the gods of the higher heavens can see progressively longer distances. The empyrean gods of the five highest heavens of spiritual conquest can see from the bottom to the top of the cosmos.

gati-śarīra-parigrahâ-bhimānato hīnāḥ

4.22 (SS 4.21) **Desires for visits to different regions, height and possessions, and egotism gradually decrease.**

The Saudharma and Aiśāna gods of the first and second heavens are seven cubits tall, whereas the Ānata, Prāṇata, Āraṇa and Acyuta of the ninth to twelfth heavens are three cubits. The Graiveyaka gods are two cubits tall and in the five heavens of spiritual conquest, the gods are only one cubit.

Whereas each Saudharma god possesses 3,200,000 space vehicles, the gods in Ānata to Acyuta have 700, the gods of the nine Graiveyakas have

111 and the gods of the five highest heavens have only five each. The lessening of possessions is accompanied by a lessening of egotism.

pīta-padma-śuklaleśyā dvi-tri-śeṣeṣu

4.23 (SS 4.22) The colouring of the first two types of empyrean god is red (fiery), of the next three, yellow (filament), and of the remaining types, white.

The gods of Saudharma and Aiśāna are red. Those of the third to fifth heavens – Sānatkumāra, Māhendra and Brahmaloka – are yellow. Those from Lāntaka, the sixth heaven, up to Sarvāthasiddha, the highest heaven, are white.

prāg graiveyakebhyaḥ kalpāḥ

4.24 (SS 4.23) The types of empyrean gods up to the Graiveyakas are graded.

From the first heaven, Saudharma, to the twelfth, Acyuta, the empyrean gods have ranks such as chief, co-chief, etc. Above this they have no ranks.

brahmalokālayā lokāntikāḥ

4.25 (SS 4.24) The terminal gods, who are destined to end their worldly existence soon, live in Brahmaloka.

This sutra introduces a special type of god, the terminal (lokantika) gods, who are close to liberation and live near the side border, fairly close to the top of the heavenly region. The SB explains that there are eight varieties of terminal gods who live, respectively, in the eight directions surrounding the Brahmaloka, the fifth heaven. However, the SBT says that the gods live near the black gaps which are in certain parts of the Brahmaloka (see figure 12, p. 109).[3]

sārasvatâ-ditya-vahny-aruṇa-gardatoya-tuṣitâ-vyabādha-maruto 'riṣṭāś ca

4.26 (SS 4.25) The varieties of terminal gods are: Sārasvata, Āditya,

[3] The black gaps are black matter which have an enormous power of attraction. The gods dare not go near in their space vehicles for fear of being pulled in. Details are given in the Inner Corpus, book 5, 6.106.

The Black Gaps

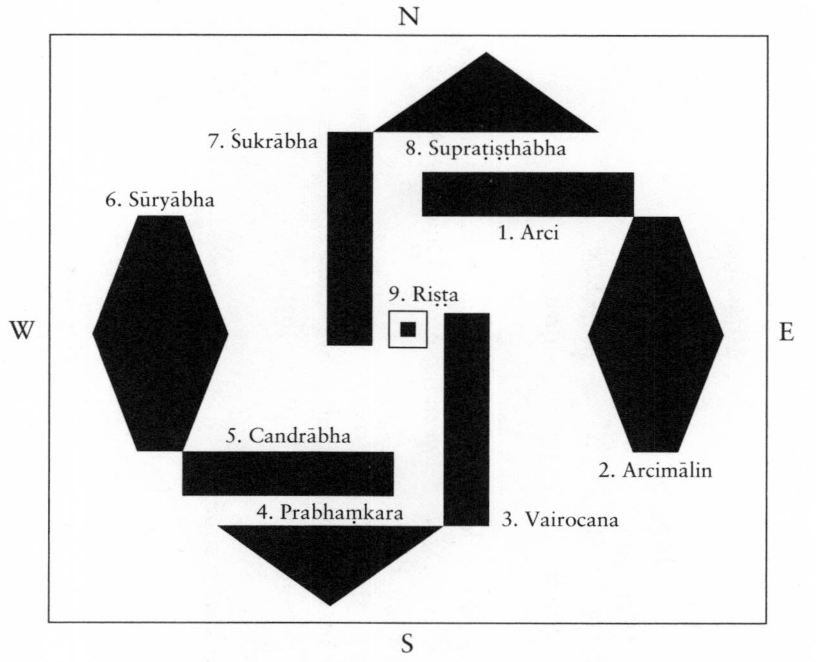

Figure 12

Vahni, Aruṇa, Gardatoya, Tuṣita, Avyābādha, Marut and Ariṣṭa.

The SBT reconciles the nine varieties of terminal gods listed here with the eight mentioned in the commentary of the previous sutra by explaining that the ninth variety refers to the gods living in the space vehicle called Ariṣṭa which is in the centre. The directions in which the gods live are as follows:

VARIETY OF GOD	DIRECTION
Sārasvata (Eloquent)	north-east
Āditya (Bright Orb)	east
Vahni (Fire)	south-east
Aruṇa (Dawn)	south
Gardatoya (Splashing Stream)	south-west
Tuṣita (Gratified)	west
Avyābādha (Unimpeded)	north-west
Marut (Wind)	north
Ariṣṭa (Unhurt)	centre

Although the SS does not name the Maruts as a distinct variety in the sutra, it says that they live between the Avyābādhas and Ariṣṭas. The SS places the Ariṣṭas in the north.

The terminal gods are known as divine saints because they are without sexual drives. They attain liberation after, at most, another seven or eight births and sometimes only two or three.

vijayādiṣu dvicaramāḥ

4.27 (SS 4.26) In the heavens of Vijaya (Victory) and so on, the gods have only two more births as humans before attaining liberation.

This sutra describes the condition of the gods in the first four of the five heavens of spiritual conquest (Vijaya, Vaijayanta, Jayanta, Aparājita, see 4.20). These gods have three more lives remaining, two of which will be human ones, before liberation. Each is re-born as a human, then as a god again in any one of the five highest heavens of spiritual conquest and then as a human who attains liberation. The SBT notes and rejects the view that the last re-birth in the celestial realm *must* be in Sarvārthasiddha, the highest and most sublime of the five highest heavens. Nevertheless, those who are born in Sarvārthasiddha are assured of only one further life as a human being in which they will attain liberation.

aupapātika-manuṣyebhyaḥ śeṣās tiryag-yonayaḥ

4.28 (SS 4.27) **All beings other than humans and those born by descent are subhumans.**

This sutra identifies subhumans as all life distinct from the gods and infernals (born by descent) and humans. "Subhumans" therefore includes animals, all small and microscopic life, vegetation and earth-, water-, fire- and air-bodied beings. They exist throughout cosmic space and so their habitat is not defined. Their lifespans are given in SS 3.39.

sthitiḥ

4.29 (not in SS) **The lifespans of gods are now explained.**

bhavaneṣu dakṣiṇārdhādhipatīnāṃ palyopamam adhyardham

4.30 (not in SS) **The maximum lifespan of the chiefs of the southern half, among the mansion-dwelling gods, is 1.5 pit-measured periods.**

śeṣāṇāṃ pādone

4.31 (not in SS) **The maximum lifespan of the other chiefs is 1.75 pit-measured periods.**

asurendrayoh sāgaropamam adhikaṃ ca

4.32 (not in SS) **The maximum lifespans of the two chiefs of the fiendish youths are respectively one ocean-measured period and a little more than one ocean-measured period.**

There are two chiefs for each of the ten types of mansion-dwelling gods, one for the north and one for the south of the area they inhabit. The chiefs of the south live for 2.5 pit-measured periods (p.m.p.). Those in the north live for 1.75 p.m.p. The exceptions to this are the chiefs of the first type of mansion-dwelling gods, the fiendish youths (see 4.6). Camara, the chief of the south, lives for one ocean-measured period (o.m.p.) and Bali, the chief of the north, lives a little longer.

sthitir asura-nāga-suparṇa-dvīpa-śeṣāṇāṃ sāgaropama-tripalyopamā-rdhahīnamitā

(SS 4.28, variant of 4.29–4.32) **The maximum lifespan of the fiendish**

youths is one ocean-measured period [o.m.p.], of the serpentine youths is three pit-measured periods [p.m.p.], of the vulturine youths is 2.5 p.m.p., of the island youths is 2 p.m.p. and of the remaining six types [of mansion-dwelling gods] is 1.5 p.m.p.

saudharmādiṣu yathākramam

4.33 (not in SS) **The maximum lifespans of the empyrean gods in the heavens of Saudharma and so on are now described in succession.**

sāgaropame

4.34 (not in SS) **Two ocean-measured periods.**

This refers to the lifespan of the gods in the first heaven, Saudharma.

adhike ca

4.35 (not in SS) **The maximum lifespan in the Aiśāna, the second heaven, is a little more than two ocean measured periods.**

saudharmai-śānayoḥ sāgaropame adhike

(SS 4.29, variant of 4.33–4.35) **The maximum lifespan of the Saudharma and Aiśāna gods is a little more than two ocean-measured periods.**

sapta sānatkumāre

4.36 (not SS) **In Sānatkumāra, the maximum lifespan is seven ocean-measured periods.**

viśeṣa-tri-sapta-daśai-kādaśa-trayodaśa-pañcadaśabhir adhikāni ca

4.37 (not SS) **In Māhendra and the higher heavens, the maximum lifespans are somewhat more than seven ocean-measured periods, and then successively more than seven by 3, 7, 10, 11, 13 and 15 o.m.p.**

In the Māhendra heaven, the maximum lifespan is somewhat more than seven ocean-measured periods (o.m.p.); in Brahmaloka, 7 + 3 = 10 o.m.p.; in Lāntaka, 7 + 7 = 14 o.m.p.; in Mahāśukra, 7 + 10 = 17 o.m.p.; in Sahasrāra, 7 + 11 = 18 o.m.p.; in Ānata and Prāṇata, 7 + 13 = 20 o.m.p., in Āraṇa and Acyuta, 7 + 15 = 22 o.m.p.

sānatkumāra-māhendrayoḥ sapta

(SS 4.30, variant of 4.36) The maximum lifespan of Sānatkumāra and Māhendra is somewhat more than seven ocean-measured periods.

tri-sapta-navai-kādaśa-trayodaśa-pañcadaśabhir adhikāni tu

(SS 4.31, variant of 4.37) The maximum lifespan of Brahmaloka and Brahmottara is a little more than ten ocean-measured periods; of Lāntava and Kāpiṣṭha, somewhat more than 14 o.m.p.; of Śukra and Mahāśukra, somewhat more than 16 o.m.p.; of Śatāra and Sahasrāra, somewhat more than 18 o.m.p.; of Ānata and Prāṇata, somewhat more than 20 o.m.p.; of Āraṇa and Acyuta, 22 o.m.p.

āraṇâ-cyutād ūrdhvam ekaikena navasu graiveyakeṣu vijayādiṣu sarvārthasiddhe ca

4.38 (SS 4.32) In the heavens above Āraṇa and Acyuta, there is a successive increase of one ocean-measured period in the maximum lifespans of the nine varieties of Graiveyaka (Neck-dwelling) gods, the gods in the Vijaya (Victory) heavens and Sarvārthasiddha.

The nine heavens of the Graiveyaka (Neck-dwelling) gods are above the heavens of the Āraṇa (Deep) and Acyuta (Unswerving) gods which have a lifespan of 22 o.m.p. Therefore, the maximum lifespan for the first variety of Neck-dwelling gods is 23 o.m.p. With successive increases of one ocean-measured period for each Neck-dwelling heaven, the gods in the ninth of these heavens have maximum lifespans of 31 o.m.p. In the four heavens of spiritual conquest above this, beginning with Vijaya (Victory), the lifespan is 32 o.m.p. and in the highest heaven, Sarvārthasiddha (Fully Accomplished), it is 33. The SB notes that in Sarvārthasiddha the minimum lifespan is also 33 o.m.p.

The SS includes the category of nine subdirectional heavens (4.20) after the nine heavens of the Neck-dwelling gods. The gods in these are said to have a lifespan of 32 o.m.p. and the gods in the highest heavens, including Sarvārthasiddha, are said to have a lifespan of 33 o.m.p.

aparā palyopamaṃ adhikam ca

4.39 (not SS) The minimum lifespan for a god is one pit-measured

period and also somewhat more than this.

According to the SB/SBT, in the first heaven, Saudharma (Abode of the Righteous), the minimum lifespan is one pit-measured period. In the next heaven, Aiśāna (Abode of the Great Lord), it is somewhat higher.

sāgaropame

4.40 (not SS) **In Sānatkumāra, the minimum lifespan is two ocean-measured periods.**

adhike ca

4.41 (not SS) **In Māhendra, the minimum lifespan is somewhat more than two ocean-measured periods.**

parataḥ parataḥ pūrvā pūrvā'nantarā

4.42 (not SS) **Beyond Māhendra, the minimum lifespan is identical with the maximum lifespan of gods in the heaven immediately below.**

According to the SB/SBT, the maximum lifespan in the fourth heaven, Māhendra (Abode of the Supreme Lord), is somewhat more than seven ocean-measured periods, so this is the minimum lifespan of the gods in the next heaven up, Brahmaloka (Abode of the Big Lord), and so it proceeds through to the twelfth heaven and the nine Neck-dwelling heavens above this.

Above these in the four heavens beginning with Vijaya (Victory), the maximum lifespan is 32 o.m.p. and so the minimum in each is 31. This is followed by Sarvārthasiddha (Fully Accomplished) where the minimum should be 32, but it is not so. This anomaly is dealt with by the SS, see SS 4.33–4.34.

aparā palyopamam adhikam

(SS 4.33, variant of 4.39) **The minimum lifespan is somewhat more than one pit-measured period.**

parataḥ parataḥ pūrvā pūrvā' nantarā

(SS 4.34, variant of 4.40–4.42) **Beyond this, the minimum lifespan is identical with the maximum lifespan of gods in the heaven immediately below.**

In the SS, the maximum lifespan in Saudharma and Aiśāna is given as somewhat more than two ocean-measured periods. Accordingly, the minimum lifespan of the Sānatkumāra and Māhendra gods is the same as this. Similarly, as the maximum lifespan of the Sānatkumāra and Māhendra gods is more than seven ocean-measured periods, the minimum lifespan of Brahmaloka and Brahmottara is more than 7 o.m.p. All five highest heavens have a maximum lifespan of 33 o.m.p. The minimum for Sarvārthasiddha is also 33, which is in line with the principle of the minimum being the same as the maximum in the heaven below.

nārakāṇāṃ ca dvitīyādiṣu

4.43 (SS 4.35) **In the second hell and below, the minimum lifespan of infernal beings is identical with the maximum in the hell immediately above.**

The lifespans of infernal beings is now dealt with. The maximum lifespan in the first hell, called gem-coloured, is one ocean-measured period (see 3.6). Therefore, the minimum lifespan in the second hell is 1 o.m.p. Similarly, the maximum lifespan in the second hell is 3 o.m.p., and so the minimum lifespan of the infernal beings of the third hell is 3 o.m.p. and so on, down to the seventh hell.

daśavarṣasahasrāṇi prathamāyām

4.44 (SS 4.36) The minimum lifespan of infernal beings in the first hell is 10,000 years.

bhavaneṣu ca

4.45 (SS 4.37) **The minimum lifespan of the mansion-dwelling gods is also 10,000 years.**

vyantarāṇāṃ ca

4.46 (SS 4.38) **The same applies to the forest gods.**

parā palyopamam

4.47 (not SS) **The maximum lifespan of the forest gods is one pit-measured period.**

jyotiṣkāṇām adhikam

4.48 (not SS) **The maximum lifespan of the luminous gods is more than one pit-measured period.**

The lifespan of the sun god is one pit-measured period and 1000 years; of the moon god one pit-measured period and 100,000 years.

parā palyopamam adhikam

(SS 4.39, variant of 4.47) **The maximum lifespan of the forest gods is somewhat more than one pit-measured period.**

jyotiskāṇāṃ ca

(SS 4.40, variant of 4.48) **This is the same for the luminous gods.**

The lifespan of the luminous gods is slightly more than one pit-measured period.

grahāṇām ekam

4.49 (not in SS) **The maximum lifespan of the planets is one pit-measured period.**

nakṣatrāṇām ardham

4.50 (not in SS) **The maximum lifespan of the constellations is half a pit-measured period.**

tārakāṇāṃ caturbhāgaḥ

4.51 (not in SS) **The maximum lifespan of the stars is one-quarter of a pit-measured period.**

jaghanyā tv aṣṭabhāgaḥ

4.52 (not in SS) **The minimum lifespan of the stars is one-eighth of a pit-measured period.**

caturbhāgaḥ śeṣāṇām

4.53 (not SS) **The minimum lifespan of luminous gods other than the stars is one-quarter of a pit-measured period.**

tadaṣṭabhāgo 'parā

(SS 4.41, variant of 4.53) The minimum lifespan of the luminous gods is one-eighth of a pit-measured period.

laukāntikānām aṣṭau sāgaropamāṇi sarveṣām

(SS 4.42) The lifespan of all the terminal gods is eight ocean-measured periods. They are all five cubits tall with white colouring.

CHAPTER FIVE

Substances

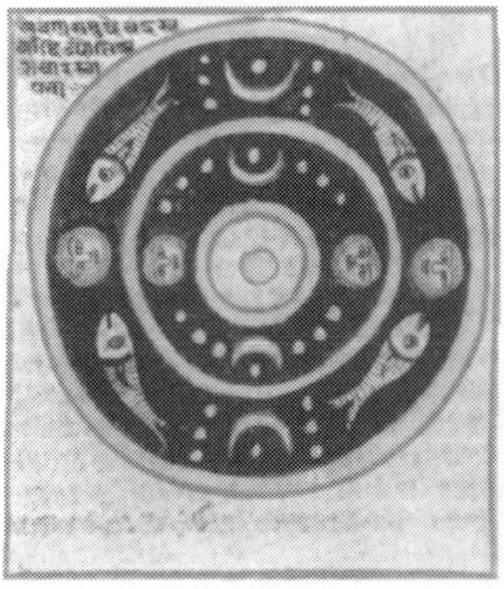

Contents

Existence

The first category of truth, sentient beings or souls, was dealt with in chapters 1–4. Now attention is given to the five non-sentient entities which, together with the soul, constitute the six substances of the universe.

ajīvakāyā dharmâ-dharmâ-kāśa-pudgalāḥ

5.1 The media of motion and of rest, space and matter are extended non-sentient entities.

These four entities are extended in space. The first two entities each consist of an innumerable number of indivisible units (see 5.7), whereas the third has an infinite number of units (5.9). Here, "unit" is used as the term for the smallest indivisible part of any one of the substances. Material clusters can have a numerable, innumerable or infinite number of units (5.10). The smallest particle of matter, the atom, consists of only one unit of matter (5.11) and is a conglomerate of the qualities of colour, taste, smell and touch.

dravyāṇi jīvāś ca

5.2 (SS 5.2–5.3) These entitities are substances. Souls are also substances.

In all there are five substances: the four non-sentient entities listed in the previous sutra, and souls.

The SS defines substance as that which passes through modes and qualities or is passed through by modes and qualities. There is an identity between a substance and its modes and qualities, but there is also difference. There is an identity because they are never perceived separately. There is difference because they can be defined differently and they serve different purposes.

nityāvasthitāny arūpāṇi ca

5.3 (SS 5.4) These substances are eternal, their number is fixed and they are devoid of material attributes.

rūpiṇaḥ pudgalāḥ

5.4 (SS 5.5) The clusters of matter and single atoms, however, have material qualities.

Of the five substances, medium of motion, medium of rest, space, matter and soul, only the fourth, matter, has the qualities of touch, taste, smell and colour. The others are without material qualities. The SS says there are six substances (see SS 5.39).

ā ākāśād ekadravyāṇi

5.5 (SS 5.6) The first three substances are each a single indivisible whole, that is, they are each one substance.

Here begins the description of the distinctive features of the first three substances: the media of motion and of rest, and space. All three are homogenous wholes, whereas matter exists in clusters and as single atoms throughout cosmic space. Similarly, souls are independent entities, infinite and inexhaustible in number despite the fact that individual souls have been attaining liberation throughout beginningless time.

The number of material clusters and free atoms is infinite times infinite, which is infinite times greater than the number of souls (see appendix 1).

niṣkriyāṇi ca

5.6 (SS 5.7) Each of the three substances referred to above is motionless.

The media of motion and of rest, and space are all stationary whereas material bodies and souls are capable of moving from one place to another.

Despite remaining in one place, which is all cosmic space, the three substances are, like all substances, dynamic. They are constantly changing but without losing their identity.

Some commentators interpreted "motionless" as immutability, but the SBT rejects this interpretation on the grounds that, according to the Jaina scripture, all substances are subject to the three cardinal phases of origination, cessation and continuity. There is nothing that is absolutely permanent or absolutely impermanent.

TRANSLATOR'S NOTE

It is the modes of a substance that begin and end and these on-going beginnings and ends make up the continuity of the substance. For example, a book is a makeshift substance. In reality, the book is a mode of four substances in combination: material particles, space units, units of the medium of motion or of rest and time units. The book begins and ends its modes in every passing moment but continues to serve the purpose of being a book.

asaṅkhyeyāḥ pradeśā dharmādharmayoḥ

5.7 (**SS 5.8 in part**) **In the substances called medium of motion and medium of rest, there are an innumerable number of units.**

The units of these substances are non-detachable, indivisible and continuous constituents. They are not like parts of a material body, but of the whole within which they exist.

jīvasya

5.8 (SS 5.8 in part) There are innumerable soul units in a soul.

The size of the soul varies from individual to individual, but the number of units in any soul is innumerable (see appendix 1). The SS explains that there are three levels of "innumerable" – low, middling and high. In the case of the media of motion and rest, and of the soul, the quantity of units is in the middle range of innumerable (equivalent to no. 8 in the series of 1–20 in figure 13 given in appendix 1).

Of these three substances, the first two are immobile (see 5.6) and pervade all cosmic space. However, despite its innumerable units, the soul can occupy a body of any size in accord with the body-making karma bound to it in its previous life.

When the soul pervades the cosmos (just prior to liberation), its eight central soul units, which are stable, coincide with the rectangular space made up of eight space units on Mount Meru in the centre of cosmic space (3.10). The other units of the soul expand to pervade cosmic space totally.

ākāśasyānantāḥ

5.9 There are an infinite number of space units in space.

Space is divided into two parts, cosmic and transcosmic. Cosmic space is that part which is occupied by souls and matter and which is co-extensive with the media of motion and of rest. There are innumerable space units in cosmic space. It is only in space taken as a whole, both cosmic and transcosmic, that there are infinite space units.

saṅkhyeyâsaṅkhyeyāś ca pudgalānām

5.10 The number of units in clusters of matter may be numerable, innumerable or infinite.

nâ-ṇoḥ

5.11 There is no additional unit in an atom of matter.

Clusters of matter may be constituted of as few as two atoms and as many as an infinite number of atoms. The atom is the single unit of matter and occupies only one unit of space. Therefore it cannot be conceived as having beginning, middle or end. The number of space units occupied by a cluster of matter may be equal to the number of atoms in that cluster. However, no clusters can occupy an infinite number of space units. This will be discussed in 5.14.

lokākāśe'vagāhaḥ

5.12 All four substances mentioned above are contained in cosmic space.

dharmâ-dharmayoḥ kṛtsne

5.13 The medium of motion and medium of rest both occupy all cosmic space.

The three substances, medium of motion, medium of rest and cosmic space, are co-existent and co-extensive. Their units penetrate each other without offering any kind of resistance; there is a one-to-one correspondence between the units of the three substances. The SS compares this pervasion of the two media throughout cosmic space to the pervasion of oil in the sesame seed. This is contrasted to the location of a jar in a particular place in the room.

Beyond cosmic space is transcosmic space which is a receptacle without contents. Cosmic space is a plenum, transcosmic space is a vacuum.

ekapradeśādiṣu bhājyaḥ pudgalānām

5.14 A cluster of matter may occupy one space unit or numerable or innumerable space units. An atom occupies only one space unit.

Depending on its contracted or expanded condition, a cluster of one, two, three or more atoms occupies at least one space unit and, at most, as many space units as there are atoms in the cluster. This maximum may be as innumerable as the space units in all cosmic space if the cluster has as many atoms as there are space units. A cluster can never occupy infinite space units because there are only innumerable space units in cosmic space.

The SS explains that atoms and clusters can penetrate each other just like the non-material substances, the media of motion and of rest. This penetration is likened to a number of lamps lighting the same space without any mutual resistance. The SS quotes the scripture: "The entire cosmic space is densely packed with diverse and infinite times infinite subtle and gross clusters of matter."

TRANSLATOR'S NOTE

This sutra reveals a conundrum of Jaina philosophy. A space unit is measured as a space occupied by one atom, yet it is possible for an infinite number of atoms to occupy one space unit.

asaṅkhyeyabhāgādiṣu jīvānām

5.15 A soul can occupy space that is one innumerablth part, or more, of cosmic space.

pradeśasaṃhāra-visargābhyāṃ (visarpābhyām) pradīpavat

5.16 Like the light of a lamp, the soul assumes the size of the body it happens to occupy on account of the contraction and expansion of its space units.

The soul is an extended substance with innumerable units which contract and expand to fit the body determined for it by its karma. However, the units of the soul are not like the units of a cluster of matter; the soul is an indivisible substance, its units are non-detachable, it is devoid of the qualities of touch, taste, smell and colour.

In normal conditions, the soul is co-extensive with the body in which it lives. When the soul extends itself to cover the entire cosmic space in order to enjoy all the sensation-producing karma at once, the innumerable units of the soul coincide one-to-one with the innumerable units of cosmic space.

The SB compares the pervasion of the entire body by the soul and the latter's contraction or expansion according to available body size, with the pervasion of the light of a lamp to fill an available area such as a large or small hall, large or small jar, etc. The area occupied by a soul is also occupied by the medium of motion, medium of rest, space and matter. This is possible because four of these five substances are devoid of obstructive structure. They are able to penetrate the only obstructive substance – matter. The SS states that the five substances do not lose their identity even though they exist in a state of interpenetration with each other.

The question why the contraction of the soul only reduces to an innumerablth part of cosmic space rather than a single space unit is answered in the SB by the fact that the worldly soul is always accompanied by the karmic body which is composed of infinite times infinite atoms (see appendix 5) which must occupy innumerable space units. The liberated soul cannot contract itself to a single space unit either, because it eliminates only one-third of the body occupied during its last worldly existence and that reduced size is maintained in the liberated state.

A very pertinent question is raised and answered by the SS in this connection. If an individual soul occupies an innumerablth part of the cosmic space, how can the infinite times infinite souls in existence, each with their own body, be accommodated in cosmic space which only has innumerable space units? The answer is that souls fall into two classes, subtle-bodied and gross-bodied. Subtle-bodied souls do not offer resistance to each other or to gross-bodied ones. They are able to co-exist in space units. Besides this, an infinite times infinite number of souls can jointly inhabit the space units occupied by the sub-microscopic body of the least developed soul.

gati-sthityupagraho dharmâ-dharmayor upakāraḥ

5.17 The function of the medium of motion is to act as the supporting cause for motion and the function of the medium of rest is to act as the supporting cause for rest.

This sutra begins the description of the functions of the five substances, starting with the media of motion and of rest.

While the soul is the efficient cause and the body the material cause of motion, the medium of motion is the supporting cause. Without it, motion is not possible. The same applies to the medium of rest in respect of rest.

The SS illustrates the function of the medium of motion by likening it to the water through which a fish swims. The function of the medium of rest is likened to the earth as the general support upon which the horse stands. When they are moving, body (matter) and soul derive support from the medium of motion. When they are stationary, they derive support from the medium of rest.

The SS examines the view that, rather than space, the medium of motion and the medium of rest existing as three substances, there is only the single ubiquitous substance of space which serves the purpose of all three. This view is rejected on the grounds that space is the necessary receptacle for all other substances (see 5.18). If space was the receptacle as well as being the media of motion and of rest, then matter and soul would be capable of motion and rest everywhere in space, both in cosmic space and in transcosmic space (5.9). Nor can earth, water, etc. be viewed as the supporting causes of motion and rest because, unlike the media of motion and rest, they have other purposes to serve. The media of motion and rest have no other purpose but the support of motion and rest, respectively.

ākāśasyâ-vagāhaḥ

5.18 Space acts as the receptacle of other substances.

Here the function of space is detailed. Space is the receptacle of all substances. The units of the media of motion and of rest coalesce with the units of cosmic space. The coalescence is a kind of mutual co-operation as the condition for each other's existence. In addition to these three substances mutually supporting each other, the other two substances, soul and matter, are also housed by space. Space is, therefore, the condition of all substances.

The SS clarifies that the specific characteristic of space is to accommodate other substances and also itself. In transcosmic space, the other substances do not exist and therefore space only has to accommodate itself. In other words, it is the receptacle of itself.

śarīra-vāṅ-manaḥ-prāṇâ-pānāḥ pudgalānām

5.19 Matter functions as the material cause of body, speech, mind and breath.

Having defined the function of the first three substances (space, medium of motion and medium of rest) in the previous sutras, the primary function of matter is now defined.

The commentaries all explain the interaction between soul and matter which is the nature of worldly life. Every worldly soul has one or more bodies (gross and/or subtle) that are made of special classes of material clusters (see 2.37). Whatever a soul possesses, whether speech organ, respiratory system or mind, is a result of its interaction with matter. Thus, the worldly existence of the soul is vitally dependent on matter (see appendix 5 for the nature of the clusters of matter that constitute body, speech, mind and breath).

The SBT explains that speech is possible only for souls who have attracted clusters of matter suitable for the body to make the speech organ, transform the clusters into sound and pour them out as language through the properly developed vocal chords etc. The physical mind is a cluster of matter that sustains the psychic mind which is of the nature of sentience and knowledge, capable of thought and memory.

The SS goes on to detail the psychic and physical aspects of speech. There are three processes that generate the *power* of speech which is the psychic aspect of speech: (1) partial elimination and partial suppression of the energy-obstructing karma, (2) partial elimination and partial suppression of the karma which obstructs empirical and articulate knowledge, (3) the fruition of the body-making karma concerned with major and minor organs (including the organ of speech). The material nature of physical speech, that is, the sound of the words, is proved by the fact that other material bodies such as a wall or the wind flowing in the opposite direction can obstruct it.

Similarly, the mind, both as a physical and psychic product, is the result of soul and matter interacting. The psychic mind (which has the essential characteristic of knowledge, see SS 2.11) is the power potential (2.18) and also sentience determined by knowledge-covering karma. As such, it has a material nature. The physical mind is the brain itself, produced by the processses of knowledge-covering, energy-obstructing and body-making karma. This organ provides the material cause for the mental faculties of discrimination, memory and attention (2.25).[1] The proof of the mind's material nature is in the effects that material things have on it, such as

[1] Although affected by karma, the psychic mind is of the soul. It is beyond intellect which is part of the physical mind. The psychic mind creates the physical mind as the vehicle for thought.

being frightened by thunder and lightning and maddened by alcohol.

Breathing is due to the partial elimination and partial suppression of the energy-obstructing and knowledge-covering karma and the rise of body-making karma. The breath itself is composed of material particles of air which are the vital condition for life. The material nature of breath is proved by the fact that it can be obstructed by material objects.

The SS draws the conclusion that the activation of the material bodies such as mind, speech and breath is due to a non-material activator, the soul, which exists behind the phenomena.

sukha-duḥkha-jīvita-maraṇopagrahaś ca

5.20 The production of pleasure, pain, life and death is also due to matter.

This sutra enumerates the other vital functions of matter. The objects that produce pain and pleasure are made of matter. Matter as nourishment sustains life and as toxin brings about death.

The SS explains this sutra with an emphasis on karmic matter. Pleasure and pain are due to the internal condition of pleasure-giving and pain-giving karmas coming to fruition, and to the appropriate external objects and conditions. The matter that produces life and death is the lifespan karma and vitality karma. Under special circumstances (see 2.52), death, premature to that ordained by karma, may be caused by external matter such as poison, weapon, fire, etc.

parasparopagraho jīvānām

5.21 Souls render service to one another.

Now, the function of souls is defined. Souls influence each other through service which may be favourable or unfavourable, beneficial or harmful. They cannot live independently of one another. They have to share their pleasure and pain with others. As partners in good and evil acts, they are jointly responsible although they must bear the karmic results individually for the part they play. They create a common environment and live together in weal and woe.

vartanā pariṇāmaḥ kriyā paratvâ-paratve ca kālasya

5.22 The functions of time are: becoming, change, motion and the

sequence of before and after.

This is the first mention of the substance time. All the substances dealt with previously were extended bodies, that is, they took up space. But time has no extension in space; its existence is extrapolated from the phenomena of becoming, change, motion, before and after. The concept of time is considered in 5.38.

sparśa-rasa-gandha-varṇavantaḥ pudgalāḥ

5.23 The clusters of matter and atoms have the qualities of touch, taste, smell and colour.

The nature of matter is now explained. There are eight kinds of touch: hard, soft, heavy, light, cold, hot, viscous (sticky), dry (rough). There are five kinds of taste: bitter, sour, astringent, acidic and sweet. There are two kinds of smell: pleasant and unpleasant. There are five kinds of colour: black, blue, red, yellow and white. Of the eight kinds of touch, only four – cold, hot, viscous and dry – are possible in an atom (see 5.25).

śabda-bandha-saukṣmya-sthaulya-saṃsthāna-bheda-tamas-chāyâ -tapô-ddyotavantaś ca

5.24 The clusters of matter possess the following modes: sound, integration, subtlety, grossness, shape, disintegration, darkness, shadow, heat and light.

Sound is of two kinds, linguistic and non-linguistic, according to the SS. Linguistic sound can be further categorized into articulate and inarticulate. The articulate variety is the lore composed in the Aryan and non-Aryan languages. The inarticulate variety is apparent in the extra-ordinary faculties of animals with two or more senses.[2] Both linguistic varieties are made by effort. Non-linguistic sound is also of two varieties, that which is natural and that which is made by effort. The natural one is illustrated by thunder, the sound of clouds colliding. The variety that is made by effort is fourfold: (1) sound produced by instruments made of hide, e.g. drum, (2) sound produced by string instruments, e.g. sitar, (3) sound produced by metal instruments, e.g. cymbals, (4) sound produced

[2] For instance, the abilities of animals to know there is going to be rain and to behave appropriately before it falls.

by wind instruments, e.g. flutes, conches.

Integration is of two kinds: natural and by effort. The integration which occurs independently of human effort is natural. For example, the integration of atoms due to their complementary viscosity and dryness, and the integration of atoms in the phenomena of lightning, fire, rainbows etc. The integration effected by human effort is illustrated by the joining of the parts of furniture and also the binding of material karma by a soul.

Subtlety is twofold: absolute and relative. The subtlety of atoms is absolute, the subtlety of composite bodies is relative.

Grossness is also twofold: absolute and relative. The grossness of the material cluster that is co-extensive with cosmic space is absolute. The grossness of other material bodies is relative.

Shape is twofold: definite and indefinite. Definite shapes are mainly of five types: circular, triangular, quadrangular, rectilinear and ringed. The shape of clouds is indefinite because it is ever-changing.

Disintegration is possible in six ways: by scratching, grinding, cutting into pieces, breaking into parts, dividing into layers and emitting sparks.

Darkness is the mode of matter in which a preponderance of black atoms obstructs vision.

Shadow is the mode of matter which is caused by covering light.

Heat, like that of fire, is the warmth caused by the sun and the like.

Light, soothing like water and shining like fire, is the lustre of the moon, gems, etc.

aṇavaḥ skandhāś ca

5.25 Matter has two varieties, atoms and clusters.

The function and modes of matter having been described, the varieties of matter are now described.

Regarding the atom, the SS quotes *Niyamasāra*, verse 6, by the great Jaina philosopher Kundakunda: "An atom is a particle which is not divisible any further; itself is the beginning, itself is the middle and itself is the end of the atom. The atom is not known by the senses. It is indivisible."

The SB quotes an ancient verse: "An atom is the ultimate cause, subtle, eternal and possessed of one taste, one smell, one colour and two kinds of touch. The two kinds of touch are hot or cold and viscous or dry." The four other kinds of touch (hard, soft, heavy, light, see 5.23) are the qualities of composite bodies only, not atoms.

To calculate how many different varieties of atoms there are, we need to calculate the different combinations of qualities possible. There are five groups of atomic qualities: (1) two kinds of touch (hot or cold), (2) two kinds of touch (viscous or dry), (3) five kinds of taste, (4) two kinds of smell, (5) five colours. Every atom has five qualities, one from each group. So, by the rule of permutations, we get $2 \times 2 \times 5 \times 2 \times 5 = 200$ varieties of atoms.

saṃghāta-bhedebhya utpadyante

5.26 Clusters of matter are produced in three ways: by integration, disintegration and by a combination of integration and disintegration.

bhedād aṇuḥ

5.27 An atom is produced by disintegration

The final product of disintegration is an atom.

bheda-saṃghātābhyāṃ cākṣuṣāḥ

5.28 The visibility of the clusters is produced by the combination of disintegration and integration.

Here visibility means perceptibility. Not all classes of material clusters are detectable by the senses. Perceptibility does not depend on the number of atoms in the cluster but on a special combination of atoms involving the joint process of integration and disintegration. According to the SBT, neither disintegration nor integration alone can produce perceptibility.

The problem of perceptibility is essentially connected with the integration of atoms which is a difficult issue. An atom has no parts. How can two atoms, both of which are partless, combine together to make a single cluster? How can many imperceptible units create a perceptible one? The SBT discusses this problem at length (5.1, 5.11, 5.25, 5.26) and attempts to solve the issue by distinguishing two aspects of atoms: an atom as partless matter (matter without parts) and an atom as the integrated qualities of touch, taste, smell and colour. These two aspects are respectively called "matter-atom" and "quality-atom". The integration of the qualities of touch, taste and so on, to a point of saturation, may result in perceptibility.

sad dravyalakṣaṇam

(SS 5.29) Existence is the character of a substance.

Existence is not substance exclusively. Existence comprises both substance and modes. Existence and reality are interchangeable terms.

utpāda-vyaya-dhrauvyayuktaṃ sat

5.29 (SS 5.30) Origination, cessation and persistence constitute existence.

All substances are real as they have existence. But what is existence? The answer given by this sutra is that existence is a combination of appearance, disappearance and persistence. What appear and disappear are modes. What persists is substance. The modes are impermanent, but the substance is permanent. Existence is the combination of impermanence and permanence, modes and substance.

The SB discusses the impossibility of the absolute permanence of the soul. If the soul were absolutely permanent, it could not undergo transformation from the life of a human to that of a god and vice versa. The acceptance of absolute permanence would, moreover, obliterate the distinction between worldly life and the state of liberation and, consequently, the spiritual discipline for the achievement of liberation would lose all meaning. Worldly life and liberation imply three distinct states of the soul: (1) ending of worldly life, (2) attainment of liberation, (3) persistence of soul. In other words, to be real, an entity must persist as substance and undergo change through the modes which begin and end.

In this connection, the SBT brings out the positive aspects of the four kinds of traditional non-existence:

1. pre-origination non-existence is existence in another form, e.g. before a golden pot originates, the gold exists.
2. post-cessation non-existence is also existence in another form, e.g. after the golden pot is destroyed, the gold exists.
3. the mutual non-existence of two things is because of their existence, e.g. this gold pot is not that gold pot and that gold pot is not this gold pot.
4. absolute non-existence refers to that which can never exist by definition of what does exist, e.g. the "square circle" is understood as impossible because both square and circle exist independently.

These four kinds of traditional non-existence are used to show the continuity between origination, cessation and persistence, between modes and substance. In the cessation of one mode there is the origination of another and through this, substance persists.

TRANSLATOR'S NOTE

The logical dilemma of partless, indivisible, imperceptible units making something – many zeros making one – has perplexed Indian philosophy for centuries. One conclusion was that reality is an illusion, there are only modes but no substance. This sutra and commentary expresses the Jaina non-absolutist solution which rejects absolutist philosophies of impermanence and permanence. The atom is understood as a combination of one substance and many qualities; the qualities have no independent existence but must be contained by the substance.

tadbhāvāvyayaṃ nityam

5.30 (SS 5.31) **What remains as it is and does not pass away is eternal.**

Having defined existence in the previous sutra, this sutra addresses the question of whether or not existence is eternal by explaining the meaning of "eternal".

The SS explains that recognition of the object in future proves the persistence of the object. Had there been only total cessation or absolutely new origination, recognition and memory could not be.

The SBT contends that origination and cessation co-exist with persistence. Origination and cessation would have no foundation without persistence and persistence would be void without origination and cessation.

The eternal soul, worldly or liberated, has modes that appear and disappear, leaving the soul intact.

arpitâ-narpita-siddheḥ

5.31 (SS 5.32) **The ungrasped [unnoticed] aspect of an object is attested by the grasped [noticed] one.[3]**

Jainism denies absolute existence or absolute non-existence, absolute permanence or absolute impermanence (see 5.29) and defends non-absolutism. An object or "real" has two fundamental aspects: eternal and non-eternal. It is permanent with respect to its essential substance and

[3] This sutra is based on the Inner Corpus, book 3, 10.46 of the Jaina scripture which gives criteria for considering the nature of substance.

impermanent with respect to the modes through which it is ceaselessly passing.

The SS explains that a particular attribute or mode of an object is brought to light by the observer for a specific purpose, relegating the other attributes and modes to the background. Such attributes and modes are designated as "the grasped ones", while the unspoken attributes and modes are the "ungrasped ones". So when a person speaks of the eternal aspect (the substance) of an object, the non-eternal aspect (the modes) is left unsaid and vice versa.

Similarly, one mode may be grasped at the expense of others. The soul is born a son, perhaps becomes an older brother, then a husband, a father, an uncle and so on. These modes are constantly coming and going depending on who the soul is interacting with. When someone speaks of a man as "my father", the man's fatherhood of another is left ungrasped, as is his sonhood, his brotherhood etc.

The SB explains that eternality ("what remains as it is and does not pass away", 5.30) and existence ("origination, cessation and persistence", 5.29) are established by means of the grasped and ungrasped aspects of the substance. It classifies the real under four aspects that are perceived or "grasped": (1) substance, (2) classification of substance, (3) object in its mode that has originated and (4) object in its mode that is passing away. The first two fall under the philosophical standpoints related to substance and the last two under the standpoints related to modes (1.6, 1.34–1.35).

The SB gives the seven attributes that may be predicated of a real:

1. existence
2. non-existence
3. inexpressibility
4. existence and non-existence
5. existence and inexpressibility
6. non-existence and inexpressibility
7. existence, non-existence and inexpressibility.

From this material provided by the SB, the SBT extrapolates the three important theories of Jaina philosophy: the Doctrine of Non-Absolutism, the Doctrine of Philosophical Standpoints and the Sevenfold Predication.

The Doctrine of Non-Absolutism. Non-absolutist philosophy finds no contradiction in a "real" being both permanent and impermanent, existent and non-existent, because it does not predicate being without becoming, or becoming without being.

To understand this, the problem of change, which has received the keen attention of all Indian thinkers, is analysed. There are two fundamental and opposing views of reality: (1) only what is eternal and unchanging is real, and (2) only what is incessantly changing is real. The former is called the Philosophy of Being and the latter the Philosophy of Becoming. In the former, change is considered as absolutely unreal, while in the latter, change is the essence of things. According to the former, it is only the substance that is real, while in the latter, it is only the modes that are real.

The Philosophy of Being is identified with the doctrine of an abiding entity such as that of the Vedānta tradition, which believes that change is only an illusion emanating from the eternal unchanging Brahman. The Philosophy of Becoming denies such an entity as, for example, in Buddhism which does not believe in substance, but only in change. Other traditions fall somewhere in between these two extremes, such as the Sāṅkhya-Yoga tradition in which the eternal substance, the soul, is absolutely constant while the primordial matter changes.

The Jaina Philosophy is distinct from these theories because the eternal substance and the changing modes are viewed as real and integral. It is not that the modes alone are subject to change while the eternal substance is static and unchanging; the substance is also liable to change, though not to absolute cessation and disappearance like the modes. The substance is renewed as the modes change. Transformation is defined as "the continuity of one's own nature through change" (5.41). This is confirmed by the SBT which says an entity is a single whole and it has the dual aspect of change and permanence; the categorization of it as substance and mode is only a device for the enlightenment of the novice.

The SBT then discusses the Law of Contradiction and shows the absence of any opposition between permanence and impermanence, existence and non-existence as attributes of the same entity. It is our experience, not abstract logic, that is the proof of the compatibility or incompatibility between attributes.

The Doctrine of Philosophical Standpoints. The philosophical standpoints are angles of vision or ways of approach and observation. These angles and ways give partial truths which contain grains of everlasting truth. The cumulative philosophical experience provided by the standpoints is extraordinarily wide-ranging and coherent and deep, and generates faith that truth is understandable.

The SBT shows how the standpoints can be used to examine a concrete real such as "spectacles". When considered through the first standpoint, common person's view, the spectacles can be described as a substance, which is one aspect of their existence (the other aspect being the modes). Considered through the seventh standpoint (actuality view), which recognizes an object as correctly identified only if it satisfies the action implied by the root-meaning of its name, spectacles are assessed in terms of their ability to *specere* meaning "to look at" (for further details on the standpoints, see 1.6 and 1.35).

The philosophical standpoints have an unlimited area of application, there being as many standpoints as there are thinkers. There is no viewpoint that is perfect as there is no science that is complete. And as there can be reality that science does not encompass, so there can be problems that are not solved by philosophy which is an endless quest. The philosophical standpoints, moreover, spread over all fields of thought and language. According to the doctrine, all philosophies are imperfect although they are the glorious blocks that build the grand edifice of philosophy.

The Sevenfold Predication. This is an investigation of the notions of existence, non-existence and inexpressibility that can be attributed to a real. A real changes constantly and therefore it is not possible to attribute absolute existence to it. What can be attributed to it is non-absolute existence which is liable to change at the next moment. Thus we get the first two predicates of the Sevenfold Predication using, as an example of a real, a pen:

1. The pen exists in some respect.
2. The pen does not exist in some other respect.

At any instant in its existence, the pen has modes that are originating, and modes that are passing away. There is simultaneous origination and cessation. So the pen "exists" with respect to one framework of substance, place, time and mode. The pen "does not exist" with respect to another framework of substance, place, time and mode.

The pen has infinite modes which, as such, are neither knowable nor expressible. As it is also impossible to conceptualize or to express simultaneously the existence and non-existence of something, we are forced to think of and express them sequentially. So we reach the third predicate:

3. The pen is inexpressible in some respect.

Now the three predicates of a real, (1) that it exists, (2) that it does not exist and (3) that it is inexpressible, become seven predicates through the law of combination which allows four different configurations of the three:

4. The pen exists and does not exist in some other respect.
5. The pen exists and is inexpressible in some other respect.
6. The pen does not exist and is inexpressible in some other respect.
7. The pen exists, does not exist and is inexpressible in some other respect.

These are the seven predicates that constitute the Sevenfold Predication.

TRANSLATOR'S NOTE

It was due to the Doctrine of Philosophical Standpoints that Jainism became a veritable repository of philosophies that originated and flourished in India.

The arguments advanced in the SBT, in regard to the Doctrine of Non-Absolutism and the Sevenfold Predication, are very much like those of Hegel who objected to the principle that A is A or, what for him amounts to the same thing, that A cannot at the same time be A and not-A, because "no mind thinks or forms conception or speaks in accordance with this law, and . . . no existence of any kind whatever conforms to it." (*The Encyclopaedia of Philosophy*, Macmillan and Free Press, 1972, vol. 4, p. 415.) Further details of the Sevenfold Predication are available in *TV*, IV.42.

snigdha-rūkṣatvād bandhaḥ

5.32 (SS 5.33) The integration of atoms is due to their tactile qualities of viscosity and dryness.

na jaghanyaguṇānām

5. 33 (SS 5.34) There cannot be integration of atoms that possess the minimum one degree of viscosity or dryness.

Viscosity and dryness vary in their degrees of intensity, from as little as one, two, three etc. to numerable, innumerable and infinite. Atoms with only one degree of viscosity or dryness cannot integrate with one another. According to SB and SBT, the implications of this sutra are that atoms of two or more degrees can integrate with each other whether they are both of the same quality, or one is viscous and one dry.

The SBT also points out the implication that a one-degree atom can integrate with a two-degree atom of a different quality. However this is rejected categorically by the SS which says that one-degree atoms cannot integrate under any conditions.

guṇasāmye sadṛśānām

5.34 (SS 5.35) Atoms which have the same degree of viscosity or same degree of dryness cannot integrate.

The SBT illustrates this law with the example of two wrestlers. As two wrestlers of equal strength cannot win in wrestling, so two equally viscous atoms or equally dry atoms cannot integrate with each other. However, the SS interprets the sutra to mean there cannot be integration of atoms of the same degree even if one is dry and one viscous.

Here, the SBT also rejects the view that a one-degree atom can integrate with a two-degree atom of the same quality.

dvyadhikādiguṇānāṃ tu

5.35 (SS 5.36) Two viscous or two dry atoms can integrate if the viscosity or dryness of one is two or more degrees higher than the other.

This sutra explains further the limits on integration. Two atoms of similar quality cannot integrate if there is only one degree difference between them. The SB gives a few examples of possible integration such as a one-degree viscous atom integrating with a three-degree viscous atom, a one-degree dry atom integrating with a three-degree dry atom and so on.

However, according to the SS, integration *only* occurs between atoms, whether similar or different in quality, if their intensity differs by exactly two degrees. So, for example, a two-degree viscous atom can only integrate with a four-degree atom, either viscous or dry.

The tables below summarize the views of the three commentators on atomic integration.

ATOMIC INTEGRATION: SB AND SBT

DEGREES OF INTENSITY	SAME QUALITY	DIFFERENT QUALITY
One + one	No	No
One + two	No	Yes
One + three	Yes	No
One + three or more	Yes	Yes
Two or more + equal number	No	Yes
Two or more + one degree higher	No	Yes
Two or more + two degrees higher	Yes	Yes

Two or more + three or more degrees higher	Yes	Yes

ATOMIC INTEGRATION: SS

DEGREES OF INTENSITY	SAME QUALITY	DIFFERENT QUALITY
One + one	No	No
One + two	No	No
One + three	No	No
One + three or more	No	No
Two or more + equal number	No	No
Two or more + one degree higher	No	No
Two or more + two degrees higher	Yes	Yes
Two or more + three or more degrees higher	No	No

bandhe samādhikau pāriṇāmikau

5.36 (not SS) **In integration, the atom with the equal or higher degree of viscosity or dryness transforms the intensity of the dissimilar atom to its own.**

When there are two dissimilar atoms with the same intensity, one will transform the other to its own quality. It is not possible to predict which will transform the other.

A higher degree raises a lower degree to its own level if the integration is between similar atoms.

bandhe'dhikau pāriṇāmikau ca

(SS 5.37, variant of 5.36) **In integration, the atom with greater degree of intensity transforms the intensity of the atom which is two degrees less to be like itself.**

guṇa-paryāyavad dravyam

5.37 (SS 5.38) **That which possesses qualities and modes is a substance.**

The nature of substances enumerated in 5.2 is now defined.

The SS quotes an ancient verse which defines quality as the divider of one substance from another and mode as the transformation of substance. A substance is never devoid of qualities and modes, their association being natural and eternal (see also 5.40 for a further definition of quality).

Substances are distinguished from one another by their qualities. For instance, the quality of sentience distinguishes a soul from a non-sentient object. Similarly, the qualities of colour, smell, etc., distinguish matter from a soul which is devoid of such qualities. Qualities are persistent attributes of substances. Modes, on the other hand, are evanescent phases of those substances and their qualities.

A substance is partially identical with its qualities and modes and also partially different from them.

TRANSLATOR'S NOTE

A substance is partially identical with its qualities and modes because each quality or mode is part of it, e.g. a lemon is yellow, wet (juicy), tastes bitter, and is hanging from a tree. It is partially different from these qualities and modes precisely because of this partial identity which means that no quality or mode is the whole of it, e.g. the lemon is partially different from yellow because it is also bitter and wet and hanging from a tree, which are qualities or modes that differ from the quality of yellowness. The substance is not merely qualities and modes but something more that integrates them.

kālaś cetyeke

5.38 (not SS)   Time is also a substance, according to some teachers.

kalaś ca

(SS 5.39, variant of 5.38)   Time is also a substance.

It was said in 5.22 that time is dealt with separately from other substances because, unlike them, it has no extension in space. Although it does not move, time is not a single substance like the medium of motion, medium of rest, and space (see 5.5). The time units are conceived as gems, with one placed on every cosmic space unit. Despite this metaphor, time units are without shape as they are not matter; they lack the qualities of touch, taste, colour and smell.

The SS proves the existence of time as an independent substance by arguing that time satisfies the definition of an existent (substance) because it has modes and qualities. Its modes are origination, cessation and persistence; the present ends and begins again at every moment, and through this time persists. Its qualities, which it has in common with other substances, are non-sentience and the absence of material qualities. Its unique qualities are its functions of causing becoming, change, motion, the sequence of before and after (5.22).

The SBT quotes the scripture to prove that time is a substance:

> "How many substances are there, O Lord?"
> Mahāvīra replied: "O Gautama, there are six substances, the extended substance of the medium of motion, the extended substance of the medium of rest, the extended substance of space, the extended substance of matter, the extended substance of the soul, and the unit of time.
>
> (Inner Corpus, book 5, 25.109)

The SBT asks whether time units can exist as isolated substances. It asserts that there must be unbreakable connections between all the time units. So time has two aspects: as an integrated and indivisible substance and as individual units spread over the cosmos.

The SBT quotes a scriptural text where time is identified with the modes of sentient and non-sentient entities.

so'nantasamayaḥ

5.39 (SS 5.40) Time consists of an infinite number of time units.

See appendix 2 for details on the nature and infinite number of time units.

dravyāśrayā nirguṇā guṇāḥ

5.40 (SS 5.41) Those which have substances as their foundation, and are not themselves the foundation of anything, are qualities.

tadbhāvaḥ pariṇāmaḥ

5.41 (SS 5.42) Transformation means the continuity of one's own nature through change.

Transformation is the continuity of the essential nature of substances and of qualities through change.

TRANSLATOR'S NOTE

Modes appear and disappear, but substances and qualities do not. Qualities change in their intensity, but do not change in their essential nature. The change that takes place in substances is more fundamental and can be defined only in reference to time units which are more subtle.

anādir ādimāṃś ca

5.42 (not in SS) Transformation is twofold: transformation with a beginning and transformation without beginning.

There is no beginning in the transformation of substances that are without material qualities, that is, the media of motion and of rest, space and souls (and time, for those who accept it as a substance).

rūpiṣv ādimān

5.43 (not in SS) The transformation in material entities has a beginning.

The transformation in material objects is diverse, such as the transformation of touch, of taste and so on. The transformation of the intensity of the qualities of touch, taste, etc., of an atom may take place spontaneously without any external cause.

yogopayogau jīveṣu

5.44 (not in SS) The activities and modes of sentience in souls have a beginning.

Although souls are substances without material attributes, their transformations do have a beginning. For instance, the soul's activities of body, speech and mind have a beginning. Similarly, the modes of sentience in the soul, such as empirical knowledge, articulate knowledge etc., have a beginning as particular events, not as general qualities of the soul.

CHAPTER SIX

The Inflow of Karma

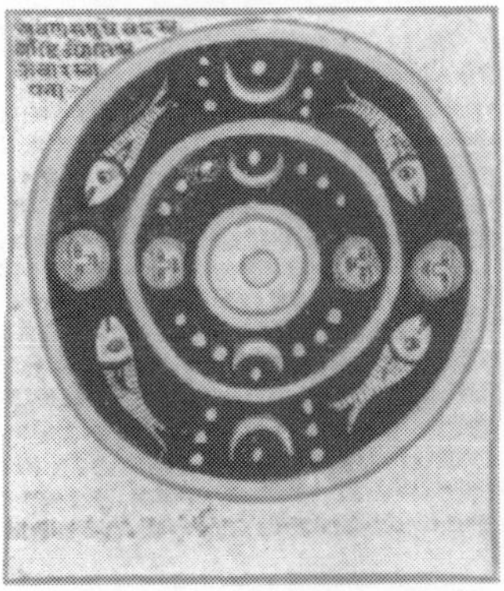

Contents

The first two of the seven categories of truth, sentient and non-sentient entities, have been explained. Now, the next category, the inflow of karma, is considered.

kāya-vāṅ-manaḥkarma yogaḥ

6.1 The operation of the body, speech and mind is action.

sa āsravaḥ

6.2 The threefold action is the cause of the inflow of karma.

The soul's beginningless karmic body channels the infinite power of the soul and in so doing causes itself and the soul to vibrate incessantly. The body-making karma creates further bodies (fiery, gross, conveyance and protean) which also vibrate and intensify the soul's vibration.

The partial elimination and partial suppression of the power-obstructing karma (see 8.14) supplies the channelled, limited power that is the energy (life-force) which activates the body, speech organ and mind.

The speech organ uses the speech material (clusters of matter in the mode of sound) created by the rise of body-making karma. The psychic mind uses the physical mind created by the body-making karma. It also has available for use the mind-power channelled from the soul by the partial elimination and partial suppression of the mind-covering karma (a sub-species of knowledge-covering karma).

In the case of the omniscient soul, this process of partial elimination and partial suppression of karma is overtaken by the complete elimination of all types of destructive karma. Infinite unchannelled knowledge and power are realized.

śubhaḥ puṇyasya

6.3 (SS 6.3 in part) Good actions cause the inflow of beneficial karma.

aśubhaḥ pāpasya

6.4 (SS 6.3 in part) Evil actions cause the inflow of harmful karma.

Violence, stealing, incontinence and so on are negative, evil activities of the body. Inflammatory speech, lies, harsh words, back-biting and so on are evil activities of speech. Lust, animosity, envy and so on are evil activities of the mind. Such activities cause the inflow of harmful karma. The good activities, which are counter to these, cause the inflow of beneficial karma. Good actions can, moreover, lead to the weakening of karmic binding if they are not undermined by evil actions such as violence and indulgence.

The SS explains that the good or evil nature of an activity depends on the good or evil intention of the person. The general effect of good activity is pleasure and that of evil activity is pain. However, karmic bondage produced by a good activity contains an element of karma which is not beneficial – knowledge-covering, intuition-covering, deluding and obstructive.

sakaṣāyâ-kaṣāyayoḥ sāmparāyike-ryāpathayoḥ

6.5 (SS 6.4) The activities of a person driven by passions cause long-term inflow (bondage) while the activities of a person free of passions cause instantaneous inflow (bondage).

The actions of a person free of passion cause karmic bondage in which the karma takes one time unit to bind, one time unit to be experienced and one to wear off. The SBT adds that an ascetic with very thin passions also experiences this instantaneous inflow, provided he meticulously observes the monastic code. Activities accompanied by passion cause karmic bondage that, in turn, causes the soul's long-term worldly wanderings.

avrata-kaṣāye-ndriya-kriyāḥ pañca-catuḥ-pañca-pañcaviṃśati-saṃkhyāḥ pūrvasya bhedāḥ

6.6 (SS 6.5) The different "doors" (causes) for the inflow of long-term karma are the five senses, four passions, five indulgences and twenty-five urges.[1]

The five senses are skin (touch), tongue (taste), nose (smell), eye (sight) and

[1] The translation follows the order of doors given in SS 6.5.

ear (hearing). The four passions are anger, pride, deceit and greed. The five indulgences are causing injury, lying, stealing, incontinence and possessiveness. The twenty-five urges are:

1. urges that lead to enlightened world-view
2. urges that lead to deluded world-view
3. evil urges of body, speech and mind
4. the inclination of the ascetic to abstain
5. urges that produce instantaneous inflow
6. physical enthusiasm
7. using instruments of destruction
8. malicious activity
9. torturous activity
10. murderous activity
11. urges for visual gratification
12. urges for tactile gratification
13. inventing and manufacturing lethal weapons
14. evacuating bowels or vomiting at gatherings of men and women
15. occupying uninspected and unswept places and leaving things there[2]
16. undertaking others' duties out of anger or conceit
17. approving of an evil act
18. divulging the sins of others
19. arbitrary interpretation of scriptural teachings
20. disrespect for the scriptural teachings
21. damage to the environment such as digging earth, tearing leaves, etc.
22. possessive clinging
23. deceitful actions
24. promotion of deluded views
25. harbouring passions and possessiveness.

The senses, passions, indulgences and urges collaborate in the production of karmic inflow. Any passionate act, whether good or evil, causes the inflow of long-term karma.

tīvra-manda-jñātâ-jñātabhāva-vīryâ-dhikaraṇa-viśeṣebhyas tadviśeṣaḥ

6.7 (SS 6.6) The nature of karmic bondage caused by inflow varies according to the particular physical and psychological conditions of the

[2] Places are inspected and swept before occupation by oneself or any object to ensure there are no small beings who may be inadvertently crushed.

subject. The conditions are: high or low intensity of the passions, whether the act is done knowingly or unknowingly, the enthusiasm [energy] with which the act is done and the instrument used in the act.

Every inflow is followed by the binding of the karmic particles to the soul, which is called karmic bondage. The nature and strength of this bondage are determined by the particular conditions given above. If the passions of the subject are intense, the bondage is deep and long-lasting. If the passions are mild, the bondage is light and short-term. If there is no passion, the bondage is instantaneous. The effects of the other conditions are similarly explained.

adhikaraṇaṃ jīvâ-jīvāḥ

6.8 (SS.6.7) The instruments of long-term karmic inflow are both sentient and non-sentient entities.

The sentient instrument (and efficient cause) of karmic inflow is the soul and its different modes, such as the intention to act, the preparation for the act and the act itself. The non-sentient instruments of karmic inflow are the body and the implements used in the act.

ādyaṃ saṃrambha-samārambhâ-rambha-yoga-kṛta-kāritâ-numata-kaṣāyaviśeṣais tris-tris-triś catuś caikaśah

6.9 (SS 6.8) The modes of the sentient instruments of inflow are: the three stages of intention, preparation and commission; the three actions of body, speech and mind; the three types of acts, those done by oneself, those in which one convinces others to undertake the act, and those undertaken by others but approved by oneself; and the four passions of anger, pride, deceit and greed.

By the formula of permutation, the total number of modes of the sentient instrument of karmic bondage is $3 \times 3 \times 3 \times 4 = 108$.

The ultimate spring of long-term karmic inflow and bondage is the four passions which drive the body, speech and mind to plan, prepare and perpetrate an act, by oneself or through others, or to be a party to an act simply by approving of someone else's initiative in acting.

nirvartanā-nikṣepa-saṃyoga-nisargā dvi-catur-dvi-tribhedāḥ param

6.10 (SS 6.9) The non-sentient means of long-term karmic inflow and

bondage are: two karma-created apparatus, four wrong ways of placing things, two wrong ways of mixing and three wrong ways of casting body, speech and mind.

The two types of karma-created apparatus are: (1) the five types of body (see 2.37) including the speech organ, mind and respiratory system, and (2) dolls, paintings and weapons.[3] The former are made by karma while the latter are karma-created in a secondary sense, having been manufactured by humans who are karma-created. All these apparatus are the means of karmic bondage because they are the instruments used for good and evil actions.

The remaining three non-sentient instruments of long-term karmic bondage are transgressions of strict monastic rules.

The four wrong ways of placing things are: (1) in uninspected places, (2) in unswept places, (3) hastily, and (4) absent-mindedly.

The two wrong ways of mixing are: (1) mixing food or drink to make it delicious, and (2) exchanging monastic equipment to suit oneself.

The three wrong ways of casting body, speech and mind are: (1) to cast away one's body by suicide, (2) to cast forth words that are not relevant to the scripture, and (3) to cast forth perverse thoughts.

tatpradoṣa-nihnava-mātsaryâ-ntarāyâ-sādanô-paghātā jñāna-darśanāvaraṇayoḥ

6.11 (SS 6.10) Slander, concealment, envy, obstructiveness, and disregard or condemnation of the scripture, its keepers and instruments, cause the inflow of knowledge-covering and intuition-covering karma.

This sutra deals with knowledge-covering and intuition-covering karma, the first two of the eight principal types of karma (see below for others). Knowledge and intuition are two stages of the act of perception. Intuition is the perception of the pure existence of an object. Knowledge perceives the details of the object (see 2.9). The knowledge-covering and intuition-covering karmas which obscure these faculties are produced by acts that hinder the quest for knowledge and support superstition and ignorance.

[3] These were the manufactured objects of the time used, respectively, for pleasure, arousal and harm.

duḥkha-śoka-tāpâ-krandana-vadha-paridevanāny-ātma-paro-bhayasthānāny asadvedyasya

6.12 (SS 6.11) **Causing pain, grief, agony, crying, injury or lamenting in oneself, or others or both, attracts pain karma.**

The SS clarifies that the mere infliction of pain, grief and so on does not cause an inflow of pain-producing karma. It is the evil motive behind the infliction of pain that attracts evil inflow. The doctor may inflict pain on the patient when performing surgery. But such infliction of pain does not cause evil inflow. Similarly, an ascetic practises austerities which pain his body but such austerities are motivated by the desire to eliminate karma and attain liberation.

bhūta-vratyanukampā dānaṃ sarāgasaṃyamādi yogaḥ kṣāntiḥ śaucam iti sadvedyasya

6.13 (SS 6.12) **Compassion through charity for all living beings, especially those observing religious vows, self-restraint of a person with attachment and the like, blameless activity, forbearance, and purity [freedom from greed] cause the inflow of pleasure karma.**

The SBT emphasizes that compassion expresses itself as acts of charity to all beings including ascetics, householders and beggars, but especially ascetics (see translator's note).

Self-restraint also plays an important role in generating the inflow of pleasure-producing karma. Self-restraint with no vestige of passion inhibits inflow but, when practised by a person with attachment, generates an inflow of pleasure-producing karma. The SB includes here a lay person's partial restraint and partial indulgence. If self-restraint and greed are equally present, as when a person lives by the "small" (lay) vows (see 7.2), the power of the pleasure-producing inflow is weakened. The SB also includes involuntary self-restraint due to unavoidable circumstances (e.g. a famine) which causes a pleasure-producing inflow, provided the passions do not interfere. Further types of self-restraint, misguided acts of self-imposed hardship and austerity by misguided people (including ascetics), such as courting death by jumping from a mountain or walking through fire, are also considered conducive to pleasure-producing inflow, provided they are performed out of religious conviction and not out of anger or despair.

Blameless activity refers to that which is approved by the community and does not infringe moral and religious mores.

Forbearance is the antidote of anger achieved by contemplating the merits of tolerance.

Purity arises when the mind is purged of greed. The practice of contentment is the antidote of greed. Scrubbing out greed is a crucial stage in the path of spiritual advancement. Absolute elimination of greed leads to perfect spirituality.

TRANSLATOR'S NOTE

In the Inner Corpus, book 5 (*Bhagavatī*), 7.114, the inflow of pleasure-producing karma is attributed solely to compassion for living things by desisting from inflicting pain. Here, the *Tattvārtha Sūtra* extends this description of compassion to include positive acts of charity and also adds further factors, self-restraint etc., as causes of the inflow of pleasure-producing karma. In *Tattvārtha Sūtra*, 6.20, and in *Bhagavatī*, 8.428, these same factors are given as the causes of birth in the realm of gods. The additional factors and the expansion of the meaning of compassion are intriguing issues related to the parts of the scripture that are extant and the parts that have met the ravages of time (see appendix 6, p. 289).

kevali-śruta-saṅgha-dharma-devâ-varṇavādo darśanamohasya

6.14 (SS 6.13) The inflow of view-deluding karma is caused by maligning the Jinas, their scripture, religious order and doctrine, and the gods and goddesses.

The enlightened world-view is obscured by the view-deluding karma. Persistent disregard for the experience of wise men and the scripture deepens scepticism and destroys the capacity to see the truth.

The Jinas are completely free of knowledge-covering karma. The religion taught by them and handed down to their immediate disciples, people of extraordinary intelligence and supernatural powers, is contained in the scripture. The religious order is constituted of ascetics practising the three gems of enlightened faith, enlightened knowledge and enlightened conduct. The religion taught in the scripture is the doctrine of non-violence. The gods are of four classes (see 4.1). Maligning is the practice of attributing blameworthy acts to the virtuous.

According to the SS tradition, the view that the Jinas live on gross food is to malign the omniscients. According to all Jaina traditions, to say the scriptures approve of meat-eating is to malign the scriptures. To say the religious order is full of low-caste people is to malign the order. Abusing the religion of the Jinas as worthless and its followers as destined to be reborn as demons is to malign the doctrine. Declaring that the gods consume wine and meat is to malign the gods.

kaṣāyodayāt tīvrātmapariṇāmaś cāritramohasya

6.15 (SS 6.14) The inflow of conduct-deluding karma is caused by the highly-strung state of the soul due to the rise of passions.

The rise of passions and quasi-passions blocks the entry to the spiritual path; the person fails to rise above selfish desires and follow the way of the wise. This causes an inflow of conduct-deluding karma.

The four passions are: anger, pride, deceit and greed. The nine quasi-passions are: laughter, relish, ennui, grief, fear, abhorrence, feminine sexuality, masculine sexuality, hermaphroditic sexuality (see 8.10).

Passions beget passions. A soul under the sway of passion attracts an inflow of conduct-deluding karma which perpetuate that passion. The chief causes of these passion karmas are: provoking passion in others, speaking ill of the ascetics, bad habits and bad vows.

As regards the quasi-passions, the inflow of laughter karma is effected by sneering at enlightened faith, laughing at people in distress and so on. The inflow of relish (non-restraint) is caused by addiction to unwholesome sports and distaste for vows and mores. The inflow of ennui (with the practice of self-restraint) is caused by stirring dissatisfaction in others, undermining their satisfaction, associating with a bad crowd and the like. The inflow of grief is caused by one's own grief and encouraging others' grief. The inflow of fear is effected by frightening oneself and others. The inflow of abhorrence is caused by deriding the praiseworthy conduct of others. The inflow of feminine sexuality is effected by lying, cheating, criticizing, excessive lust and so on. The inflow of masculine sexuality is effected by the calming of anger, absence of addiction, fidelity and the like. The inflow of hermaphroditism is effected by intense passions, hurting the sexual parts of the body, rape and so on.

The enlightened world-view is the first step to spiritual life, which is followed by cultivation of dispassion so that the mind can be cleansed of anger and greed. Deluding karma is the breeding ground of perversities of both view and conduct. The entire spiritual discipline is directed towards elimination of this karma.

bahvārambha-parigrahatvaṃ ca nārakasyâ-yuṣaḥ

6.16 (SS 6.15) Virulent aggression and extreme possessiveness lead to birth in the infernal realm.

This aphorism begins the description of the causes of lifespan karma which determines a soul's next birth in one realm or another.

Continual participation in violence, depriving others of their possessions, excessive attachment to worldly things, a dark aura, wrathful thoughts on the eve of death, and the like attract karma which causes birth in the infernal realm.

māyā tairyagyonasya

6.17 (SS 6.16) Deceitfulness leads to birth in animal realms.[4]

Deceitfulness in thought, word and deed is crookedness of the soul caused by the effective rise of a particular kind of conduct-deluding karma. It expresses itself through the preaching of false doctrines, amorality, treachery, deceit and forgery in working life, a blue and grey aura, mournful thoughts on the eve of death, and the like.

alpārambha-parigrahatvaṃ svabhāvamārdavâ-rjavaṃ ca mānuṣasya

6.18 (not SS) Attenuated aggression, attenuated possessiveness, and a soft-hearted and straightforward nature, lead to birth in the human realm.

alpārambha-parigrahatvaṃ mānuṣasya

(SS 6.17, variant of 6.18 in part) Attenuated aggression and attenuated possessiveness lead to birth in the human realm.

svabhāvamārdavaṃ ca

(SS 6.18, variant of 6.18 in part) So does a soft-hearted nature.

niḥśīla-vratatvaṃ ca sarveṣām

6.19 Amorality and self-indulgence are the common cause of birth in all realms mentioned above [infernal, sub-human and human].

[4] The term "animal" in this sutra includes microscopic and sub-microscopic beings and also plants and one-sensed beings, i.e. earth-bodied, water-bodied, etc.

sarāgasaṃyama-saṃyamāsaṃyamâ-kāmanirjarā-bālatapāṃsi daivasya

6.20 Self-restraint accompanied by attachment, partial restraint [lay vows], involuntary purging of karma and the austerities of misguided people lead to birth in the realm of gods.

samyaktvaṃ ca

(SS 6.21) So does the enlightened world-view.

The SS tradition contends that amorality and self-indulgence do not stand in the way of birth in the realm of gods because inhabitants in the earthly realms of Deva Kuru and Uttara Kuru enjoy a life of supreme plenty (SS 3.37) without abstinence and are subsequently born in heaven. This view is endorsed by the SBT which adds association with a benevolent friend, listening to religious teachings and their exaltation, the practice of austerities and so on, as leading to birth in the realm of the gods. It also includes the enlightened world-view.

As a result of their actions in past lives, infernal beings inherit cruelties, animals inherit dumbness, humans gentleness and gods a joyous life. The inhabitants create their own environment in accord with their inherited dispositions.

yogavakratā visaṃvādanaṃ cāśubhasya nāmnaḥ

6.21 (SS 6.22) Crooked and misleading actions attract inauspicious body-making karma.

Action can be mental, vocal or physical. Crooked action is an expression of deceit primarily concerned with self, whereas the deceit of misleading action, as for example teaching a false spiritual path, involves other souls. Deluded views, back-biting, a restless mind, using false weights and measures, defaming others, praising oneself and so on are examples of actions which attract inauspicious body karma.

viparītaṃ śubhasya

6.22 (SS 6.23) The opposite causes the inflow of auspicious body karma.

The opposite, that is, straightforwardness, harmony, not cheating and so on, attract beneficial karma. Normal physical and mental health are signs of straightforward and harmonious behaviour in past lives. Physical deficiency and mental disability indicate crookedness of thought, word and deed.

darśanaviśuddhir vinayasampannatā śīlavrateṣv anaticāro'bhīkṣṇaṃ jñānopayoga-saṃvegau śaktitas tyāga-tapasī saṅgha-sādhu-samādhi-vaiyāvṛttyakaraṇam arhad-ācarya-bahuśruta-pravacanabhaktir āvaśyakāparihāṇir mārgaprabhāvanā pravacanavatsalatvam iti tīrthakṛttvasya

6.23 (SS 6.24) The sixteen causes of body karma leading to the life of a Jina are: (1) purity of world view, (2) humility, (3) obeying the mores and abstinences, (4) persistent cultivation of knowledge, (5) dread of worldly existence, (6) charity and (7) austerity according to one's capacity, (8) establishing harmony and peace in the monastic order, (9) rendering service to the nuns and monks, (10) pure devotion to the adorable one, (11) pure devotion to the spiritual teacher, (12) pure devotion to learned monks, (13) pure devotion to the scripture, (14) regard for compulsory duties, (15) proper practice and promotion of the spiritual path, (16) adoration of the learned ascetics in the scripture.

These sixteen virtues lead to the most exalted state of embodied spirituality and finally to liberation. They are discussed in further detail:

1. Purity of world view is explained by the SS as the predilection for the path of liberation taught by the Jina. Such purity is characterized by eight factors: (1) absence of suspicion, (2) absence of misguided tendencies, (3) absence of doubt, (4) absence of delusion, (5) strong conviction, (6) firmness, (7) affection for the doctrine, and (8) belief in the greatness of the doctrine.
2. Humility means proper respect and honour for the path of liberation and the teachers.
3. Obeying the mores and abstinences means faultlessly observing the vows of non-violence, truthfulness, etc., and avoiding the passions of anger, greed, etc.
4. Persistent cultivation of knowledge is the constant application of the mind to the seven categories of truth: souls, non-sentient things, the inflow of karmic particles (to the soul), binding of the karmic particles (to the soul), stopping the inflow of the karmic particles, the falling away of the karmic particles, and liberation from worldly (karmic) bondage (see 1.4).

5. Dread of worldly existence is constant anxiety about suffering.
6. Charity means offering food to self-restrained ascetics, inspiring fearlessness and imparting knowledge.
7. Austerity is mortification of the body in accord with the path of liberation.
8. Establishing harmony in the monastic order is necessary in times of difficulty and disorder which may overtake the monks or nuns in their practice of religious discipline.
9. Rendering service to the monks and nuns means giving food etc. to them strictly according to the scriptural injunctions.

10 –13. Pure devotion is unconditional loyalty to the worthy ones (Jinas), spiritual teachers, monks and nuns of learning and scripture.

14. Regard for compulsory duties refers to the regular performance of six compulsory practices: (1) maintaining equanimity for a set period of time, (2) praise of the twenty-four Jinas (ominiscient teachers of this time cycle), (3) paying homage, (4) reflection upon and recoiling from past bad deeds, (5) abandoning attachment to the body for a set period of time, (6) taking a vow to prevent future faults.
15. Proper practice and promotion of the spiritual path means preaching the path correctly in regard to knowledge, austerities, charity, worship of the Jina, and so on.
16. Adoration of the learned ascetics in the scripture is cultivation of affection for them on account of their religious exaltation.

These virtues fulfil their purpose equally well if cultivated individually or *en masse*. In the scripture, there is a list of twenty causes which lead to the life of a Jina (Inner Corpus, book 6, chapter 8.18). Of the sixteen causes given above, the last, adoration of the learned ascetics in the scripture, is not included. The extra five are:

16. affection for liberated souls
17. affection for elderly monks
18. affection for ascetics
19. open-mindedness
20. high regard for the scripture.

parâ-tmanindā-praśaṃse sadasadguṇācchādano-dbhāvane ca nīcairgotrasya

6.24 (SS 6.25) **Defaming others and praising oneself, hiding others' merits and finding fault, cause the inflow of karma leading to low status.**

tadviparyayo nīcairvṛtty-anutsekau cottarasya

6.25 (SS. 6.26) The opposites of the above causes, together with humility and modesty, cause the inflow of karma leading to high status.

vighnakaraṇam antarāyasya

6.26 (SS 6.27) Being obstructive causes the inflow of obstructive karma.

Obstructing the five kinds of potential – beneficence, gain, satisfaction, comfort and power (see 2.5) – causes the inflow of obstructive karma.

CHAPTER SEVEN

The Vows

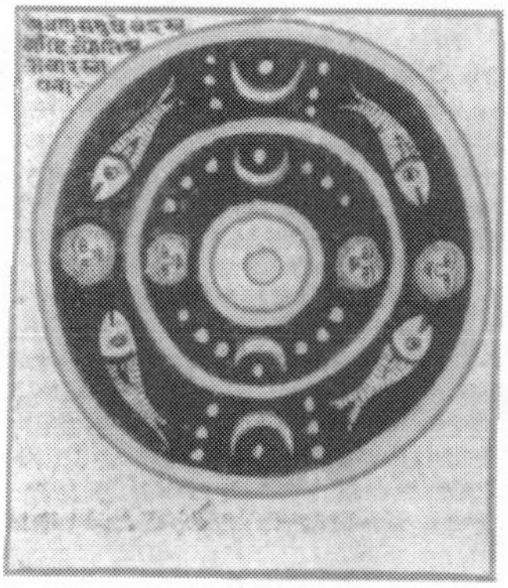

Contents

The first three categories of truth – souls, non-sentient entities and karmic inflow – have been described in the previous six chapters. Now the observance of vows which determine the variety of the karmic inflow is described.

hiṃsâ-ṇrta-steyâ-brahma-parigrahebhyo viratir vratam

7.1 Abstinence from violence, falsehood, stealing, carnality and possessiveness – these are the vows.

Violence, falsehood and the like, influence behaviour so deeply that they are seen as entrenched habits which require vows to root them out. Non-violence is mentioned first, because it is the principal vow, the basis of all other vows. In the same way that a fence is meant to protect a field, the last four vows are meant to protect the primary vow of non-violence.

A vow is a self-imposed obligation as to what one ought to do, and not do. It must be practised in thought, word and deed with full commitment to its careful observance at all times. Vows may generate the positive activities which generate the inflow of beneficial karma (see 6.3).

The SS raises a problem here which highlights the idea of a vow as both "ought not" and "ought to". It points out that self-restraint, that is, observing the vows, is named as a type of morality (9.6) which is, in turn, named as one of the ways of inhibiting karmic inflow (9.2–9.3). Yet in the commentaries to this sutra, including that of the author himself (the SB), a vow of self-restraint is given as the cause of (beneficial) karmic inflow. How can a vow both inhibit and generate karmic inflow?

The answer, says the SS, is the dual nature of each vow: its detached and attached aspects. To practise non-violence with detachment is to not be violent whereas to practise non-violence with attachment is to be compassionate in the worldly sense. The detached aspect of non-violence inhibits the inflow of karma while the attached aspect generates beneficial karma.

TRANSLATOR'S NOTE

The teaching on the dual aspects of non-violence leads to the principle that one should avoid acts of non-violence with attachment as such acts obstruct liberation.

deśa-sarvato'ṇumahatī

7.2 Partial abstinence is a small vow and complete abstinence is a great vow.

When the five vows given in the first sutra are accepted and partially practised according to one's capacity, they are called small vows. When they are accepted and practised completely and absolutely without relaxation, they are great vows.

tatsthairyārthaṃ bhāvanāḥ pañca pañca

7.3 There are five supporting practices for stabilizing each of the great vows.

vāṅ-manoguptî-ryâ-dānanikṣepaṇasamity-ālokitapānabhojanāni pañca

(SS 7.4) Controlling speech, controlling the mind, moving about carefully, handling implements carefully, inspecting food and drink properly to ensure they are acceptable.

These first five supporting practices stabilize the vow of non-violence. All are concerned exclusively with the "great vows" of the ascetics. They have little bearing on the "small vows" of lay people.

Sutras 7.4–7.8 are not included in the SB version of the sutras but they do appear in the commentary for 7.3 with slight variations. The supporting practices for the vow of non-violence are given as: moving about carefully, controlling the mind, seeking alms carefully, handling implements carefully, inspecting food and drink properly in daylight to ensure they are acceptable.

krodha-lobha-bhīrutva-hāsyapratyākhyānāny-anuvīcībhāṣaṇaṃ ca pañca

(SS 7.5) Giving up anger, greed, fear and jokes, and resorting to thoughtful speech.

These five supporting practices stabilize the vow of truthfulness. The SB gives the same in a different order.

śūnyāgāra-vimocitāvāsa-paroparodhākaraṇa-bhaikṣaśuddhi-sadharmāvisaṃvādāḥ pañca

(SS 7.6) **Staying in a secluded place such as a mountain cave, staying in a deserted house, not obstructing access to other ascetics, seeking food exactly as prescribed in the scripture, avoiding disputes with fellow ascetics about articles of common use.**

These five supporting practices for the vows of non-stealing are all related to the items for which the monastic order begs.

In the SB, the practices are given as: seeking shelter at a place only after due permission and careful consideration, doublechecking regularly that the shelter is still available, ascertaining the limits of the shelter which is offered, seeking shelter with a fellow monastic, only accepting food and drink when approved by the spiritual teacher.

strīrāgakathāśravaṇa-tanmanoharāṅganirīkṣaṇa-pūrvaratānusmaraṇa-vṛṣyeṣṭarasa-svaśarīrasaṃskāratyāgāḥ pañca

(SS 7.7) **To avoid: listening to lewd stories about women, looking at sexually arousing parts of a woman's body, recalling past sexual experience, stimulating or delicious food and drink, decorating one's own body.**

These five supporting practices stabilize the vow of celibacy.

In the SB, the things and activities to avoid are: places inhabited by women, animals and hermaphrodites, listening to lewd stories about women, looking at the sexually arousing parts of a women's body, recalling past sexual experiences, stimulating food and drink.

manojñâ-manojñe-ndriyaviṣayarāga-dveṣavarjanāni pañca

(SS 7.8) **To give up attachment to the agreeable, and aversion to the disagreeable, objects of the five senses.**

These five supporting practices, one for each of the senses, stabilize the vow of non-possessiveness. The SB gives the same list.

hiṃsādiṣv ihāmutra câ-pāyâ-vadya-darśanam

7.4 (SS 7.9) **The observer of the vows should contemplate the pitfalls and blemishes of violence, falsehood, and so on, in this life and the next.**

The list of supporting acts for each vow is followed up with the practices for strengthening the vows generally. The first of these practices is reflection upon the damaging effects in this life and the next of violence, falsehood and so on, so that the full horror of these deeds becomes apparent. The great value of the vows is then clearly grasped and the practitioner derives the moral strength needed to fulfill them.

duḥkham eva vā

7.5 (SS 7.10) **Acts of violence and so on are nothing but unmitigated suffering.**

Violence, falsehood and so on are the universal sources of suffering. The perpetrators of these acts harm both self and others. The merits of the vows are brought home to the practitioner when he feels the miseries inflicted by evil acts on his own life and the lives of his fellow beings.

maitrī-pramoda-kāruṇya-mādhyasthyāni ca sattva-guṇādhika-kliśyamānâ-vineyeṣu

7.6 (SS 7.11) **The observer of vows should cultivate friendliness towards all living beings, delight in the distinction and honour of others, compassion for miserable, lowly creatures and equanimity towards the vainglorious.**

The vows are strengthened by their practical application in daily life. Friendliness and non-violence strengthen each other. Friendliness softens the heart and nourishes the capacity for forgiveness and forbearance. The SB asks one to make the famous scriptural resolve: "I forgive all creatures. I cultivate friendliness with all. I harbour resentment against none."

Delighting in the honour and distinction of others corrodes one's own pride and conceit while compassion for their misfortune fosters a charitable heart. The cultivation of equanimity has the power to chastize vainglory in self and others.

jagat-kāyasvabhāvau vā saṃvega-vairāgyārtham

7.7 (SS 7.12) **The observer of vows should reflect upon the nature of the world outside and inside his own body in order to quicken fear of, and disinterest in, worldly life.**

To rid the soul of the ignorance that distorts its world-view and motivates it to pursue selfish ends detrimental to observance of vows, it is necessary to reflect upon the impermanence of the world and the fragility of the body. Such contemplation inspires disgust for evil deeds and disinterest in worldly goods.

The SB describes the world as "transformation of substances". Some transformations have a beginning and some do not. It gives creation, dissolution and conservation as synonyms for origination, cessation and continuity. The body is ephemeral, miserable, worthless and impure. As well as generating fear and disgust for the world, reflection upon this truth inspires regard for religion, religious people and the state of liberation.

The SS emphasizes the soul's transmigration from birth to birth in the different regions of cosmic space (see 3.1–3.6), subjecting itself to interminable miseries. There is nothing that is abiding and permanent. The body is likewise impermanent, full of suffering, devoid of any essence and contaminated with foul matter. Such contemplation of the body produces profound aversion and repugnance which nourish spirituality.

pramattayogāt prāṇavyaparopaṇaṃ hiṃsā

7.8 (SS 7.13) **Taking life away out of passion is violence.**

Here "passion" is the powerful emotions of anger, pride, deceit and greed. An injury to life motivated by passion is violence.

The SS explains the implication of an act performed "out of passion" by pointing out that injury to life does not of itself constitute an evil act. As the scripture says:

> One may deprive a creature of his life and not be touched by the act of killing provided one has been following the moral code and meticulously observing the religious norm.
>
> (*Siddhasenadvātriṃśikā*, 3.16)

It has also been said:

> A tiny insect may be trampled to death on the track under the foot of an ascetic of restrained movement. However, according to the scripture, because there is no attachment or hatred, no bondage whatsoever is created. Just as the sense of clinging, not the actual ownership of things, has been declared possessiveness in the scripture, even so, it is only the passion that is said to be the cause of bondage and not the act if it is free of passion and laxity.
>
> (*Pravacanasāra*, 3.16)

By the same logic, the passion to kill, even without an actual killing, has been called violence.

> A creature may die or not (from an action), but it is a definite act of violence if the perpetrator has acted without restraint. Mere injury does not produce bondage in a self-restrained person acting with complete care and caution.
>
> (*Pravacanasāra*, 3.17)

There is violence in the spiritual sense, even when there is no injury as a physical event. It has therefore been said:

> A person under the sway of passion kills himself at the outset even though another creature might or might not have been killed as a consequence.

asadabhidhānam anṛtam

7.9 (SS 7.14) To speak what is not true is falsehood.

Speaking untruthfully out of passion and preaching false doctrines are both falsehoods. But even speaking out truthfully is despicable when it leads to violence. Harsh words and back-biting, whether or not they are true, are blameworthy.

The SB distinguishes three kinds of untruth: denial of truth, whimsical statements, and despicable comments. Denial of truth means contradicting it by false assertion. For example, saying there is no soul, there is no life after death, the soul is the colour (brightness) of the sun, and so on. When a person identifies a cow as a horse and a horse as a cow, he is making a whimsical statement. Hurtful remarks, harsh words, back-biting, and so on, are examples of despicable comments.

adattādānaṃ steyam

7.10 (SS 7.15) Taking anything that is not given is stealing.

The SB clarifies that to take anything whatsoever, even a blade of grass, that is not offered, or that does not belong to the donor who offers it, is theft, if it is taken with the motive of theft.

The SS explains that the use of open roads and common facilities are not cases of theft. The crucial factor in theft is the motive of theft. Whether one accepts a thing or not, it is the contamination of the mind that determines the immorality of the act.

maithunam abrahma

7.11 (SS 7.16) Coupling is carnality.

Coupling is explained in the SS as the desire to touch each other, which arises in the minds of two people charged with lust from the rise of conduct-deluding karma. The desire leads to copulation.

Celibacy promotes the virtues of non-violence, truth and so on, while copulation augments their opposites because it is bound to involve killing mobile and immobile beings, speaking falsely, commiting theft and indulging in possessiveness.

TRANSLATOR'S NOTE

The implication is that coupling refers to free sexual activity outside marriage.

mūrcchā parigrahaḥ

7.12 (SS 7.17) Clinging is possessiveness.

Possessiveness is clinging to the animate and inanimate. It may refer to clinging to something in the external world or to feelings within the self. The SB describes it as desire, coveting, craving, longing, yearning, greed, clinging.

The SS explains clinging as earning money, maintaining one's possessions and up-grading livestock, precious things and properties. Nourishing the passions of the mind is also a form of emotional clinging. In fact, clinging is essentially a state of mind. Even in the absence of any actual external possession, a person obsessed with the sense of mineness has possessiveness.

The SS raises an interesting contention as to whether the "properties" of knowledge, intuition, and so on, are possessions because they may also generate possessiveness. However, the contention is rejected on the grounds that knowledge, intuition and so on, if enlightened, are not due to passion and, therefore, are not possessions. The absence of clinging is the criterion of non-possessiveness. Enlightened knowledge, intuition and so on are intrinsic qualities of the soul and as such are devoid of possessive instinct. Lust, hatred and so on, however, are due to karma, and are not properties of the soul and so are unworthy of being entertained and cosseted.

The sense of mineness necessitates maintaining the possession, which is bound to involve violence, falsehood, theft and concupiscence and, ultimately, suffering due to birth in a hell realm or the like.

niḥśalyo vratī

7.13 (SS 7.18) **One who is free of any thorns is an observer of the vow.**

Now that the vows have been explained, "observer of the vow" is explained. The observer of the vow must be free of the *thorns* of deceit, anxiety to fulfil desires through the practice of austerities, and deluded world-view. It is not possible to observe any vow properly in the presence of these thorns which annihilate the bliss of liberation.

agāry anagāraś ca

7.14 (SS 7.19) **Observers of the vows fall into two classes: the householders and the homeless monks who have renounced violence and possessiveness.**

The householders are also called "learners" and the homeless monks (and nuns), "ascetics".

aṇuvrato'gārī

7.15 (SS 7.20) **The householder is the observer of the small vows.**

It is difficult for the householder totally to avoid injury to life in the daily routine of cultivating land, cooking food, grinding corn, cleaning the toilet and so on. To accommodate this, the SS explains observance of the first small vow of non-violence as avoiding injury to mobile beings which have two or more senses. The SBT says that the householder observing this vow should desist from "intended" acts of violence.

Similarly, as the householder cannot always refrain from all forms of falsehood, he takes the second small vow of truthfulness to avoid false statements out of extreme affection for people or property, hatred and a deluded outlook which might lead to destruction of homes and villages.

The third small vow of the householder is to refrain from taking anything without the owner's consent, including something which has been abandoned by another person and may lead to punishment by the king or to censure by the people.

The fourth small vow of the householder is to desist from sexual activity with anyone other than one's spouse.

The fifth small vow of the householder is to voluntarily limit the possession of cattle, corn, land and so on.

dig-deśâ-narthadaṇḍavirati-sāmāyika-pauṣadhopavāsô-pabhogaparibhogaparimāṇâ-tithisaṃvibhāgavratasampannaś ca

7.16 (SS 7.21) The seven supplementaries which enrich the observer of the small vows are: refraining from movement beyond a limited area, restricting movement to an even more limited area, refraining from wanton destruction of the environment by thought, word or deed, keeping aloof from sinful conduct for a set period of time, fasting on sacred days and observing special restrictions at secluded places, limiting the use of consumable and non-consumable goods, offering alms to wandering ascetics.

The seven supplementaries are also known as the "mores".

In SBT, the first, third and sixth supplementaries are called subsidiary vows which are accepted for permanent life-long observance. The second, fourth, fifth and seventh are trainee's vows to be practised on relevant occasions, daily or on particular days. In SS, the first three supplementaries are called "subsidiary vows" and the remaining four, "trainee's vows".

The SB elaborates further on the vows:

1. Refraining from moving outside a limited area requires the householder to restrict his sphere of activity as the only way to avoid all harmful activities beyond the specified area.

2. Further restricting movement requires the householder to commit himself to activity in an even smaller area so as to expand the area of immunity from his exploitative activities. This commitment grants fearlessness of him to all beings outside that area.

3. Wanton destruction is described by the SB as destroying the consumable and non-consumable necessities of a householder's life. The SS identifies five varieties of wanton destruction: (1) evil thoughts of conquest, subjugation, killing, mutilating, hurting and so on, (2) evil counsel to torture animals and indulge in harmful activities, (3) negligent conduct such as recklessly cutting trees, digging or flooding fields, (4) supplying lethal weapons, (5) malicious sermons.

4. Keeping aloof from sinful conduct for a set period means desisting from all injurious activities during that time.

5. The sacred days for fasting are prescribed as the eighth, fourteenth or

fifteenth day of the fortnight. During the fast period, the householder abstains from bathing and using cosmetics and, ever refraining from violence and so on, remains constantly aware of his vows. The SS says that fasting on sacred days should be observed at clean places occupied by monks, temples or one's own place of religious practice.

6. Limiting use of consumable and non-consumable goods refers to food, drink, cosmetics, rich clothes and jewellery, beds, chairs, vehicles and so on.

7. Offering alms to ascetics must be undertaken with care to follow the strict prescriptions of the scriptures. The ascetics should be offered suitable food and drink with devotion and humility befitting the custom and etiquette of the place and occasion. The SS lists food, religious equipment, medicine and shelter as necessities to be offered to ascetics. The SBT recommends food, drinks, dainties, delicacies, clothes, towels, shelter, beds and medicine as alms that can be given.

The householder observing these vows is described as partially self-restrained.

māraṇāntikīṃ saṃlekhanāṃ joṣitā

7.17 (SS 7.22) The householder should become a practitioner of the penitential rite of emaciation of the passions by a course of fasting which spans a number of years and ends in death.

The rite of fasting to death is undertaken only when the practitioner perceives clear signs of approaching death or feels his utter incapacity to fulfill his religious vows. He does not undertake the vows out of passion or deluded belief. He finds joy in such fasting and meets death fearlessly.

The SB gives details of the practice of this rite at some length. The practitioner starts by reducing his diet, then fasts regularly for progressively longer periods, adopts the observance of the ascetic's self-restraint and finally gives up all food and drink to fast to death while engaged in reflections (see 9.7) and meditations (9.27, 9.30, 9.37–9.46).

The SS defines death as the ending of the lifespan, karmically bound in the previous life, due to the wearing out of the senses and vitality. The rite of emaciation is undertaken by the householder for the attenuation of the external body and the internal passions. It is adopted with full joy and calmness of mind and not impetuously. It is not suicide because it is undertaken without duress or passion. To commit suicide is to kill oneself out of anger, agony, malice or frustration, whereas fasting to death purges the soul of its passions and perversities by conquering the fear of death.

śaṅkā-kāṅkṣā-vicikitsâ-nyadṛṣṭipraśaṃsā-saṃstavāḥ samyagdṛṣṭer aticārāḥ

7.18 (SS 7.23) The transgressions of the enlightened world-view are: suspicion, misguided inclination, doubt, praise for the heretical doctrines, and familiarity with the heretical doctrines.

The observer of vows has been described as free of the thorn of deluded world-view (see 7.13), in other words, in possession of the enlightened world-view. Confusion and doubt will undermine the observance of the vows by weakening the enlightened world-view that is the first step to religious life.

The SB brings out the connotations of the five attitudes warned against. Suspicion means a sense of uncertainty about the truth of the doctrine propounded by the Jinas. Misguided inclination refers to irrational hankering for the heretical doctrines concerning worldly and other-worldly favours. Doubt refers to intellectual illusion about fundamental truths and the fruit of spiritual exertion. Praise for the heretical doctrines is the unfounded appreciation of the merits of heterodox disciplines and doctrines. Familiarity with these doctrines means cultivating intimacy with their real and imagined merits.

The SB gives two broad divisions of the heretical doctrines, the speculative and the non-speculative, and a further four sub-divisions of these: activism, inactivism, agnosticism and egalitarianism. There are 363 varieties of these four sub-divisions (8.1).

vrata-śīleṣu pañca pañca yathākramam

7.19 (SS 7.24) There are five transgressions of each of the five small vows and seven mores.

bandha-vadha-cchavicchedâ-tibhārāropaṇâ-nnapānanirodhāḥ

7.20 (SS 7.25) Tethering, beating, piercing the skin, overloading, and withholding food and drink.

These are the five transgressions of the small vow to abstain from violence. The first three transgressions are concerned with all creatures, mobile and immobile, and the last two with men, and beasts of burden such as elephants, bulls, buffaloes.

mithyopadeśa-rahasyābhyākhyāna-kūṭalekhakriyā-nyāsāpahāra-sākāramantrabhedāḥ

7.21 (SS 7.26) Wrong instruction, divulging secrets, forging documents, misappropriating funds entrusted to one's care, and disclosing confidential deliberations.

These are the five transgressions of the small vow to abstain from falsehood.

stenaprayoga-tadāhṛtādāna-viruddharājyātikrama-hīnādhikamānonmāna-pratirūpa-kavyavahārāḥ

7.22 (SS 7.27) Abetting theft, dealing in stolen goods, evading customs in foreign lands, misrepresenting the weight of goods one is buying or selling, and dealing in counterfeit goods.

These are the five transgressions of the small vow to abstain from stealing.

paravivāhakaraṇê-tvaraparigṛhītâ-parigṛhītāgamanâ-naṅgakrīḍā-tīvrakāmābhiniveśāḥ

7.23 (SS 7.28) Matchmaking, promiscuity, sex with whores, unnatural sexual practices, and intense sexual passion.

This sutra lists the five transgressions of the small vow to abstain from carnality.

kṣetra-vāstu-hiraṇya-suvarṇa-dhana-dhānya-dāsī-dāsa-kupyapramāṇātikramāḥ

7.24 (SS 7.29) The failure to keep within the set limits of tillable land and buildings, silver and gold, livestock and grain, male and female slaves, and of base metals, earthenware and wooden furniture.

This sutra lists the five transgressions of the small vow to abstain from possessiveness.

ūrdhvâ-dhas-tiryagvyatikrama-kṣetravṛddhi-smṛtyantardhānāni

7.25 (SS 7.30) Going beyond the limits of the set area upwards,

downwards, horizontally; adding to the set area, and forgetting the limitations made.

The exposition of the transgressions of the five small vows completed, the above sutra lists the five transgressions of the first of the seven supplementary vows, the vow to refrain from movement beyond a limited area.

ānayana-preṣyaprayoga-śabda-rūpānupāta-pudgalakṣepāḥ

7.26 (SS 7.31) **Importing from beyond the limits of the set area, deputing a servant to bring something from beyond these limits, calling another beyond the limits, gesturing to another beyond the limits, exporting beyond the limits.**

This sutra gives the five transgressions of the second supplementary vow, the vow to restrict movement to an even more limited area than observed in the practice of the first supplementary vow (see above).

kandarpa-kautkucya-maukharyâ-samīkṣyādhikaraṇô pabhogādhikatvāni

7.27 (SS 7.32) **Erotic talk, erotic gesture, garrulity, unmindful deeds beyond the set limit, and excessive use of consumer goods.**

This sutra lists the five transgressions of the third supplementary vow, the vow to refrain from wanton destruction of the environment.

yogaduṣpraṇidhānâ-nādara-smṛtyanupasthāpanāni

7.28 (SS 7.33) **Improper physical activity, improper speech, improper thought, lack of enthusiasm for the vow, and an unmindful attitude to the vow.**

This sutra lists the five transgressions of the fourth supplementary vow, the vow to keep aloof from sinful conduct for a set period of time.

apratyavekṣitâ-pramārjitotsargâ-dānanikṣepa-saṃstaropakramaṇâ-nādara-smṛtyanupasthāpanāni

7.29 (SS 7.34) **Evacuating excreta in uninspected and unswept places, picking up things or leaving them in uninspected and unswept places, spreading mats in uninspected and unswept places, disregard for the vow, and an unmindful attitude towards the vow.**

This sutra lists the five transgressions of the fifth supplementary vow, the vow to fast on sacred days at secluded places.

No vow should be observed disrespectfully or unmindfully. Proper inspection and sweeping places clean of all animate material are necessary in order to avoid hurting or killing insects.

sacitta-sambaddha-saṃmiśrâ-bhiṣava-duṣpakvāhārāḥ

7.30 (SS 7.35) **Eating animate food,[1] eating things in contact with animate food, eating things mixed with animate food, drinking alcohol, and eating half-cooked food.**

This vow lists the five transgressions of the sixth supplementary vow, the vow to limit use of edible goods and of non-edible goods which are placed in contact with animate ones.

sacittanikṣepa-pidhāna-paravyapadeśa-mātsarya-kālātikramāḥ

7.31 (SS 7.36) **Placing alms on animate objects [such as green leaves], covering alms with animate objects, pretending that the food belonged to others, offering competitively against other donors, and untimely offering of food.**

This sutra lists the five transgressions of the seventh supplementary vow, the vow to offer alms to wandering ascetics. It focuses upon dubious motivations of the donors.

jīvita-maraṇāśaṃsā-mitrānurāga-sukhānubandha-nidānakaraṇāni

7.32 (SS 7.37) **Hope for longer life, hope for shorter life, attachment to friends, clinging to pleasures, and craving for reward.**

The enumeration of the transgressions of the seven supplementary vows complete, this sutra deals with the five transgressions of the vow of emaciation of the passions by gradual fasting (see 7.17).

Observers of the vow to gradually fast to death should be free of all desires and cravings for rewards as a result of fasting. They must practise absolute detachment from worldly things.

[1] This refers to any food that is still living or has living beings (e.g. bacteria) on it. All flesh and eggs and some plants are considered permanent supporters of microscopic life even when cooked.

anugrahārthaṃ svasyātisargo dānam

7.33 (SS 7.38) Charity consists in offering alms to the qualified person for one's own benefit.

The giver gives for his own benefit with a sense of gratitude to the recipient. Charity practised with a pure heart helps weaken karmic bondage. (For the qualifications of the giver and recipient, see 7.34.)

vidhi-dravya-dātṛ-pātraviśeṣāt tadviśeṣaḥ

7.34 (SS 7.39) The worth of a charitable act is determined by the manner of giving, the nature of the alms offered, the disposition of the giver and the qualification of the recipient.

The giver's motives and enthusiasm and the quality of the alms offered determine the worth of the act of charity. The genuinely monastic life of the recipient adds dignity to the act. The worth of the charity is enhanced if the giver gives with a sense of duty and the recipient accepts what is a bare necessity of monastic life.

The SB clarifies that the manner of giving includes propriety of place and time of giving, the enlightened faith of the giver, the sense of honour and regard with which the offering is made, the priority and acceptability of the thing given. The nature of the alms offered relates to the good smell, taste and so on of the food and drink as well as their class and quality. The disposition of the giver relates to his freedom from envy, feeling of pleasure and joy, sense of honour, good intention, freedom from expectation, deceit and eager desires.

The qualification of the recipient relates to his enlightened faith, knowledge, conduct and practice of austerities.

The SS offers a slightly different explanation of the four constituents of giving. The manner of giving relates to the regard or disregard in the mind of the giver for the recipient. The merit of the thing given depends on its usefulness in the practice of austerities and religious studies of the recipient. The merit of the giver is his freedom from envy and lack of depression. The fitness of the recipient is his commendable practice of the spiritual discipline of self-restraint.

CHAPTER EIGHT

Karmic Bondage

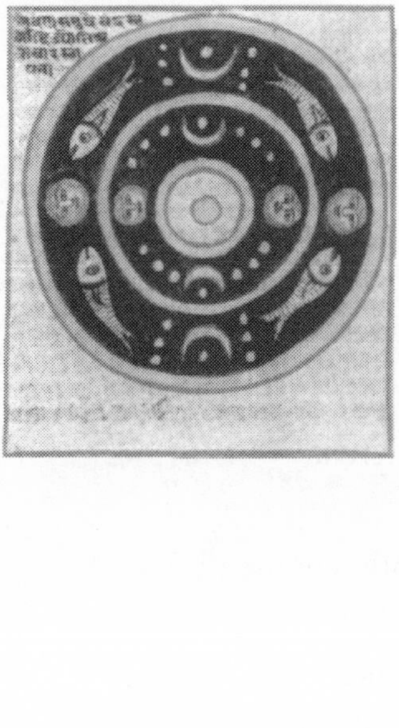

Contents

The third category of truth, karmic inflow, was explained in the sixth chapter and the means of determining its variety through vows was explained in the seventh. Now, the fourth category of truth, the binding of karma, is explained.

mithyādarśanâ-virati-pramāda-kaṣāya-yogā bandhahetavaḥ

8.1 The five causes of bondage are: deluded world-view, non-abstinence, laxity, passions and the actions of the body, speech and mind.

1. The first cause of bondage, deluded world-view, falls into two principal types, speculative and non-speculative, according to the SB tradition. Deluded views, which are reached by unwarranted imagining and abstraction, are speculative (committed). There are 363 varieties of speculative deluded views mentioned in the scripture. Views entertained by the common folk on blind faith are non-speculative (uncommitted). Doubt is a third type of deluded world-view.

The SS describes the two broad divisions of deluded views as those which are natural and those produced by formal instructions or instigation of others. Natural deluded views are due to the rise of view-deluding karma. Deluded views produced by others' instructions are divided into four or five types.

The four types are: (1) activism,[1] of which there are 180 varieties, (2) inactivism,[2] of which there are eighty-four varieties, (3) agnosticism, of which there are sixty-seven varieties, (4) equal validity of all doctrines, of which there are thirty-two varieties.

The five types of deluded views are given as: (1) absolutist, (2) perverse, (3) sceptical, (4) egalitarian, and (5) agnostic. Absolutism is illustrated by

[1] Belief in liberation but not in the other categories of truth.

[2] Disbelief in the distinction between beneficial and harmful karma.

doctrines such as: "Whatever exists is the cosmic person", "All existents are permanent", and so on. Examples of perverse views are: "The unbound (ascetics) may keep the bonds (clothes and other equipment)", "The omniscient consumes food", "Women can achieve liberation", etc.[3] Views deluded by scepticism are exemplified by doubts like: "Enlightened world-view, enlightened knowledge and enlightened conduct may or may not lead to liberation."[4] The deluded view of egalitarianism is illustrated by the doctrine that considers all deities and all philosophical views as equally valid. Agnosticism denies the possibility of a distinction between good and bad doctrines.

In this connection, the SBT names as upholders of deluded doctrines about thirty great non-Jaina philosophers of ancient times, such as Bādarāyaṇa and Jaimini, the famous Vedānta and Mīmāṃsā advocates. The doctrines were deluded because they were absolutist, allowing for no other viewpoints.

2. The second cause of bondage, non-abstinence or indulgence, is the opposite of abstinence which was explained in 7.1.

3. The third cause of bondage, laxity, consists of absentmindedness, lack of enthusiasm for beneficial karma, and improper actions of body, speech and mind.

4. The fourth cause of bondage, passions, will be explained in 8.10.

5. The fifth cause of bondage, action, was explained in 6.1.

Of these five causes of bondage, each cause presupposes the succeeding one, but the succeeding one does not presuppose the one before.

sakaṣāyatvāj jīvaḥ karmaṇo yogyān pudgalān adatte

8.2 (SS 8.2 in part) **Because of its passions, the soul attracts and assimilates the material particles of karmic bondage.**

Of the five causes of bondage mentioned in the previous sutra, the passions are assigned special significance because of their exclusive role in the production of long-term bondage. The karmic particles, attracted by the soul through actions motivated by passions, are assimilated and firmly bound to the soul.

[3] These views are an area of controversy between the Jaina sects.

[4] This is doubting the validity of the Jaina doctrine of liberation, see 1.1.

sa bandhaḥ

8.3 (SS 8.2 in part) The result is bondage.

Laden with karmic matter throughout its beginningless existence, the soul is always vibrating. This vibration draws fresh karmic matter which is bound to the soul by passions. The binding is called bondage. The soul has no hands to draw, nor body to hold karmic matter. It is the beginningless karmic matter which draws fresh karmic matter into the soul from all directions. The "entry" of the karma into the soul is metaphorical; the material particles, capable of becoming karma and situated everywhere, are merely converted into the different types of karma by the soul (see 8.25).

prakṛti-sthity-anubhāva-pradeśās tadvidhayaḥ

8.4 (SS 8.3) There are four aspects of bondage: type, duration, intensity (quality) of fruition, and mass of material particles assimilated.

Now that the causes of bondage have been explained, this sutra begins the description of the nature of bondage.

1. Type of bondage: There are eight types of bondage (see 8.5) created from karma assimilated into the soul. In the SS, the type of bondage is explained as the nature of bondage and is compared with the bitter taste of the colocynth fruit or the sweet taste of sugar.
2. Duration of bondage: This is the period of time from the moment of karmic binding until the time the karma falls away after its fruition. The SS likens the varying duration of different karmic bondages to the varying duration of the sweetness in goat, cow and buffalo milk.
3. Intensity of bondage: This is the varying degrees of depth (and variety) of karmic fruition. The SS compares the intensity of the bondage with strong, medium or mild tasting milk.
4. Mass of material particles assimilated: This refers to the quantity of particles assimilated.

ādyo jñāna-darśanāvāraṇa-vedanīya-mohanīyâ-yuṣka-nāma-gotrâ-ntarāyāḥ

8.5 (SS 8.4) There are eight principal types of karmic bondage: knowledge-covering, intuition-covering, sensation, deluding, lifespan, body, status, and obstructive.

This sutra describes the first aspect of bondage – type. The eight types are explained as follows:

1. Knowledge-covering karma hinders knowledge of objects.
2. Intuition-covering karma hinders intuition of objects.
3. Sensation karma produces sensations of pleasure and pain.
4. View-deluding karma distorts enlightened appreciation of the categories of truth; conduct-deluding karma produces passions and quasi-passions.
5. Lifespan karma determines lifespan.
6. Body karma produces the bodies of infernals, subhumans (animals, plants and microscopic beings), humans and gods.
7. Status karma determines the family, class and society into which one is born.
8. Obstructive karma hinders the properties of beneficence, gain, satisfaction, comfort and power (see 2.4). It can also partially or completely obstruct the spiritual energy of self-restraint (2.5).

pañca-nava-dvy-aṣṭāviṃśati-catur-dvicatvāriṃśad-dvi-pañcabhedā yathākramam

8.6 (SS 8.5) Of the eight types of karmic bondage, there are five sub-types of knowledge-covering, nine intuition-covering, two sensation, twenty-eight deluding, four lifespan, forty-two body, two status, and five obstructive.

matyādīnām

8.7 (SS 8.6) There are five sub-types of knowledge-covering karmic bondage with respect to empirical knowledge [cognition], articulate knowledge, clairvoyance, mind-reading and omniscience.

The SS raises an interesting problem. Covering a type of knowledge presupposes the existence of that type of knowledge in the soul. In these sutras, five sub-types of knowledge-covering karma, one for each type of knowledge, are accepted as existent in each soul. But there are souls who are intrinsically incapable of attaining liberation and, therefore, cannot have the power of mind-reading and omniscience, the two types of knowledge which are possible only in souls capable of attaining liberation. Consequently, the problem arises as to whether it is logical to accept the existence of a type of knowledge which will never manifest. The problem is solved by admitting two kinds of existence, existence that is potential and existence that manifests. Thus considered, the five sub-types of knowledge exist potentially in all souls, although they will not all necessarily manifest.

cakṣur-acakṣur-avadhi-kevalānāṃ nidrā-nidrānidrā-pracalā-pracalāpracalā-styānagṛddhivedanīyāni ca

8.8 (SS 8.7) The nine sub-types of intuition-covering karmic bondage relate to: the four varieties of intuition – visual, non-visual, clairvoyant and omniscient – and the five varieties of sleep – dozing, sleeping, drowsing, sleepwalking and torpidity.

Dozing is light sleep for alleviating fatigue. Drowsing is a state of sleep while upright. Torpidity is a dormant or hibernating state where, according to the SS, a special kind of energy may give vent to cruel acts of great intensity in dreams.

TRANSLATOR'S NOTE

Sleep appears to be included here because it involves a state of indistinct perception which is a form of intuition but in which passion (conduct-deluding karma) may also play a part in dreams.

sad-asadvedye

8.9 (SS 8.8) The two sub-types of sensation karmic bondage are the producers of pleasure and pain.

darśana-cāritramohanīya-kaṣāya-nokaṣāyavedanīyākhyās tri-dvi-ṣoḍaśa-navabhedāḥ samyaktva-mithyātva-tadubhayāni kaṣāya-nokaṣāyāv anantānubandhy-apratyākhyāna-pratyākhyānāvaraṇa-saṃjvalanavikalpāś caikaśaḥ krodha-māna-māyā-lobhā hāsya-raty-arati-śoka-bhaya-jugupsā-strī-puṃ-napuṃsakavedāḥ

8.10 (SS 8.9) The twenty-eight sub-types of deluding karma are bondage with respect to three kinds of delusion of view and twenty-five kinds of delusion of conduct.

The three kinds of delusion of view are: the near-perfect enlightened world-view, deluded world-view and a mixture of the two.

The twenty-five conduct-deluding karmas are the sixteen passions and nine quasi-passions. The sixteen passions are: the four passions of anger, pride, deceit and greed, each being either tenacious, non-abstinent,

partially abstinent or flickering. The nine quasi-passions are: laughter, relish, ennui, grief, fear, abhorrence, and the female, male and hermaphroditic dispositions.

The enlightened world-view is attained for varying durations by the elimination, suppression, or partial elimination and partial suppression of the view-deluding karma (see 2.3–2.5). The perfect enlightened world-view is only attained when the view-deluding karma is totally eliminated.

A near-perfect enlightened world-view is the first of the three types of deluded view referred to in this sutra. Suppressing the view-deluding karma results in an enlightened world-view which is imperfect because it only lasts one intra-hour before fading. However, it is destined to reappear. Partial suppression and partial elimination of the view-deluding karma is accompanied by the rise (fruition) of some of the deluding karma. This enlightened world-view is also less than perfect because it has an end, although it does last a long time and will ultimately be converted into a permanent possession of the soul. In the meantime, it is also a kind of bondage.

Completely deluded world-views are the second type of delusion and the third occurs when enlightened and deluded world-views are mixed and there is a kind of oscillation between them.

The SS explains the bondage of a completely deluded world-view as the state of karma which, when it rises, produces aversion to the religious path revealed by the Jina, indifference to belief in the categories of truth, and inability to distinguish between beneficial and harmful attitudes to life. This completely deluded world-view turns into a near-perfect enlightened world-view when the delusion is checked and becomes incapable of destroying the disinterest in worldly life which the soul has developed. Deluded and enlightened world-views mix, when, like the inferior species of rice which has only partially lost its power of fermenting a beverage, the soul has purged itself only partially of delusion.

The sixteen kinds of passion and the nine quasi-passions are synonymous with conduct-deluding karma.

When the four passions of anger, pride, deceit and greed are of great intensity, they keep the soul immersed in the darkness of delusion leading to deluded conduct and unending worldly wanderings. They are called tenacious. The SB describes them as the destroyers of the enlightened world-view. However, these passions become weak when the soul attains the enlightened world-view and are then called non-abstinent passions. The SB describes them as the destroyers of the inclination for abstinence. Such passions prevent the soul from observing the vows. When those passions are further weakened, they are called partially abstinent because they allow the soul to undertake the small vows of a layperson. The SB explains that they cover the capacity for complete abstinence. When these passions get rid of their gross nature and become subtle forces, they are called flickering passions which disturb the soul's higher states of spiritual development. The SB explains that they are detrimental to the practice of perfect conduct which requires complete absence of passion.

The SB compares the four types of anger, tenacious, non-abstinent, partially abstinent and flickering, respectively, to a rift in rock, earth, sand and water. The four types of pride are compared respectively with a pillar of rock, bone, wood and straw. The four types of deceit are compared respectively with the degree of crookedness of a bamboo-root, a ram's horn, cow's urine and a chalk-mark by the carpenter. The four types of greed are compared respectively with the stain made by lac, mud, dirty grease and turmeric. The antidotes of anger, pride, deceit and greed are, respectively, forgiveness, humility, straightforwardness and contentment.

The nine kinds of quasi-passion karma are so called because they are incapable of harming the soul in the absence of the full passions of anger, pride, deceit and greed. The SS defines the bondage of the quasi-passions in terms of their results at the time of fruition. The bondage of the quasi-passion of laughter produces laughter, the bondage of the quasi-passion of relish produces relish, and so on. The SB compares the persistence of the male, female and hermaphroditic dispositions respectively with those of the straw fire, wood fire and cow dung fire, which last for comparatively longer periods. The SBT compares the hermaphroditic disposition to the conflagration of a township. (For the inflow of quasi-passions, see 6.15.)

nāraka-tairyagyona-mānuṣa-daivāni

8.11 (SS 8.10) **The four sub-types of lifespan karma lead to birth as infernal beings, subhumans, humans and gods.**

Lifespan karma determines both longevity and the realm of birth.

gati-jāti-śarīrâ-ṅgopāṅga-nirmāṇa-bandhana-saṅghāta-saṃsthāna-saṃhanana-sparśa-rasa-gandha-varṇâ-nupūrvy-agurulaghū-paghāta-parāghātâ-tapo-ddyotô-cchvāsa-vihāyogatayaḥ pratyekaśarīra-trasa-

subhaga-susvara-śubha-sūkṣma-paryāpta-sthirâ-deya-yaśāṃsi setarāṇi tīrthakṛttvaṃ ca

8.12 (SS 8.11) The forty-two sub-types of body karma determine:

(1) realm of birth
(2) species of birth
(3) bodies
(4) primary and secondary organs of the body
(5) formation of the organs
(6) cohesion of the parts of the body
(7) integration of the body
(8) configuration of the body
(9) bone-joints
(10) touch
(11) taste
(12) smell
(13) colour
(14) linear propulsion in space
(15) balanced body weight [neither too heavy nor too light]
(16) vulnerability
(17) bellicosity
(18) heat
(19) lustre
(20) respiration
(21) flight in the sky (graceful or clumsy)
(22–23) unique and common body
(24–25) mobile and immobile body
(26–27) pleasing and ugly appearance
(28–29) sweet and harsh voice
(30–31) auspicious and inauspicious body
(32–33) subtle and gross body
(34–35) mature and immature body
(36–37) stable and unstable body
(38–39) presentable and unpresentable body
(40–41) good and bad reputation
(42) the qualities of a Jina

The bondage of body karma determines the realms of birth and also the shape of the bodies of the inhabitants of those realms. The forty-two sub-types listed above give an idea of the results of the bondage of body karma.

1. There are four realms of birth, those of infernals, subhumans (animals, plants and micro-organisms), humans and gods.

2. There are five species of beings: one-sensed, two-sensed, three-sensed, four-sensed and five-sensed ones (see 2.13–2.14). The one-sensed beings are earth-bodied, water-bodied, fire-bodied, air-bodied, or plant-bodied. These kinds have further distinctions. For example, earth-bodied beings include pure earth, pebbles, sand, salt, iron, copper, lead, silver, gold, diamond, and so on. Water-bodied beings include moisture, frost, fog, snow, ice, pure water, and so on. Examples of fire-bodied beings are charcoal, flame, fire-brand, ray of light, burning chaff, pure fire, and so on. Air-bodied beings include breeze, cyclone, hurricane, gale and whirlwind. Examples of plant-bodied beings are bulb, root, trunk, bark, wood, leaf, tendril, flower, fruit, bush, joint, creeper, moss and so on.

There are also sub-microscopic varieties of vegetation which are the least developed organisms. These souls share a common body. They possess only one sense, touch, like other one-sensed creatures. Large clusters of these are born together as colonies which die an infinitesimal fraction of a second later.

3. There are five kinds of bodies: gross, protean, conveyance, fiery and karmic (2.37), up to four of which may be possessed simultaneously by a soul (2.44).

4. There are many varieties of primary and secondary organs, determined by karma, which are used for the gross, protean and conveyance bodies. Primary organs include head, breast, back, arms, feet and so on. The secondary organs are within the primary; for example, the brain and forehead are secondary organs within the head.

5. The formation of the organs refers to the anatomy of the sexes and other organs generally.

6. The cohesion of the parts of the five types of body is the holding together of the different organs.

7. Integration means the working together of the diverse organs in each of the five types of body as one whole personality.

8. Configuration refers to the general shape of the body, its symmetry, arrangement of its parts and deformities. There are six kinds of configurations of which the first is most auspicious. In order of their excellence, the configurations are: (1) symmetrical body, (2) symmetrical body above navel only, (3) symmetrical body below the navel only, (4) hunch-backed body, (5) dwarfish body, (6) entirely asymmetrical body.

9. The bone-joints determine the strength and stamina of the body. There are six kinds of bone-joints of which the first is the most auspicious. They are: (1) interlocking of bones on both sides, strengthened with pin and plate, (2) interlocking of bones on one side with half-pin and half-plate or interlocking of bones with pin, (3) interlocking of bones on both sides, (4) interlocking bone on one side and pin on the other, (5) pin between two bones, (6) two bones bound by skin, sinews and flesh.

10–13. There are eight kinds of touch, five kinds of taste, two kinds of smell and five kinds of colour, determined by body karma (5.23).

14. The soul moves from one life to the spot of its next birth by linear propulsion in space which is of four kinds depending to which of the four realms it is travelling.

15. The property of being neither too heavy nor too light enables the body to maintain its balance, without falling over because of the weight of its own body nor flying up because of its lightness.

16–20. These types of body karma are self-explanatory.

21. The body karma which determines power of flight in the sky also determines the grace or clumsiness of gait in general.

22–23. As well as individual bodies occupied by one soul, there are common bodies occupied by many souls.

24–33. These are also self-explanatory.

34–35. The mature and immature body needs further explanation. According to the SB, there are five varieties of maturation: (1) alimentary, (2) bodily, (3) sense, (4) respiratory and (5) speech. Maturation means completion of the constitution of these five factors through which the soul builds its body. The SBT refers to the six varieties of maturation mentioned in the scripture, the sixth one being the mind. It explains the discrepancy with the SB by pointing out that the mind is a kind of sense organ and, therefore, can also be understood as part of the senses, the third constituent of maturation. In fact, later on, the SB acknowledges that according to others the mind is a variety of maturation.

The soul begins all six varieties of maturation simultaneously but completes them consecutively in the order given above. The alimentary maturation involves the attraction of the various types of material particles suitable for constructing the body, senses, respiration, speech and mind. The bodily maturation is the transformation of the attracted particles into the bodies (renewed karmic, new gross and/or protean, new fiery and possibly conveyance). The transformation of the attracted particles into senses of touch, taste and so on, is the maturation of the senses. The transformation into the respiratory system of the particles, which confer the power of inhaling and exhaling, is the maturation of respiration. The development and use of the capacities to attract particles capable of producing speech organs and to attract particles capable of producing the physical mind are the maturations of the speech and mind, respectively. The maturations are progressively subtler in nature, from the maturation of the aliment up to the maturation of the mind which is the subtlest and last maturation.

The completion of the six maturations is compared by the SB with the completion of a building. The maturation of aliment is the collection of the building materials. The maturation of the body is the construction of the framework. The maturation of the senses, respiration, and speech are the construction of the entrances and exits. The maturation of the rational mind is the deliberation over the arrangement and use of the building, where the lounge, bedroom, dining room and so on, will be.

36–41. Self-explanatory.

42. The last type of effect from karmic bondage is birth into a life in which one will become a founder of religion (6.23).

uccair nīcaiś ca

8.13 (SS 8.12) The effects of the two sub-types of status karma are high and low status in life among the same species.

The status of a person is determined by the quality of his or her lineage, place of birth, family, wealth, power etc.

There are people who enjoy high status in society such as the people born in the Āryan countries of Magadha, Aṅga, Vaṅga, Kaliṅga and so on and those in the families of Hari, Ikṣvāku, etc. They are offered respect and honour because of their wealth and power. On the other hand, there are people like the Chandalas (lower-caste and outcaste people), boar-hunters, pig-dealers, butchers, fishermen who occupy a low place in community life.

TRANSLATOR'S NOTE

The countries and families named in this commentary reflect the distribution of power and wealth at the time. The distinction between Āryan and non-Āryan refers to those people and countries descended from the Āryan tribes who swept down into north India in the second millenium BCE. The caste system is believed to have arisen from the integration of these warriors and their priests with the native people of India.

dānādīnām

8.14 (SS 8.13) The five sub-types of obstructive karma obstruct beneficence, gain, satisfaction, comfort and power.

āditas tisṛṇām antarāyasya ca triṃśatsāgaropamakoṭīkoṭyaḥ parā sthitiḥ

8.15 (SS 8.14) Bondage to knowledge-covering, intuition-covering, sensation and obstructive karmas lasts up to 30×10^{14} ocean-measured periods.

The description of the first category of bondage – the types – completed, this sutra begins the description of the second aspect of bondage: duration.

The duration of bondage is the length of time the karma takes to produce its entire result. The four types of karma cited above start taking effect after a maximum dormant period of $30 \times 100 = 3000$ years and continue to have effect for up to 30×10^{14} o.m.p. According to the SS, this maximum duration applies to the five-sensed rational beings with mature organs and a deluded world-view.

saptatir mohanīyasya

8.16 (SS 8.15) Bondage to deluding karma lasts up to 70×10^{14} ocean-measured periods.

The maximum dormant state of this bondage before the karma begins to take effect is $70 \times 100 = 7000$ years.

nāma-gotrayor viṃśatiḥ

8.17 (SS 8.16) Bondage to body and status karma lasts up to 20×10^{14} ocean-measured periods.

According to the SS, this maximum duration applies to five-sensed rational beings with mature organs and deluded world-view. The dormant state of karma that endures for this maximum period is $20 \times 100 = 2000$ years.

The SS asks the reader to consult the scripture for further information on the duration of karmic bondage of other beings.

trayastriṃśatsāgaropamānyāyuṣkasya

8.18 (SS 8.17) Bondage to lifespan karma lasts up to thirty-three ocean-measured periods.

The SBT clarifies that the maximum duration is actually a little more than 33 o.m.p., the excess period being ⅓ × 8,400,000 × 8,400,000 × 10^7 years (see SS 3.31). The dormant stage of this maximum duration is the same as the excess period.

aparā dvādaśamuhūrtā vedanīyasya

8.19 (SS 8.18) Sensation karma lasts at least twelve Indian hours.[5]

This minimum duration is only true of long-term bondage. Instantaneous bondage lasts a mere two time units (see 6.5).

nāma-gotrayor aṣṭau

8.20 (SS 8.19) Body and status karma last at least eight Indian hours.

śeṣāṇām antarmuhūrtam

8.21 (SS 8.20) The remaining five karmas – knowledge-covering, intuition-covering, deluding, birth, and obstructive karma – can last less than one Indian hour.

vipāko'nubhāvaḥ

8.22 (SS 8.21) The maturing or ripening of karma is the intensity [quality] of the fruition.

The description of the types and duration of bondage completed, the third aspect of bondage, the intensity (quality), is now described.

The maturing of bondage refers to the intensity or quality of its fruition, felt mildly or deeply by the soul. When they are mature, the material particles assimilated by the soul during bondage begin rising up to produce a multiple result. The SB mentions an important aspect of maturation – "transfer" in which the result of one sub-type shifts to another sub-type of the same type of karma (for types and sub-types, see 8.5–8.14). This transfer takes place without any special effort on the part of the soul. It is

[5] One Indian hour equals forty-eight Western minutes.

simply due to the current activity of the soul. The transfer is only possible between sub-types of the same type, not from one principal type of karma to another. However, there are also some sub-types which cannot transfer. View-deluding and conduct-deluding karmas cannot transfer their results to each other although they are both deluding karmas. Nor can the near-perfect enlightened world-view karma transfer to the karma that is a mixed enlightened and deluded world-view (8.10). However, the transfer can happen in the opposite direction. Thus the mixture of enlightened and deluded world-view, which is never bound as it is a transitional phase of the enlightened world-view during its fall (see appendix 4, third stage), can be transferred to the enlightened world-view. Similarly, the deluded world-view can be transferred to the enlightened world-view and the mixed world-view but the transfer cannot work in the opposite direction. There is also no transfer between the four sub-types of lifespan karma, infernal, subhuman, human and celestial.

The SS explains the multiplicity of mature karma in a different way. The varieties of maturity are due to the different degrees of passions in the soul at the time of binding the karma. The variety is also due to the state of the soul, place and time of karmic maturity, the realm of birth and the spiritual condition of the soul. When there is an intense rise of beneficial karma, the bondage of the harmful karma becomes weak and subordinate to the result of the beneficial karma. Similarly, when there is an intense rise of harmful karma, the bondage of the beneficial karma becomes weak and subordinate to the result of the harmful karma. But as already stated, the effects of the principal types of karma cannot be mutually transferred.

sa yathānāma

8.23 (SS 8.22) **The maturation is named according to the bondage that produces the effect.**

When the bondage of knowledge-covering karma matures, the maturing is called "knowledge-covering". When the bondage of intuition-covering karma matures, the maturing is called "intuition-covering", and so on. This designation does not, however, express the whole character of the maturation which has different intensities and qualities.

tataś ca nirjarā

8.24 (SS 8.23) **Maturing also causes the karma to fall off the soul.**

The SBT and SS identify two varieties of karmic "ripening" or falling off. The first is due to the usual process of maturity in which the karma bound in the past produces its result at the destined time and then ceases to exist. Sometimes, however, by special effort, the soul enjoys the result of the karma before the destined time. This second variety of maturity is like the artifical ripening of mangoes and jackfruits.

The "also" in the sutra indicates that there is another factor besides maturation which causes karma to drop off. This other factor is austerities.

nāmapratyayāḥ sarvato yogaviśeṣāt sūkṣmaikakṣetrāvagāḍhasthitāḥ sarvātmapradeśeṣv anantānantapradeśāḥ

8.25 (SS 8.24) The material particles attracted to the soul cause eight different types of bondage, enter from all sides (at all times past, present and future), cause bondage qualified by the activities of the soul, are subtle clusters of matter, are in the space occupied by the soul, are stationary, are assimilated by all the units of the soul, and are constituted of an infinite times infinite number of atoms.

Here, the fourth and last aspect of bondage, the mass of material particles assimilated, is described, throwing light on eight characteristics of the soul's karmic bondage.

The material clusters of karma which are attracted into the soul to become the karmic body are the most compact and fine matter (see 2.40 and appendix 5). The description of the clusters "entering" the soul from all directions and at all times, to become one of the eight types of karma is, of course, a metaphorical description. The karmic particles are everywhere. They do not come from a particular place to the soul; they are immediately present and available. The "entry" is simply conversion of the particles into particular types of karma according to the causes of bondage (8.1).

sadvedya-samyaktva-hāsya-rati-puruṣaveda-śubhāyur-nāma-gotrāṇi puṇyam

8.26 (not SS) Pleasure, [near-perfect] enlightened world-view, laughter, relish, male disposition, auspicious birth, auspicious body, and auspicious status are beneficial karmic bondage.

sadvedya-śubhāyur-nāma-gotrāṇi puṇyam

(SS 8.25, variant of 8.26) **Pleasure, auspicious lifespan, auspicious body and auspicious status are beneficial karmic bondage.**

ato 'nyat pāpam

(SS 8.26) **Other bondages are harmful.**

The two broad categories of karmic bondage, beneficial and harmful, are now considered with particular reference to the beneficial. The causes of the inflow of karma that produces pleasure were described in 6.13. The (near-perfect) enlightened world-view was described as a kind of bondage in 8.10. Laughter, relish and male disposition were described as varieties of quasi-passions in the same sutra. In addition to these five "fruits", there are also the "fruits" which come from auspicious lifespan karma, auspicious body karma and auspicious status karma.

The SBT finds difficulty in accepting the (near-perfect) enlightened world-view as beneficial karma because it is one of the four destructive karmas; it is due to the rise of purified view-deluding karma (see 8.10). The SBT is also discomforted by laughter, relish and male disposition – identified in 8.10 as quasi-passions (conduct-deluding karma) – being designated beneficial karma. Neither the scripture nor the ancient literature on karma mentions these four types of beneficial karma. Nor does SS 8.25 acknowledge these four karmas as beneficial. Only the forty-two varieties of bondage listed below are confirmed by all traditions as beneficial.

RESULTS OF BENEFICIAL KARMAS	*NUMBER OF VARIETIES*
SENSATION KARMA	
pleasure (8.9)	1
LIFESPAN KARMA	
subhumans, humans and gods (8.11)	3
BODY KARMA	
humans and gods	2
five-sensed beings	1
five bodies (karmic, protean, gross, fiery, conveyance)	5
auspicious configuration	1
auspicious bone-joint	1

primary and secondary organs of subhumans, humans and gods	3
auspicious colour, smell, taste and touch	4
serial propulsion to realms of humans and gods	2
neither heavy nor light	1
bellicosity	1
respiration	1
heat	1
lustre	1
agreeable gait	1
mobile body	1
gross body	1
developed body	1
individual body	1
stable body	1
auspicious body	1
pleasing appearance	1
sweet voice	1
presentable body	1
good reputation	1
auspicious formation of the organs	1
qualities of a Jina	1
STATUS KARMA	
high status	1
TOTAL	*42*

As regards the harmful types of bondage, the SB says that all types of bondage other than the named beneficial ones are harmful. In its independent sutra (8.26), the SS confirms the same view.

Pleasure is accepted as the result of a beneficial bondage which is due to a beneficial inflow. There is a likeness between cause and effect. Judged by this criterion, involuntary purging of karma and austerities by deluded people which result in birth in heaven are beneficial acts. Similarly, the acts that produce bondage leading to subhuman and human life with fully developed sense-organs, good physical structure and strong bones are beneficial, irrespective of other factors such as deluded world-view and passions that may be operating at the time. In such cases, the criterion of benefit is the strong body and high position in the species to which one belongs. The line of demarcation between beneficial and harmful bondage is therefore determined by fitness or otherwise of the being with respect to the life that it is destined to lead.

These instances of benefit or goodness are primarily worldly in nature. Spiritual goodness, however, is determined by the enlightened quality of self-restraint and austerities which result in the special elimination of karmic bondage and, consequently, to a higher stage of spiritual attainment as well as births in the higher heaven as a precursor to liberation. Spiritual good is clearly distinguished from worldly welfare.

TRANSLATOR'S NOTE

As noted above, the SBT is embarrassed by the sutra's inclusion of male disposition and also the three other factors as causes of beneficial karmic bondage. The SS does not include them in its version of the sutra. It is worthy of note that Vīrasena, in his *Dhavalā on Ṣaṭkhaṇḍāgama,* XIII. 352, clearly states that the four destructive karmas are necessarily harmful whereas the four non-destructive ones are a mixture of beneficial (pleasurable) and harmful (painful) karmas. This implies that the controversial four factors cannot cause the bondage of beneficial karma. However, in another commentary, *Jayadhavalā on Kaṣāyapāḍuḍa*, Vīrasena accepts the four factors as causes of beneficial bondage. The divergence of opinion among great Jaina thinkers of ancient times on such a vital issue demands deeper study of the scriptures available in the two principal Jaina sects.

CHAPTER NINE

Inhibiting and Wearing Off Karma

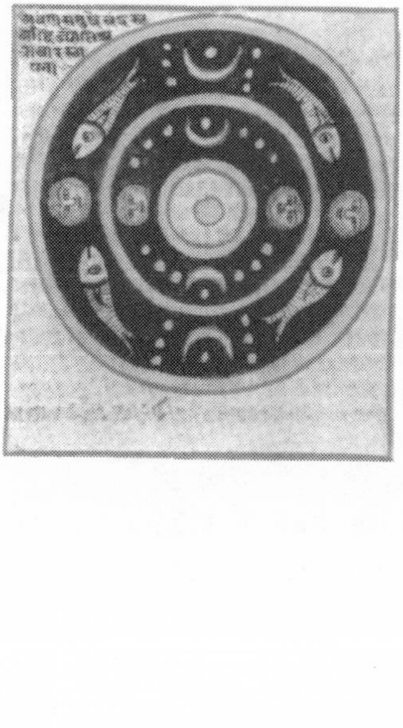

Contents

The fourth category of truth, karmic bondage, was explained in the previous chapter. Now, the fifth category, stopping incoming karma, and the sixth, the wearing off of karma, are considered.

āsravanirodhaḥ saṃvaraḥ

9.1 Stopping the inflow of karma is inhibition.

There are forty-two "doors" of karmic inflow – three instantaneous (see 6.2, 6.5) and thirty-nine long-term (6.6). The instantaneous doors are the activities of body, speech and mind which are absolutely free of passion. Stopping all forty-two doors completely or partially is inhibition. Complete inhibition is only possible at the spiritual stage immediately before liberation. Progress in spiritual development depends on progress in inhibition.

Inhibition has two aspects, psychic and physical. Psychic inhibition is when the mind disengages from worldly action. Physical inhibition is when the karmic inflow actually ceases because of this mental detachment.

The SS uses the fourteen stages of spiritual development to explain how inflow is stopped. The stages are:

1. deluded world-view
2. lingering enlightened world-view, resembling an aftertaste
3. combination of enlightened and deluded world-view
4. enlightened world-view unaccompanied by any sort of self-restraint
5. enlightened world-view with partial self-restraint
6. enlightened world-view with complete self-restraint but with laxity in early stages
7. complete self-restraint free of laxity
8. complete self-restraint with gross passions attended by various novel experiences
9. complete self-restraint with gross passions and similar but progressively purer experiences

10. complete self-restraint with subtle flickering greed
11. complete self-restraint with suppressed passions but rise of knowledge-covering karma
12. complete self-restraint with eliminated passions but rise of knowledge-covering karma
13. omniscience accompanied by mental, verbal and physical activity
14. omniscience with no activity.

At each stage of spiritual development, there are kinds of karmic inflow which are inhibited at the next stage. In the first stage, 117 out of a total 120 kinds of karma may enter and bind. The following sixteen kinds of karma, which are due to deluded world-view, confine the soul to the first stage of spiritual development, that of deluded world-view:

1. deluded world-view (kind of deluding karma, 8.10)
2. hermaphroditic disposition (deluding karma)
3. lifespan in hell (kind of lifespan karma, 8.11)
4. birth in hell (lifespan karma)
5. birth as a one-sensed being (kind of body karma, 8.12)
6. birth as a two-sensed animal (body karma)
7. birth as a three-sensed animal (body karma)
8. birth as a four-sensed animal (body karma)
9. sixth bodily configuration: complete asymmetry (body karma)
10. the sixth bone-joint: two bones bound by skin, sinews and flesh (body karma)
11. linear propulsion of the soul towards the infernal realm (body karma)
12. hot body (body karma)
13. immobile body (body karma)
14. subtle body (body karma)
15. immature body (body karma)
16. common body (body karma).

The inflow of these sixteen kinds of karma is inhibited at the second stage of spiritual development, that of lingering enlightened world-view resembling an aftertaste, to which the soul falls from a higher stage (see appendix 4). Here only 101 kinds of karma may enter and bind (117 − 16 = 101), out of which the following twenty-five kinds are due to the rise of non-restraint caused by the tenacious passions:

1. sleeping (kind of intuition-covering karma, 8.8)
2. sleepwalking (intuition-covering karma)
3. torpidity (intuition-covering karma)
4. tenacious anger (kind of deluding karma, 8.10)

5. tenacious pride (deluding karma)
6. tenacious deceit (deluding karma)
7. tenacious greed (deluding karma)
8. female disposition (deluding karma)
9. animal lifespan (kind of lifespan karma, 8.11)
10. birth in the animal realm (lifespan karma)
11. the second configuration of the body: symmetrical body above the navel (kind of body karma, 8.12)
12. the third configuration of the body: symmetrical body below the navel (body karma)
13. the fourth configuration of the body: hunchbacked (body karma)
14. the fifth configuration of the body: dwarfish (body karma)
15. the second type of bone-joints: interlocking bones on one side with half-pin and half-plate or with pin (body karma)
16. the third type of bone-joint: interlocking bones on both sides (body karma)
17. the fourth type of bone-joint: interlocking bone on one side and pin on the other
18. the fifth type of bone-joint: pin between two bones (body karma)
19. linear propulsion towards the animal realm (body karma)
20. lustrous body (body karma)
21. graceful flight (body karma)
22. ugly appearance (body karma)
23. harsh voice (body karma)
24. unpresentable body (body karma)
25. low status among one's own species (kind of status karma, 8.13).

These karmas are inhibited at the third stage of spiritual development, that of partly enlightened and partly deluded world-view. At this stage, two lifespan karmas, human and celestial, also do not enter and bind. Thus the total number that bind is seventy-four (101 – (25 + 2) = 74).

Out of the seventy-four kinds, the following ten are due to the rise of non-restraint caused by non-abstinent passions:

1. anger (kind of conduct-deluding karma that is non-abstinent, 8.10)
2. pride (non-abstinent conduct-deluding karma)
3. deceit (non-abstinent conduct-deluding karma)
4. greed (non-abstinent conduct-deluding karma)
5. human lifespan (kind of lifespan karma, 8.11)
6. birth in the human realm (lifespan karma)
7. gross body (kind of body karma, 8.12)

8. limbs of the gross body (body karma)
9. the first type of bone-joint: interlocking bones on both sides with pin and plate
10. linear propulsion towards the human realm.

At the fourth stage, that of enlightened world-view accompanied by non-abstinence, seventy-seven kinds of karma may enter and bind: the seventy-four mentioned above as well as Jinas' body karma, human propulsion karma and celestial propulsion karma (8.12). At the fifth stage, the ten kinds of karma listed above are inhibited, making the number of karmas that bind at this stage sixty-seven (77 − 10 = 67). Of these, four are due to the rise of partially abstinent passions:

1. anger (kind of conduct-deluding karma that is partially abstinent, 8.10)
2. pride (partially abstinent conduct-deluding karma)
3. deceit (partially abstinent conduct-deluding karma)
4. greed (partially abstinent conduct-deluding karma).

At the sixth stage, that of self-restraint with laxity, these four passions are inhibited. Thus at this stage, sixty-three kinds of karma enter and bind (67 − 4 = 63). Of these, six are due to laxity:

1. pain (kind of sensation karma, see 8.9)
2. ennui (kind of deluding karma, see 8.10)
3. grief (deluding karma)
4. unstable body (kind of body karma, see 8.12)
5. inauspicious body (body karma)
6. disreputed body (body karma).

These six karmas are inhibited at the seventh stage of spiritual development, that of self-restraint without laxity. At this stage fifty-nine kinds of karma (63 − 6 = 57, together with the major and minor organs of the conveyance body) may enter and bind. Of these, the celestial lifespan is caused by self-restraint with or without laxity, but no lifespan karma is bound beyond the seventh stage.

At the eighth stage, that of self-restraint with gross passions and novel experiences, the celestial lifespan karma is inhibited. Hence, in the beginning of the eighth stage, only fifty-eight kinds of karma (59 − 1 = 58) may enter and bind. At this stage, there is no laxity and there are only the flickering passions of anger, pride, deceit and greed (8.10) which may be intense, medium or mild. Of these fifty-eight kinds of karma, two kinds – dozing and drowsing – are inhibited in the second part of this stage. Thus only fifty-six kinds may enter and bind. At a later part of this stage, thirty kinds of karma are inhibited:

1. birth in celestial realm (kind of lifespan karma, 8.11)
2. the species of five-sensed beings (kind of body karma, 8.12)
3. protean body (body karma)
4. conveyance body (body karma)
5. fiery body (body karma)
6. karmic body (body karma)
7. the first body configuration: symmetry (body karma)
8. primary and secondary organs of the protean body (body karma)
9. primary and secondary organs of the conveyance body (body karma)
10. colour (body karma)
11. smell (body karma)
12. taste (body karma)
13. touch (body karma)
14. linear propulsion toward the celestial realm (body karma)
15. balanced body weight, neither heavy nor light (body karma)
16. vulnerability (body karma)
17. bellicosity (body karma)
18. respiration (body karma)
19. graceful flight (body karma)
20. mobile body (body karma)
21. gross body (body karma)
22. mature body (body karma)
23. individual body (body karma)
24. stable body (body karma)
25. auspicious body (body karma)
26. pleasing appearance (body karma)
27. sweet voice (body karma)
28. presentable body (body karma)
29. formations of the organs (body karma)
30. the physical qualities of a Jina (body karma).

Thus, twenty-six kinds of karma enter and bind in the last part of the eighth stage of spiritual development. Of these, the four quasi-passions of laughter, relish, fear and abhorrence are due to the intense passions.

These four passions are inhibited in the beginning of the ninth stage of spiritual development, that of self-restraint with gross passions and purer experiences. Thus, in the first part of this stage there is inflow and bondage of only twenty-two kinds of karma. Of these, two kinds – male disposition and flickering anger – are inhibited in the second part of the stage. Thus, in the remaining period, there is the inflow and bondage of only twenty kinds of karma. Of these, two kinds – flickering pride and deceit – are inhibited in the third part. Thus, there is the inflow and bondage of only eighteen kinds of karma. (The four passions that have been inhibited are all of medium intensity.)

Of the remaining eighteen kinds, one kind, flickering greed, is also inhibited in the tenth stage. Thus, at the tenth spiritual stage, that of self-restraint with subtle flickering greed, there are seventeen kinds of karma that may enter and bind:

1. empirical cognition (kind of knowledge-covering karma, 8.7)
2. articulate knowledge (knowledge-covering karma)
3. clairvoyance (knowledge-covering karma)
4. mind-reading (knowledge-covering karma)
5. omniscience (knowledge-covering karma)
6. visual intuition (kind of intuition-covering karma, 8.8)
7. non-visual intuition (intuition-covering karma)
8. clairvoyant intuition (intuition-covering karma)
9. omniscient intuition (intuition-covering karma)
10. reputable body (kind of body karma, 8.12)
11. high status (kind of status karma, 8.13)
12. obstruction of beneficence (kind of obstructive karma, 8.14)
13. obstruction of gain (obstructive karma)
14. obstruction of satisfaction (obstructive karma)
15. obstruction of comfort (obstructive karma)
16. obstruction of power (obstructive karma)
17. pleasure (kind of sensation karma, 8.9)

At this stage the passions that exist are mild. Of these seventeen kinds, all but the last are inhibited in the next three stages of spiritual development – the stages of suppressed passions, eliminated passions, and omniscience accompanied by activity. Thus, only pleasure karma enters and binds. At the fourteenth stage, that of omniscience without activity, all karma is inhibited.

TRANSLATOR'S NOTE

There are 148 kinds of karma. Of the ninety-seven listed in 8.6, the forty-two body karmas are expanded to a total of ninety-three in 8.12. Thus we get (97 – 42) + 93 = 148.

If the arising of karmas is taken into consideration, some of the karmas listed in 8.12 are grouped together. So, the five cohesions of body and the five integrations of the diverse organs are said to arise as part of the five types of bodies. This reduces the kinds of karma by ten. The smell, odour, taste and touch karmas are counted as only four kinds instead of twenty, reducing the kinds of karma by a further sixteen. The total number of (arising) karmas is then 122 (148 – (10 + 16) = 122).

Of these 122 kinds of karma, only 120 can be newly bound by the soul. The two deluding karmas – the near-perfect enlightened world-view and the mixture of the enlightened and deluded world-views (8.10) – cannot be bound because they are either phases of the deluded view when it is purified, or a combination of enlightened and deluded world-views when the soul falls from the stage of enlightened world-view (appendix 4). They are therefore subtracted from the 122 kinds of arising karma.

The number is further reduced to 117 for the kinds of karma which the soul can bind at the first stage of spiritual development, because the conveyance body and its organs and the body karma of Jinas cannot be bound there. These karmas require higher spiritual development; the conveyance body and its organs can be used at the sixth stage and bound for future use at the seventh (2.49) and the body karma of Jinas can be bound from the fourth to the eighth stage of spiritual development (*DOK*, pp. 80, 85).

sa gupti-samiti-dharmâ-nuprekṣā-parīṣahajaya-cāritraiḥ

9.2 Inflow is inhibited by guarding, careful movement, morality, reflection, conquering hardships, and enlightened conduct.

tapasā nirjarā ca

9.3 Austerities wear off karma as well as inhibiting it.

Although there are as many ways of inhibiting karma as there are causes of its inflow, there are seven principal inhibitors, which are given in the two sutras above and explained in those below. These explanations are mainly in reference to the ascetic's lifestyle.

When austerities are part of enlightened conduct, they not only wear off karma already bound to the soul but also prevent further karma accumulating.

According to the SS, the causes of inhibition have been specified in order to exclude practices and rituals such as religious pilgrimage, sacred ablution, deluded ordination, offering one's head to the deity as a gift, worship of gods and demi-gods and so on. Such practices and rituals are inspired by attachment, hatred and delusion which attract rather than inhibit karma.

samyag yoganigraho guptiḥ

9.4 Guarding is enlightened control of the threefold activities of body, speech and mind.

Each of the seven ways of inhibiting inflow is now dealt with individually, beginning with guarding. One should guard one's body, speech and mind against evil in order to control one's desires so that they are in harmony with moral principles. "Enlightened" means in the manner prescribed by the scripture.

Guarding bodily activity refers to controlling voluntary movements such as lying, sitting, standing, walking, moving articles of religious life, so that they are performed with perfect religious propriety to avoid causing harm to life.

Guarding speech means controlling speech when seeking religious necessities, requesting directions, discussing illness with a doctor and so on. According to SBT, such guarding entails covering the mouth while seeking food and drink from householders, and during verbal exchanges, to avoid injuring small lifeforms. The ascetic must observe the scriptural norm while speaking, a principle which layfollowers are also expected to follow. At its purest, guarding implies noble silence.

To guard the mind is to refrain from sinful intentions and to set oneself wholesome resolves. At the highest level, avoiding all worldly thoughts, wholesome or unwholesome, is guarding of mind.

īryā-bhāṣai-ṣaṇâ-dānanikṣepo-tsargāḥ samitayaḥ

9.5 To move carefully is to walk, speak, seek alms, handle objects of daily use and dispose of excreta in the correct manner.

This sutra explains the second of the karmic inhibitors, careful movement. "Correct manner" means as approved by monastic rules for avoiding injuring any form of life while performing the duties necessary for religious life.

1. Walking correctly involves walking cautiously and only for the purpose of performing necessary religious duties, showing restraint in movement, and looking carefully on all sides in the area one is travelling through.

2. Speaking correctly involves speaking wholesome words that are measured, indubitable, harmless and meaningful.

3. Seeking alms correctly means asking for the necessities of religious

life, such as food, drink, broom[1], pots, cloth[2] and shelter, strictly in accord with scriptural prescription. It means being free from the blemishes of faulty donation, faulty donors and faulty methods of seeking alms.

4. The correct manner of handling articles of religious use consists in properly inspecting and dusting them before moving them in order to avoid injury to small beings such as flies and insects.

5. Correct disposal of excreta means depositing stools, phlegm, spit, urine somewhere not occupied by mobile or immobile lifeforms.

uttama kṣamā-mārdavâ-rjava-śauca-satya-saṃyama-tapas-tyāgâ-kiñcanya-brahmacaryāṇi dharmaḥ

9.6 Morality is perfect forgiveness, humility, straightforwardness, purity (freedom from greed), truthfulness, self-restraint, austerity, renunciation, detachment and continence.

This sutra explains morality which is the third way of inhibiting karmic inflow. "Perfect" applies to all ten moral virtues which must be practised meticulously by ascetics.

1. Forgiveness depends upon controlling anger and practising tolerance in adverse situations. According to the SB, it requires forbearance and gratitude that worse has not happened. To practise unconditional forgiveness, we should see ourselves as the source of anger. The SB advises that angry abuse from another should be countered by looking to oneself for the cause of the anger. If the cause can be found within oneself, the other should be forgiven for his anger. Even if the fault does not lie with oneself, the other should be forgiven because his anger is due to ignorance. The ignorant should always be forgiven. If someone accuses us covertly, he should be forgiven because he did not do so overtly. If he accuses us overtly, he should be forgiven because he did not resort to physical violence. If he did resort to beating, he should be forgiven because he did not kill us. If he did attempt to kill us, he should be forgiven for not distracting us from the religious path. We should always find reason to forgive a person who harms us and should remember that whatever misfortunes confront us, they are due to our past karma.

2. Humility arises when pride about one's race, family, prosperity,

[1] Used by Jaina ascetics to sweep aside small forms of life which might otherwise be crushed.

[2] Pots and cloth are not mentioned in the SS as the orders of this tradition do not allow these items. Cf. 9.24, no. 8.

intellect, knowledge and other such attainments, is subdued. The SB describes humility as lack of self-aggrandizement, and control and destruction of pride. Pride has eight varieties, determined by its object: (1) paternal superiority, (2) maternal superiority, (3) beauty, (4) fortune, (5) exceptional intellectual and creative power, (6) scriptural learning, (7) prosperity, and (8) power.

3. Straightforwardness is sincere and honest intention. The SB also includes avoiding controversy.

4. Purity means to be free of greed. A greedy mind is always impure. The SB lists the mind-polluting passions produced by greed as anger, pride, deceit, violence, and falsehood.

5. Truthfulness includes refraining from harsh words, back-biting, garrulity, derogatory language, vituperation, and so on. The SB describes truthfulness as relating facts. It is sweet, civil, unambiguous, manifest and free from attachment and hatred.

6. Self-restraint refers to abstaining from all activities which injure any form of life, subtle or gross. The SB identifies controlling body, speech and mind and, in particular, carefully inspecting objects and places so as to avoid injuring life.

7. Austerity means mortification of the body for the regeneration of the soul. The SB identifies two types of austerity, external and internal, each with six sub-types (see 9.19–9.20). The many kinds of fasting occupy a central position among the austerities prescribed in Jaina scripture.

8. Renunciation is the abandonment of possessive attitudes towards the necessities of life. The SB itemizes external objects, such as broom, pots and so on, necessary in practising the Jina's discipline, as well as internal pollutants of speech and mind under the sway of passions, which may become objects to which the soul clings. In this respect, the body is also sometimes considered an internal possession. Renunciation is essentially freedom from clinging and hankering.

9. Detachment is letting go of attachment to the body and monastic articles. It is a refinement of renunciation in which the sense of mineness is relinquished.

10. Continence means residing with the teacher to observe the abstinences, acquire learning and erode the passions. The SB distinguishes five kinds of teachers: (1) initiator (who confers initiation), (2) teacher of the nature of animate, inanimate and mixed objects, (3) junior instructor of the scripture, (4) senior instructor of the scripture, (5) expert in teaching the heart of the scripture.

anityâ-śaraṇa-saṃsārai-katvâ-nyatvâ-śucitvâ-srava-saṃvara-nirjarā-loka-bodhidurlabha-dharmasvākhyātatvānucintanam anuprekṣāḥ

9.7 The twelve reflections are upon impermanence, helplessness, the cycle of birth and death, solitariness, otherness of the body, impurity of the body, inflow of karma, inhibiting karma, wearing off karma, the nature of the cosmos, rarity of enlightenment and the lucid exposition of the doctrine.

Here, reflection, the fourth of the seven inhibitors of karmic inflow, is explained. The twelve reflections are the process for arriving at the enlightened world-view. Although the SB is typically populist and elaborate in its description while the SS is more academic and condensed in its approach, they have essential agreement on the results of the reflections.

1. Reflecting upon impermanence of the body, which is defined as an internal apparatus, and of external apparatus such as beds, seats, clothes, encourages detachment from worldly things.

2. Reflecting upon the helplessness of the soul in a world beset with the miseries and misfortunes of birth, bereavement, old age and death, strengthens commitment to the spiritual path. The soul's encounters with worldly suffering are likened to a helpless deer cub facing a hungry lion in the lonely forest. This induces a sense of detachment from worldly affairs and deep faith in the religious discipline taught by the Jina.

3. Reflecting upon suffering, the beginningless cycle of births and deaths as infernals, animals, humans and gods brings home the truth that the relationship between individuals is constantly changing. The son becomes the father, the servant becomes the master, the foe becomes the friend and so on, obliterating the distinction between who is "one's own" and who is "not one's own". A sense of dread and distaste for worldly life is induced by such reflection along with a determination to strive for release from the cycle of transmigration.

4. Reflecting upon the solitariness of the soul in its births, sufferings and death cleans the mind of its attachment to those who are "one's own" and aversion to those who are "not one's own". The mind achieves a balanced state that is conducive to spiritual pursuits and inspired to attain liberation.

5. Reflecting upon the otherness of the soul from the body and other physical objects focuses on the soul as an eternal intelligent self and the body as an evanescent insentient object. The intrinsic purity of the soul is experienced and the bodily attachment obstructing

the spiritual path is destroyed.

6. Reflecting upon the filthy condition of the body strengthens dispassion and disgust for the body. The body is impure because it is produced by the mixture of father's semen and mother's blood which are impure. It is impure because everything it consumes turns foul and putrid. It is impure because it is the receptacle of dirt, sweat, phlegm, bile, urine and faeces. It is impure because it is impossible to change its foul smell by any kind of bath or cosmetic.

7. Reflecting upon inflow, as also on inhibiting and wearing off karma, provides insight into the causes of bondage and liberation. Reflecting on karmic inflows as the pitfalls in this life and next, and as the entrance for the harmful and exit for the beneficial, brings about an inclination to control inflow. In this connection, the SB cites the example of Gārgya Sātyaki who, in spite of his proficiency in flight and the occult sciences, met death because of his lust for women. The example of mighty elephants, enticed by objects which are pleasant to touch, being entrapped by elephant tamers is also given. Similarly, the fatal consequences for fish, black bees, moths and deer of their respective addictions to taste, smell, sight, and sound are cited to bring home the pitfalls of inflows due to sensual indulgence.

8. Reflecting upon the merits of inhibiting karmic inflow and of the great vows of the ascetic strengthens the power of inhibition necessary for liberation.

9. Reflecting upon wearing off karma enables us to purge the soul of its impurities. The wearing off may occur without conscious effort or through virtuous practices. The first is illustrated by births in hell or heaven due to the fruition of past karma which subsequently wears off. The second refers to the practice of austerities and endurance of hardships for the elimination of past karma.

10. Reflecting upon the nature of the cosmos leads to the enlightened world-view. One is able to achieve purity of thought. The cosmos is made up of five extensive substances (see 5.2) and is subject to multiple states of origination, decay, continuity, evolution and dissolution (5.29).

11. Reflecting upon the rarity of enlightenment builds up a solid foundation for spirituality. It eliminates laxity and encourages attainment of enlightenment. Overwhelmed by deluded world-views and passions, the soul is eternally experiencing miserable births and deaths in various realms. Reflection on these vicissitudes generates lucidity of thought and spiritual illumination.

12. Reflecting on the lucid exposition of the doctrine creates confidence in the mind of the aspirant. It infuses the strength needed to practise the path which is the door to enlightened world-view and the redeemer of the soul from its worldly sufferings. The five great (ascetic) vows (7.1–7.2) and the seven categories of truth (1.4) propounded in the scripture are the constituents of the path of liberation.

mārgācyavana-nirjarārthaṃ pariṣoḍhavyāḥ parīṣahāḥ

9.8 Enduring hardships prevents deviation from the spiritual path and wears off bound karma.

kṣut-pipāsā-śīto-ṣṇa-daṃśamasaka-nāgnyâ-rati-strī-caryā-niṣadyā-śayyâ-krośa-vadha-yācanâ-lābha-roga-tṛṇasparśa-mala-satkārapuraskā-ra-prajñâ-jñānâ-darśanāni

9.9 There are twenty-two hardships arising out of hunger, thirst, cold, heat, insect bites, nudity, ennui, women, travel, seat and posture for practising austerities, sleeping place, indignation for reproach, injury caused by others, seeking alms, lack of gain, physical ailment, touch of thorny grass, dirt, honour and reward, learning, lack of intelligence, and loss of faith.

Here, the fifth way of inhibiting inflow, hardships for ascetics, is described. The twenty-two hardships are prescribed to facilitate strict observance of the vows, adherence to the spiritual path and weakening of karmic bondage. They occur because of the rise of five types of karma: knowledge-covering, sensation-producing, view-deluding, conduct-deluding and obstructive (see 9.13–9.16).

Most of the commentators give a brief summary of the hardships. The SB does not comment at all. The SS gives the most detailed analysis.

1–2. Hunger and thirst: Ascetics must depend on the laity for their daily needs. They cannot cook, nor can they buy. They have to live by seeking alms. They have to bear hunger and thirst patiently if food and drink approved in the scripture are not available from the householder. The SS advises that the non-availability of food and drink should be considered a good opportunity for fasting to purge the soul of its impurities by meditation and study of the scripture. Mortification of the flesh regenerates the spirit.

3–4. Cold and heat: The life of the wandering ascetic is compared with that of the birds who have no fixed abode. The ascetic has to pass nights under trees, in caves or under the skies without cover to protect the body from cold and heat. His life is devoted to abstinence from all kinds of activity that may cause injury to any form of life, however difficult it may be to lead such life in climatic extremes.

5. Bites of insects: Insects might suck his blood but the ascetic must maintain peace of mind without any thought of protecting his body from their bites.

6. Nudity: This is an essential feature of monkhood in the SS tradition. The purpose of nudity is to gain control over the feeling of shame in the state of unconcealed genitals. The ascetic is naked as a new-born baby, without possessions, not even a piece of cloth to cover his body. His mind is always fixed on the path of liberation being absolutely free of sexual desire and devoted to the practice of perfect celibacy.

7. Ennui: An ascetic may feel bored with ascetism but must control his feelings. He remains aloof from places of dance and music. He spends his time in solitary places, deserted houses, temples and caves, practising meditation and scriptural study in order to endure the hardship of ennui.

8. Women: Celibacy is compulsory for the ascetic who must scrupulously avoid association with the opposite sex. Ascetics must guard themselves against the overtures of intoxicated women who might tempt them with lustful gestures and postures in their solitary resorts. This formidable hardship is conquered through the power of meditation which can purge his sexual predispositions.

9. Travel: Ascetics have to walk from place to place, barefooted, on paths of hard gravel, sharp thorns and the like. They must face the hardships of travel calmly and quietly, without attachment to place or climate and with strict observance of the rule and norms prescribed in the scripture.

10. Seat and posture for practising austerities: Sometimes ascetics must select places to practise austerities intensely. These practices may be interrupted by natural calamity or hostile people but the patient endurance of trials and tribulations quickens progress along the spiritual path. They should cultivate fearlessness.

11. Sleeping place: An ascetic might fail to find a suitable place to sleep, and spend nights in pain and hardship, enduring extreme heat or cold, lying as still as a statue to avoid injury to flies and insects that infest the area.

12. Indignation for reproach: Sometimes an ascetic may have to endure

the wrath and indignation of ignorant and rude people who shower abuse on him. He must tolerate insults dispassionately, seeing them as the result of harmful karma bound by him in the past.

13. Injury caused by others: People may beat an ascetic violently, but he must endure such treatment with perfect equanimity, reflecting on the natural vulnerability and impermanence of the body. He has to remain evenly disposed whether his body is flayed with a chisel or anointed with sandalwood paste.

14. Seeking alms: He does not seek food, shelter and medicine with beggarly platitudes and pitiful gestures, even if his life is at stake from lack of food and drink. He endures placidly. The practice of severe austerities reduces the ascetic's body to a skeleton of bones covered with skin and a network of veins and arteries.

15. Lack of gain: Failure to find food or drink should not incite displeasure. It makes no difference to the ascetic whether or not he receives food when seeking alms. Not receiving food is a kind of austerity that fosters spirituality. In the SS tradition, the monk has no bowl to keep food. His palms are his bowl. He takes food and drink only once a day. He is mostly silent. Sometimes, he goes without food and drink for many days at a stretch and returns from many houses without acceptable food. But he always remains unruffled; the generosity or miserliness of the benefactors is not his concern.

16. Physical ailment: The ascetic has no attachment to his body. He tolerates all varieties of ailments with equanimity, never asking for a remedy. On the contrary, he ponders the impure components of the body, the impermanence of the world and the utter lack of the power that can save the body. Whatever meagre quantity of food he accepts is for the bare maintenance of his body, like a few drops of lubricant to keep the axle turning or a quantum of ointment to cure the abscess. The ascetic's principal concern is the protection and nourishment of virtue. He never takes advantage of the supernatural powers he has acquired through his austerities to cure his ailments.

17. Touch of thorny grass: Ascetics walk barefooted. Their soles are pricked by thorns and injured by rough gravels, dry grass, hard earth and so on. These hardships are tolerated with a peaceful mind. When walking, sitting and sleeping, ascetics avoid harming small creatures such as flies, insects and mosquitoes. They are always vigilant and mindful of what they do.

18. Dirt: To avoid injuring water-bodied beings, ascetics do not take

baths. In the SS tradition, the naked bodies[3] of the male ascetics produce sweat under the scorching heat of the sun and the wind blows dust on to their skin. They endure the dirt. They do not rub their skin when they suffer from eczema or itches. They cleanse their souls of passions by observing religious vows to purify their conduct.

19. Honour and reward: Ascetics should not hanker after honour or prestige for their vast knowledge and high spiritual attainments. They do not envy the high positions held by false teachers who are worshipped with devotion by the ignorant masses. They do not seek miraculous powers as reward for their austerities.

20. Learning: An ascetic is not elated by his scriptural learning. He bears his profound knowledge with meekness and modesty.

21. Lack of intelligence: Ascetics do not despair at their failure to achieve great intellectual feats, despite their strict observance of religious life and extreme austerities. They endure censure for their limited intelligence.

22. Loss of faith: Sometimes an ascetic reaches the verge of losing his faith in his religious discipline. He must rise above this mood by reviewing his understanding of the doctrine and the progress he has made in the religious path. According to the SS, the mind of the genuine ascetic is never troubled by the thought, "Even though my heart is pure due to being in the highest state of dispassion, even though I am conversant with all the categories of truth, even though I am the worshipper of the adorable ones, of the sanctuaries dedicated to the Jina, of genuine ascetics and of true religion, and even though I am a monk of very long standing, the extraordinary state of knowledge has not arisen in me. The claim that supernatural miraculous powers arise in the practitioners of long-term fasts is a cry in the wilderness. The observance of vows is a worthless pursuit." The reason why genuine ascetics do not have this thought is that they have achieved pure faith and enlightened world-view. This is how they save themselves from the pitfall of loss of faith.

The end result of the ascetic's endurance of these hardships, which arise randomly as the result of previous karma, is that the inflow of attachment and hatred is greatly inhibited.

[3] This refers to the male ascetics of the Jaina sect who go naked as a prerequisite for attaining liberation, see p.226.

sūkṣmasamparāya-cchadmasthavītarāgayoś caturdaśa

9.10 Fourteen hardships – hunger, thirst, cold, heat, bites of gadflies and mosquitoes, travel, learning, lack of intelligence, lack of gain, sleeping place, injury, ailment, touch of thorny grass and dirt – occur at the tenth stage of spiritual development which is attended by subtle flickering greed, the eleventh stage which is attended by suppressed passions and knowledge-covering karma, and the twelfth stage which is attended by eliminated passions and knowledge-covering karma.

The hardships are now explained in terms of spiritual development. Only the fourteen hardships mentioned here occur at the tenth, eleventh and twelfth stages of spiritual development (see 9.1).

The remaining eight hardships – nudity, ennui, women, seat, indignation, seeking alms, honour and reward, and loss of faith – do not occur because of the absence of gross passions at these stages. The hardship in practising nudity does not occur because the quasi-passion of abhorrence has been mastered. The quasi-passions of ennui, sexual disposition and fear have also been controlled at these stages and so the hardships arising from ennui, women and sitting are not possible either. The conquest over anger, pride and greed at these stages prevents the occurrence of hardships arising from indignation, seeking alms, and honour and reward. Loss of faith is also not possible because the faith-deluding karma is either suppressed or eliminated by now.

ekādaśa jine

9.11 Only eleven hardships are possible in the victor.

Now the hardships possible for the "victor", that is a saint at the thirteenth and fourteenth stages of spiritual development, are enumerated.

The victor is free of all four destructive types of karma – knowledge-covering, intuition-covering, deluding and obstructive – but not yet of the four types of non-destructive karmas – sensation, lifespan, body and status.

The eleven hardships to which the victor is subject are due to the rise of harmful sensation karma. They are: hunger, thirst, cold, heat, insect bites, travel, sleeping place, injury, ailment, touch of thorny grass, and dirt. These hardships do not arouse any passion in the victor. They are simply experienced without causing any reaction.

In the SS tradition, an objection is raised that it is not proper to call them hardships because there do not exist feelings of hunger, etc., in the victor, because the rise of deluding karma, which causes pain, is not present. This, says the SS, is true but they are called hardships figuratively, even in the absence of pain, because the material particles of the sensation karma are present and rising. This is just like attributing meditation to the omniscient victor, even though the function of stopping all thought, which is the essence of meditation, does not actually exist in him. The victor's meditation is to eliminate karmic residues on the eve of attaining disembodied liberation.

Alternately, the sutra can be explained by preceding it with the supplementary clause "there do not exist", because the sutras are subject to additions based on the intention of the speaker.

bādarasamparāye sarve

9.12 All the hardships occur in an ascetic who is at the stage of complete self-restraint with gross passions.

Now the common cause of all the hardships is explained. At the sixth, seventh, eighth and ninth stages of spiritual development (see 9.1), all the hardships occur because the gross passions are present.

jñānāvaraṇe prajñâ-jñāne

9.13 The two hardships, learning and lack of intelligence, are associated with knowledge-covering karma.

Intelligence and learning are due to the partial elimination and partial suppression of knowledge-covering karma (see 2.5).

darśanamohâ-ntarāyayor adarśanâ-labhau

9.14 The two hardships, loss of faith and lack of gain, are associated with view-deluding and obstructive karma respectively.

cāritramohe nāgnyâ-rati-strī-niṣadyâ-krośa-yācanā-satkārapuraskārāḥ

9.15 The seven hardships – nudity [due to abhorrence], ennui [due to dissatisfaction], women [due to male disposition], seat [due to fear],

indignation [due to anger], seeking alms [due to pride], honour and reward [due to greed] – are associated with conduct-deluding karma.

vedanīye śeṣāḥ

9.16 The remaining eleven hardships – hunger, thirst, cold, heat, biting insects, travel, sleeping place, injury, ailment, touch of thorny grass, and dirt – are associated with sensation [pain] karma.

ekādayo bhājyā yugapad ekonaviṃśateḥ

9.17 Up to nineteen hardships may occur at one time.

An individual cannot experience more than nineteen of the twenty-two hardships at once, because cold and heat cannot occur simultaneously and because travel, sleeping and sitting are mutually exclusive hardships.

sāmāyika-cchedopasthāpya-parihāraviśuddhi-sūkṣmasamparāya-yathā-khyātāni cāritram

9.18 The five stages of conduct are: initiation, ordination, purification through service, self-restraint with subtle flickering greed, and perfect conduct.

The exposition of the twenty-two hardships, which is the fifth way to inhibit karma, having been completed, the sixth way, the five stages of conduct, is now considered.

1. An aspirant for asceticism is admitted to the order in an initiation ceremony.
2. After a specified probationary period, his or her ordination is confirmed.
3. Some aspirants practise purification through service to the order, the third of the five stages.
4. In due course, the ascetic reaches the tenth stage of spiritual development, complete self-restraint with subtle flickering greed (see 9.1).
5. Finally, the ascetic succeeds in practising perfect conduct at the eleventh and higher stages of spiritual development (9.1).

All five stages of conduct represent the gradual progress in the practice of self-restraint which is the essence of ascetic conduct.

anaśanâ-vamaudarya-vṛttiparisaṃkhyāna-rasaparityāga-viviktaśayyāsana-kāyakleśā bāhyaṃ tapaḥ

9.19 The six external austerities are: fasting, semi-fasting or reduced diet, voluntarily limiting the variety and the manner of seeking food, giving up delicacies or a stimulating diet, lonely habitation, and mortification of the body.

This sutra begins the explanation of austerities, the seventh way of inhibiting karmic inflow. There are two types of austerity, external and internal, each with its own sub-types. Here we deal with the external austerities.

1. Fasting protects self-restraint and effects elimination of karma. It means abstaining from food, or both food and drink, for a set period according to one's capacity.
2. Semi-fasting is a diet, which is gradually intensified by fixing a decreasing number of morsels of food to be consumed.
3. The varieties of food to be consumed and the places where it is sought may both be restricted.
4. Alcohol, meat, honey, butter and other stimulating food and drink are given up by the spiritual aspirant.
5. The ascetic should choose a solitary place, such as a deserted house, temple, mountain cave, for meditating and practising austerities.
6. For the mortification of the body, the aspirant may practise various positions such as the standing, lotus and milking positions, sitting by pressing the calf muscles under the thighs or on the toes keeping the heels erect, and so on. Residing under a tree or in open space and enduring cold and heat are part of this austerity.

Practising the six external austerities has five salutary effects: (1) renunciation of worldly relationship, (2) lightness of the body, (3) conquest over the senses, (4) guarding of self-restraint and (5) elimination of karma.

An austerity differs from a hardship (see 9.9) in that it is specifically created by the soul to purge itself of the impurity of passion, whereas a hardship occurs randomly.

prāyaścitta-vinaya-vaiyāvṛttya-svādhyāya-vyutsarga-dhyānāny uttaram

9.20 The six internal austerities are: penance, reverence [humility], service, scriptural study, renunciation and meditation.

Along with the external austerities (see 9.19), the internal austerities of ascetics are the seventh way of inhibiting karma.

1. Penances are prescribed to expatiate transgressions of the vows.
2. Reverence means due respect for learning and the learned.
3. Service is offered with humility to the elders and the sick ascetics.
4. Study of the scripture is compulsory for the ascetics.
5. Abandoning external objects and internal passions is an important ingredient of an austere life.
6. Meditation is restraint of body, speech and mind, to which the SBT adds that it must be according to the scriptural prescriptions. The SS defines meditation as putting an end to the distraction of the mind.

nava-catur-daśa-pañca-dvi-bhedaṃ yathākramaṃ prāg dhyānāt

9.21 There are nine kinds of penance, four kinds of reverence, ten kinds of service, five kinds of scriptural study and two kinds of renunciation.

ālocana-pratikramaṇa-tadubhaya-viveka-vyutsarga-tapaś-cheda-parihārô-pasthāpanāni

9.22 The nine penances are: confessing transgression, repenting past deeds, combined confession and repentance, careful inspection of articles received, abandoning unfit articles, austerity, lowering of ascetic seniority, segregation from the order, and reordination.

These sutras begin the detailed description of the six internal austerities. The sixth internal austerity, meditation, is not mentioned here but will be considered in 9.27.

There are nine kinds of penance, the first internal austerity.

1. Ascetics confess their lapses in religious observances to their teachers.
2. Ascetics repent their lapses, that is they regret such behaviour and determine to avoid it in the future.
3. Confession and repentance can occur together.
4. Ascetics depend on alms, but must inspect carefully articles that are offered to ensure that they are suitable.
5. Ascetics must abandon unfit articles received by mistake.
6. Practising austerities according to capacity is an important part of ascetic discipline.
7. An ascetic's failure to observe the discipline properly leads to demotion in his ascetic standing.
8. The ascetic is segregated from the order for a certain period if he is found guilty of serious aberrations.

9. When the ascetic is segregated, reordination becomes necessary. The SBT clarifies that reordination is preceded by two further states of penance: unfitness for reordination and then fitness for reordination due to the practice of requisite austerities.

These nine penances are prescribed by the spiritual teacher as purificatory measures, keeping in view the place, time, capacity, physical strength of the ascetic, the nature of the offences, the species of creatures injured and the intensity of passions with which the acts were perpetrated.

jñāna-darśana-cāritrô-pacārāḥ

9.23 The four reverences are for: learning, the enlightened world-view, good conduct, and senior ascetics.

Here, the kinds of reverence, the second internal austerity, are given. Reverence is a combination of honour and devotion. Reverence to those who are senior in enlightened world-view, knowledge and conduct, is shown by standing up and going forward to receive them, offering a seat, and so on, in accord with rules of ascetic behaviour.

ācāryô-pādhyāya-tapasvi-śaikṣaka-glāna-gaṇa-kula-saṅgha-sādhu-samanojñānām

9.24 The ten services are to: the preceptor, teacher, practitioner of austerities, learner [novice], sick, group, union, order, ascetics and fellow monastics.

Here the details of service, the third internal austerity, are given.

1. The preceptor gives the vows.
2. The teacher instructs the ascetics in the practical application of the religious code. Five kinds of teachers have been identified by the SB (see 9.6). In this connection, the SB mentions the nuns' administrator who takes care of the nuns.
3. A practitioner of austerities is one who practises prolonged fasting and other difficult austerities.
4. A trainee (novice) is a newly ordained monk.
5. The SS specifies the sick as ailing ascetics.
6. Group refers to the congregation of learned ascetics, who are the elders.
7. Union means the association of sects. The SS differs here in identifying

the union as the congregation of the disciples of an ordaining preceptor.

8. Order refers to the organization of the four constituent bodies: monks, nuns, laymen and laywomen. Service to the order is an integral part of the ascetic's daily routine. It includes providing food, drink, medicine, clothing and pots (for those orders which have them) and assistance to those travelling through dense forests and difficult regions and in times of natural and man-made tribulation. Arranging residence and furniture is also part of this service.
9. Ascetics are those who are ordained in self-restraint.
10. The fellow monastics are those who follow similar rules of conduct.

The SS explains fellow monastics as ascetics approved by the people. The ascetic order as a whole, including both monks and nuns, depends for its administration on three people, the preceptor, the teacher and the nuns' administrator.

vācanā-pracchanâ-nuprekṣâ-mnāya-dharmopadeśāḥ

9.25 The five stages of scriptural study are: teaching, questioning, reflection, correct recitation and preaching of the doctrine.

Here, the details of scriptural study, the fourth internal austerity, are given.

1. The first stage in scriptural study is teaching the disciples to read the text correctly and understand the meaning properly.
2. At the second stage, questions raised by the disciples are answered.
3. Reflection on the meaning of the text follows.
4. Then the text is correctly recited and memorized.
5. Lastly, the contents of the scripture become the subject matter of preaching.

bāhyâ-bhyantaropadhyoḥ

9.26 Renunciation means abandoning the external articles and the internal passions including the body.

Here, renunciation, the fifth sub-type of internal austerity, is explained. Absolute renunciation of all possessions and passions including the body is the aim of ascetic practice. The ascetic has to be free of the sense of mineness. Whatever he seeks for the bare maintenance of life is to be used with absolute detachment. The feeling of detachment from the body is an integral part of compulsory daily practice.

uttamasaṃhananasyaikāgra-cintānirodho dhyānam

9.27 (SS 9.27 in part) The concentration of thought on a single object by a person with good bone-joints is meditation.

Meditation, the sixth sub-type of internal austerity, is now considered.

The restless mind moves from one object to another. It is immersed in thought. When the restless mind concentrates on a single object it is meditating. This is a kind of restriction placed on the mind to still it. The stilling of the speech organs and the body is also a type of meditation. Perfect stillness of the body and all its organs is the highest state of meditation which is immediately followed by disembodied liberation. This state of meditation will be discussed in 9.42.

Good bone-joints refers to the first four types of bone-joints (see 8.12), that is, bone-joints with a pin, with a half-pin and half-plate, with interlocking bones on both sides, and with bones interlocking on one side with a pin on the other.

According to the SS, liberation is possible only for the monk possessed of the first variety of bone-joint. The SS explains "thought" as a faculty that is constantly vibrating because it focuses on a number of objects in quick succession. Concentrating on a single object entails withdrawing thought from all other objects and fixing it on this particular point. Concentration is the suspension of thought. It is a sort of negation, but not like a hare's horn, which is non-existent; it is negation in the sense that it negates the objects other than the one it is concentrating upon. But it is a solid and concrete affirmation of the object upon which it is fixed. So the negation is also a sort of affirmation. It takes positive note as a logical consequence of its negation.

ā muhūrtāt

9.28 (SS 9.27 in part) The meditative state lasts an intra-hour.

The meditative state cannot last beyond one intra-hour (less than forty-eight minutes), although it can be resumed. It is a positive state, knowledge that shines like an unflickering flame.

ārta-raudra-dharma-śuklāni

9.29 (SS 9.28) There are four kinds of meditation: mournful, wrathful,

analytic and white (pure).

pare mokṣahetū

9.30 (SS 9.29) **The last two kinds of meditation, analytic and white, lead to liberation.**

Unlike the last two kinds of meditation, the first two, the mournful and the wrathful, nourish worldly life.

ārtam amanojñānāṃ samprayoge tadviprayogāya smṛtisamanvāhāraḥ

9.31 (SS 9.30) **Dwelling on ridding oneself of contact with disagreeable objects or getting out of an unhappy situation is mournful meditation.**

vedanāyāś ca

9.32 (SS 9.32) **Dwelling on ridding oneself of unpleasant feelings is also mournful meditation.**

viparītaṃ manojñānām

9.33 (SS 9.31) **Dwelling on recovering contact with an agreeable object or repeating pleasant feelings is also mournful meditation.**

nidānaṃ ca

9.34 (SS 9.33) **Intense anxiety to fulfill unfulfilled desires in future lives is also mournful meditation.**

Four kinds of mournful meditation are given in the above four sutras. These are:

1. when a person is faced with an undesirable object or situation and fastens all attention on being rid of that object or situation and also to warding off a recurrence of such a confrontation;
2. when a person is faced with a painful feeling or ailment and fastens all attention on being rid of it and warding off a recurrence of this experience;
3. when a person loses possession of an agreeable object or a pleasurable sensation and fastens all attention on recovering it;
4. when a person develops an intense lust for an object and fastens all attention on the fulfilment of this desire in future lives.

tad avirata-deśavirata-pramattasaṃyatānām

9.35 (SS 9.34) People who are at the lower spiritual stages of non-abstinence, partial abstinence and self-restraint with laxity may fall into mournful meditation.

The stages of spiritual development mentioned here are the first six stages explained in 9.1. Of these six stages, the first four are devoid of abstinence (self-restraint). In the fifth, abstinence is partial and, in the sixth, there is self-restraint with laxity.

The SS remarks that only the first three kinds of mournful concentration are possible for the ascetic who is established in the sixth stage of spiritual development, as he is free of the anxiety to fulfill desires.

hiṃsâ-nṛta-steya-viṣayasaṃrakṣaṇebhyo raudram avirata-deśaviratayoḥ

9.36 (SS 9.35) Dwelling on the perpetration of violence, falsehood, theft and the preservation of one's possessions is wrathful meditation. People who are at the lower spiritual stages of non-abstinence and partial abstinence are subject to it.

Now, the second kind of meditation is considered. Wrathful meditation does not occur at the stage of self-restraint with laxity or those higher than that. It is accompanied by extreme cruelty. Such concentration occurs in a person who persistently indulges himself in deadly sins. His aggressive urge and possessive instinct are very deep and difficult to inhibit. This meditation has four variations according to the particular indulgence of the person: (1) violence, (2) lying, (3) stealing or (4) protection of property.

ājñâ-pāya-vipāka-saṃsthānavicayāya dharmam apramattasaṃyatasya

9.37 (not SS) Dwelling on investigating the essence of the scriptural commandments, the nature of physical and mental suffering, the effects of karma and the shape of the universe and its contents is analytic meditation. People who are at the spiritual stage of complete self-restraint free of laxity are capable of it.

ājñâ-pāya-vipāka-saṃsthānavicayāya dharmyam

(SS variant 9.36) Dwelling on investigating the essence of the scriptural commandments, the nature of physical and mental suffering, the effects of

karma and the shape of the universe and its contents is analytic meditation.

Analytic meditation is possible in people who are at the seventh stage of spiritual development, complete self-restraint free of laxity (see 9.1).

In the SS tradition, the qualification of the person capable of this meditation is given in the commentary rather than the sutra. It explains that analytic meditation is possible in people who are at the spiritual stages of non-abstinence, partial abstinence, self-restraint with laxity, and self-restraint free of laxity. In other words, according to the SS, analytic meditation is possible at the fourth to seventh stages of spiritual development, instead of exclusively at the seventh stage as explained in the SB tradition.

The four objects to be meditated upon in analytic meditation are: (1) the infallible and immaculate nature of the scriptural commandment, (2) the fact of universal suffering and its conditions, (3) the nature of the fruition of various karmas and (4) the structure of the universe and its contents.

The SS explains that meditation on the first object, the scriptural commandments, is necessary for those who are intellectually weak with a limited capacity for logic; they have to depend exclusively on their faith in the absolute veracity of the path of liberation taught by the Jina. According to another explanation mentioned in the SS, the first variety of concentration is necessary to gain a penetrating understanding of the Jina's commandments, using logic and the philosophical standpoints, so as to be able to teach them to others correctly.

upaśānta-kṣīṇakaṣāyayoś ca

9.38 (not in SS) Analytic meditation also occurs at the two spiritual stages of complete self-restraint with suppressed passions and complete self-restraint with eliminated passions.

These two further stages of spiritual development at which analytic meditation occurs are the eleventh and twelfth (see 9.1).

śukle cādye

9.39 (SS 9.37 in part) The first two varieties of white meditation are also possible in a person at the stage of complete self-restraint with suppressed passions and at the stage of complete self-restraint with eliminated passions.

The fourth kind of meditation, white medition, has four varieties: (1) multiple contemplation, (2) unitary contemplation, (3) subtle infallible physical activity and (4) the irreversible, motionless state of the soul (see further details 9.42). Of these, the first two are possible in someone at the eleventh or twelfth stages of spiritual development (9.1) at which stages analytic meditation is also possible.

The SS explains that there is analytic concentration before climbing up the ladders and there is white concentration while climbing them. "Climbing ladders" starts at the eighth stage of spiritual development. (For the concept of "ladders", see appendix 4.)

pūrvavidaḥ

9.40 (SS 9.37 in part) The first two varieties of white meditation belong to the one conversant with the early scriptures.

This (part of the SS) sutra gives a further qualification of the person qualified for white meditation. However, the early literature of the scripture is no longer extant.

pare kevalinaḥ

9.41 (SS 9.38) The last two varieties of white meditation belong to the one who is omniscient.

A person who is capable of the last two kinds of meditation – subtle infallible physical activity, and irreversible stillness of the soul – is an omniscient at the thirteenth and fourteenth stages of spiritual development (see 9.1).

pṛthaktvai-katvavitarka-sūkṣmakriyāpratipāti-vyuparatakriyânivartīni

9.42 (SS 9.39) The four varieties of white meditation are: multiple contemplation, unitary contemplation, subtle infallible physical activity and irreversible stillness of the soul.

The commentaries give fuller details of these four white meditations.

1. In the first variety of white meditation, multiple contemplation, the meditator, guided by scriptural contemplation, concentrates from different philosophical standpoints (see 1.34–1.35) on the three modes – origination, cessation and continuity – of a particular entity (for instance,

his own self). The meditator also moves mentally from the thing itself to the word which signifies it and moves from any one of the activities of the body, speech and mind to any other.

2. In the second variety, unitary contemplation, the meditator, guided by scriptural contemplation, concentrates on one of the three modes of an entity, or of the word which signifies the entity, and stops it flitting from the entity signified to the word signifying it, as also from one mental, vocal or physical activity to another. This meditation is as unflickering and steadfast as the flame of a lamp in a room through which no wind passes.

3. In the third variety of white meditation, subtle infallible physical activity, which is undertaken by the omniscient a few moments before final liberation, all the activities, gross and subtle, of the mind and speech organs and also the gross activity of the body are absolutely stopped. Only the subtle activities of the body, such as respiration and the like, persist. There is, moreover, no fall, because one does not return to the previous state when the meditation is over, but rises up to the final kind of white meditation.

4. In the fourth and final variety, irreversible stillness, even the residual subtle activities of the body are stopped and the self becomes as still as a rock. There is no reversion from this last state of meditation because it is immediately followed by disembodied liberation.

tat trye-ka-kāyayogâ-yogānām

9.43 (SS 9.40) The four varieties of white meditation are respectively accompanied by three activities, any one of the three activities, only bodily activity, and no activity.

The four varieties of white meditation are defined according to the number and quality of the meditator's activities.

1. The first variety, multiple contemplation, is practised by a meditator who is mentally, vocally and physically active.
2. The second variety, unitary contemplation, is practised by one who is engaged in any one of these three activities.
3. The third variety, subtle infallible physical activity, is practised by one whose body alone is active.
4. The fourth variety, irreversible stillness, is practised by one who has stopped all kinds of activity at the fourteenth stage of spiritual development.

ekāśraye savitarke pūrve

9.44 (SS 9.41) The first two varieties of white meditation have one particular substance as their object and are accompanied by contemplation (and movement).[4]

avīcāraṃ dvitīyam

(SS only 9.42) The second variety of white meditation is devoid of movement.

In the first two varieties of white meditation, the meditator ponders one particular object. The first variety is also accompanied by movement, while the second is motionless. Both are accompanied by contemplation.

vitarkaḥ śrutam

9.45 (SS 9.43) Contemplation is pondering over the contents of the scriptures.

vicāro'rtha-vyañjana-yogasaṃkrāntiḥ

9.46 (SS 9.44) Movement is transit between the object, linguistic symbol and the activities.

Contemplation is musing which is a type of empirical knowledge (see 1.9). This musing is based on the scripture and is free from doubt and error.

Movement is a kind of transit between the object, the word which signifies it and the activities of mind, speech and body. In meditation, a single atom or a material body may serve as the object along with the word signifying an object. The transit between an object and its signifier and vice versa in meditation penetrates into their nature to discover the truth underlying them. The transit between the mental, verbal and physical activities to delve deep into their nature is also meditation.

The SS explains that the object concentrated upon is either a substance or a mode (that is, the eternal reality or the passing phase of a substance, 5.37). The linguistic symbol is the word. Activity is the action of body,

[4] In this sutra, *savitarke*, "accompanied by contemplation", is given by the SS as *savitarka-vīcarē*, "accompanied by contemplation and movement". This is endorsed in the SB commentary.

speech and mind. Transit is change. The oscillation of the mind between the substance and mode is transit between objects. Oscillation between scriptural concepts or words is transit between linguistic symbols. Oscillation between activities of body, speech and mind is transit between activities. These oscillations of the mind are called movement, their purpose being the discovery of truth at all the three levels – the object, its symbol and its activity.

To summarize, contemplation is musing on one object whereas movement is oscillation between the objects of meditation – substances and modes, symbols and actions. The meditator penetrates deeper and deeper through these objects until he transcends all of them in self-realization in the fourth variety of white meditation which is immediately followed by disembodied liberation. This sutra ends the explanation of the sixth internal austerity and, in so doing, ends the explanation of the seven principal ways of inhibiting karma.

samyagdṛṣṭi-śrāvaka-viratâ-nantaviyojaka-darśanamohakṣapakô-paśamakô-paśāntamoha-kṣapaka-kṣīṇamoha-jināḥ kramaśo'saṅkhyeyaguṇanirjarāḥ

9.47 (SS 9.45) The suppression or elimination of karmic particles increases innumerably at each of the ten stages of spiritual development which are:

(1) the possessor of enlightened world-view
(2) the lay learner practising partial abstinence
(3) the ascetic practising complete abstinence
(4) the ascetic suppressing or eliminating the tenacious passions
(5) the ascetic eliminating view-deluding karma
(6) the ascetic suppressing conduct-deluding karma [passions]
(7) the ascetic who has suppressed conduct-deluding karma [passions]
(8) the ascetic eliminating conduct-deluding passions
(9) the ascetic who has eliminated the conduct-deluding passions
(10) the victor.

The description of the ways to inhibit and wear off karma completed (see 9.2–9.46), the progressive suppression and elimination of karma is considered according to the ten stages of spiritual development. These ten stages are an ancient forerunner of the fourteen stages mentioned in 9.1.

They give a short account of the spiritual progress from the dawning of enlightened world-view to the point when view-deluding karma has worn off and the time and circumstances are appropriate for the first rays of spiritual vision (see 1.3, 2.3), and ending with the "victor", the highest stage of a soul's spirituality while still in a body. At each stage innumerably more karma wears off than at the previous stage.

pulāka-bakuśa-kuśīla-nirgrantha-snātakā nirgranthāḥ

9.48 (SS 9.46) **There are five classes of unbound ascetics: the husk, the tainted, the deficient in mores, the unbound and the successful.**

Ascetics who are practitioners of the discipline of inhibition are called unbound. They are engaged in cleansing their souls of all impurities, intellectual and moral. The expression is commonly used for all ascetics who are followers of Mahāvīra, but also more specifically for the fourth category, noted in this sutra, of ascetics who are at the eleventh and twelfth stages of spiritual development (see 9.1).

1. The first class of monks, called "the husk", are like empty pods devoid of pith. They are genuine believers in the scripture although they live on occult powers obtained by austerity and learning.
2. The second class of ascetics, called "the tainted", are attached to articles of religious life such as clothing and pots, and to adornment. They live an easy life surrounded by their relatives. Their morality is variegated by these taints.
3. The third class of ascetics, called "the deficient in mores", have two varieties: those who are deficient in mores because they have violated supporting vows and those deficient because of the rise of flickering passions.
4. The fourth class of ascetics, called "the unbound", have either suppressed or eliminated their passions. They are at the eleventh or twelfth stage of spiritual development.
5. The fifth class of ascetics, called "the successful", have attained omniscience by eliminating their four destructive karmas (see 2.1). They are at the thirteenth or fourteenth stage of spiritual development.

Although the first three unbound ascetics possess the enlightened worldview, they are morally weak in observing their supporting vows. Their faith is strong but their conduct is lacking.

saṃyama-śruta-pratisevanā-tīrtha-liṅga-leśyô-papāta-sthānavikalpataḥ sādhyāḥ

9.49 (SS 9.47) **The five classes of unbound ascetics are examined for**

their self-restraint, scriptural learning, violation of the vows, presence in the rule of the spiritual ford-founders, equipment, psychic colouring, descent in heaven and units of self-restraint.

Now the five classes of unbound ascetics are identified according to their various attainments.

Self-restraint: The husk, the tainted and those who are deficient in mores due to violation of the supporting vows are established in the first two stages of self-restraint (stages of conduct) – initiation and ordination (see 9.18). According to the SB, those who are deficient in mores because of rising passions are established in the next two stages – purification through service and self-restraint attended with subtle flickering greed. According to the SS, those who are deficient because of rising passions are established in all of four stages mentioned above. The last two classes of ascetic, the unbound and the successful, are established in perfect conduct, the fifth and final stage.

Scriptural learning: The husk, the tainted and those deficient in mores due to violation of the supporting vows, are conversant with, at most, ten books of the early literature. Ascetics who are deficient because of rising passions, and the unbound ascetics, are conversant with, at most, fourteen books of the early literature. At the very least, the husk is conversant with the Ācāra which is the third volume of the ninth book of the early literature (see appendix 6) and the tainted, the deficient in mores and the unbound are conversant with the eight scriptural matrices – the three varieties of guarding and five varieties of careful movement (9.4–9.5). The successful (that is the omniscient) is beyond the ambit of scriptural knowledge.

Violation of the vows: The husk may be incited by others to violate any of the five great vows and the supporting vow of not eating at night. However, some commentators identify instigated violation as specific to the vow of celibacy. The tainted violate their vows in two ways, through addiction to precious articles or through addiction to adorning the body. Those deficient in mores due to violating the supporting vows do just that, at times. There is no violation of the vows by the rest of the classes of unbound ascetics – the deficient in mores because of their passions, the unbound (proper) and the successful.

Presence during the rule of the spiritual ford-founders: The view of the commentators is that all five classes of unbound ascetics exist during the rule of the tīrthaṅkaras (literally "ford-founders", the title of Jinas who have lived their last human life as one of the twenty-four founders of religion in a time-cycle). However, according to some other teachers, the husk, the tainted and those deficient in mores because of vow violation, always exist during the ford-founders' rule, while the others exist during the rule and also outside of it.

Equipment: There is external and internal equipment. All the five classes of unbound ascetics possess the internal equipment of knowledge, enlightened world-view and conduct. With respect to the external equipment of broom, mouth-cover etc. (9.4–9.6), some of them possess this equipment and some do not.

Psychic colouring: The husk has the last three colourings, red (fiery), yellow (filament-coloured) and white. All six colourings, that is, the above three as well as black, blue and grey, exist in the tainted and those deficient in mores because of their violation of vows. The last three colourings exist in those who are deficient in mores because of rising passions but who practise purification through service. Otherwise, according to the SB tradition, those deficient because of their passions have only white colouring, as do the unbound and the successful. According to the SS, this second variety of those deficient in mores all have four colourings – grey, red, yellow and white – whatever their stages of conduct. The soul at the fourteenth stage of spiritual develoment is free of psychic colour.

Descent (appearance) in heaven: At most, the descent of the husk is as far as the Sahasrāra gods (4.20) who have a lifespan of eighteen ocean-measured periods; the descent of the tainted, and those who are deficient due to violation of vows, is as far as the heaven of the Āraṇa and Acyuta gods who have a lifespan of 22 o.m.p.; and the descent of those who are deficient due to rising passions, and of the unbound, is as far as the Sarvārthasiddha gods who have a lifespan of 33 o.m.p. At the least, the descent of the first four classes of the unbound ascetics is in the heaven of the Saudharma gods with a lifespan of 2 o.m.p. (2–9 o.m.p., according to the SB). The successful attains liberation.

Units of self-restraint: These are determined by the units of passion. The suppression or elimination of the units of passion is followed by an increase in the units of self-restraint. In other words, self-restraint becomes stronger as the passions grow weaker. The husk and those deficient in mores due to rising passions have the fewest units of self-restraint. Both of these states have innumerable "stations" of self-restraint along the spiritual paths which overlap. Then the state of the husk ends and the state of deficiency due to rising passions continues for innumerable stations of self-restraint until a certain point at which there are enough for the state of deficiency of mores due to violating supplementary vows and of the tainted. These three states continue for innumerable stations of self-restraint, until the tainted ceases. After crossing innumerable stations of self-restraint, the deficiency in mores due to violation of vows ends. Then the deficiency in mores due to rising of passions arises and continues alone over innumerable stations of self-restraint until it finally ends. Then the unbound state that is devoid of passion begins. This continues across further innumerable stations of self-restraint devoid of passion until the state of the successful is reached. This is followed by liberation.

The acquisition of self-restraint by each succeeding class of unbound ascetic is infinitely more than the acquisition of the preceding class.

CHAPTER TEN

Liberation

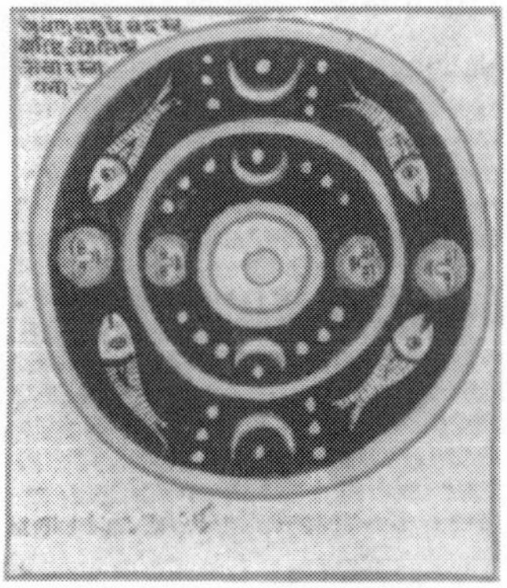

Contents

The previous chapter explained the fifth and sixth categories of truth, inhibition and wearing off of karma. Now the seventh and last category of truth, liberation, is considered. But first, omniscience that precedes liberation is explained.

mohakṣayāj jñāna-darśanāvaraṇâ-ntarāyakṣayāc ca kevalam

10.1 Omniscience arises when deluding karma is eliminated and, as a result, knowledge-covering, intuition-covering and obstructive karma are eliminated.

The elimination of deluding karma through self-restraint and austerities is followed by the simultaneous elimination of the other three destructive karmas. The SS explains in detail that the soul eliminates the three kinds of the view-deluding karma and the four tenacious passions (see 8.10) somewhere from the fourth to the seventh stage of spiritual development, and then slowly climbs to the twelfth stage of spiritual development, the state of eliminated passions (9.1). At this stage, the deluding karma is totally and finally expelled and the soul is then able to eliminate the three remaining destructive karmas all at once.

This frees the soul to attain omniscience which is pure and perfect knowledge and intuition. The one who attains this state is described by the SB (10.2) as the perfectly pure, the enlightened one, the all-knowing, the all-intuiting, the victorious, the absolutely alone.

bandhahetvabhāva-nirjarābhyām

10.2 (SS 10.2 in part) There is no fresh bondage because the causes of bondage have been eliminated and all destructive karmas have worn off.

Now the reason why the karma is no longer bound is explained. Five causes of bondage were given in 8.1 – deluded world-view, non-abstinence, laxity, passions and the actions of body, speech and mind.

Of these five, the first four have been eliminated. The last cause, action, is incapable of producing long-term inflow and bondage. It merely causes instantaneous inflow and bondage which cease in the next instant (see 6.5).

Instantaneous bondage, as explained in the *Dhavalā on Ṣaṭkhaṇḍāgama*, XIII. 47ff, is accompanied by massive elimination of karma and by transcendental bliss. It is neither bound nor unbound, neither realized nor unrealized, neither eliminated nor not eliminated, neither expelled nor not expelled. It is ineffable. It is a beatific experience at the highest level of spirituality.

Wearing off all four types of destructive karmas also prevents the binding of new karmas that could produce a deluded view or cover knowledge and intuition or stand in the way of infinite spiritual energy and bliss.

Now, only the four non-destructive karmas – sensation, lifespan, body and status – remain to be eliminated. This is achieved when the lifespan karma comes to an end at the appointed moment and is followed by liberation.

kṛtsnakarmakṣayo mokṣaḥ

10.3 (SS 10.2 in part) **The elimination of all types of karma is liberation.**

The four destructive karmas are eliminated before omniscience is attained. Then the four remaining non-destructive karmas are eliminated and the soul is detached from its body, ending its worldly existence. This is the state of liberation that is free of all karma.

aupaśamikādi-bhavyatvābhāvāc cānyatra kevalasamyaktva-jñāna-darśana-siddhatvebhyaḥ

10.4 (SS 10.3–10.4) **When the five states in all their varieties and also the state of being worthy of liberation cease, with the exception of the perfect enlightened world-view, perfect knowledge, perfect intuition and the state of being liberated, then there is liberation.**

The states that distinguish the soul from other substances were described in 2.1–2.7. What happens to these states at liberation is now explained. Three states – pure and perfect enlightened world-view, knowledge, and intuition – are due to the total elimination of karma (see 2.4); they are the intrinsic properties of the soul which never cease. Similarly, the state of being liberated also continues, unlike the state of being worthy of liberation (2.7) which ends despite also being intrinsic.

In the SS, the qualities of infinite energy and bliss are said to exist in liberated souls as inseparable companions of perfect knowledge and intuition.

The SS raises the question that if the shape and size of the soul changes according to the size and shape of the body it happens to occupy, then when the soul is liberated and therefore devoid of a physical body, should it not expand to the size of the cosmos? The explanation given is that the contraction or expansion of the soul is due to the body karma and as there is no karma of this or any sort in the state of liberation, the question of expansion to the size of the cosmos is irrelevant.

tadanantaram ūrdhvaṃ gacchaty ā lokāntāt

10.5 When all karmic bondage is eliminated, the soul soars upwards to the border of cosmic space.

Immediately after the soul has rid itself of all karma, three events take place simultaneously in one time unit: the soul's separation from the body, the soul's motion upwards and the soul's arrival at the border of cosmic space. These three events are the simultaneous effect, process and fulfilment of the cause of the upward lift.

TRANSLATOR'S NOTE

The movement from the place of death to the border of cosmic space takes place in one time unit. The soul is supposed to pass without touching the intermediate space units. This is called "touchless moving".

pūrvaprayogād asaṅgatvād bandhacchedāt tathāgatipariṇāmāc ca tadgatiḥ

10.6 The soul soars up by virtue of the antecedent impetus, separation from karmic particles, severance of the karmic bondage and its innate mode of upward flight.

āviddhakulālcakravad vyapagatalepālābuvad eraṇḍabījavad agniśikhāvac ca

(SS 10.7) **Because of these factors, it is like the potter's wheel set in motion, like the gourd with dissolved earthen layers, like the castor seeds released from the pod and like the flame of fire.**

dharmāstikāyābhāvād

(SS 10.8) **The liberated soul cannot go outside cosmic space because there is no medium of motion beyond.**

Here the motion of the soul after it has freed itself from karmic bondage is explained.

The SB explains antecedent impetus, as does the SS in the sutra, with the example of the potter's wheel which continues to revolve even after the potter has withdrawn the rod that turned the wheel. The movement which the soul derived from karma during its worldly existence furnishes the push upwards even after separation from the body.

Because of its heaviness, matter tends to pull downwards, whilst souls tend to fly upwards. This is their nature. The deviation in these tendencies is due to extraneous factors. Clods of earth fall downwards, even as wind blows horizontally and fire blows upwards. Worldly souls move down and horizontally as well as upwards because of the burden of their karmic matter. As soon as they are freed of the karmic burden, souls fly up to the place of liberation at the top of the cosmos. The tendency of the soul to fly upwards is like that of the flame which, with relatively little mass, reaches up, unlike the clod which falls downwards because of its mass.

The downward movement of worldly souls is also compared with a gourd overlaid with layers of heavy black earth sinking in water and the upward flight of the souls freed of karmic burden is compared with the gourd bobbing up to the surface of the water when the earthen layers have dissolved.

The upward motion of the soul when freed from its karma is further compared with the upward thrust of castor seeds when released from the pod.

The SB commentary and SS sutra both explain that the liberated soul cannot go outside cosmic space because there is no medium of motion beyond (5.17).

kṣetra-kāla-gati-liṅga-tīrtha-cāritra-pratyekabuddhabodhita-jñānâ-vagāhanâ-ntara-saṅkhyâ-lpabahutvataḥ sādhyāḥ

10.7 (SS 10.9) **The state of the liberated soul is considered through twelve gateways of investigation: place, time, realm of birth, gender or dress, ford, conduct, mode of enlightenment through self or others, knowledge, height, interval, number and relative numerical strength of the**

liberated souls in the preceding eleven gateways.

Now the concept of the liberated soul is explained through twelve gateways of investigation. These gateways explain the circumstances – physical, psychological and spiritual – under which the soul is liberated. A brief account of these circumstances with respect to these gateways is given below.

1. Place: The actual place of liberation is the zone of liberation at the top of cosmic space. For the places from which one can achieve liberation, see below under realms of birth.

2. Time: Generally speaking, souls can be liberated in the descending as well as the ascending time cycles (see SS 3.27). Specifically speaking, they must be born in certain aeons of these cycles to be liberated. In the descending cycle, liberation is only possible in the last part of the aeon of plenty-with-privation and any part of the aeon of privation-with-plenty. In the ascending cycle, it is only possible in the aeons of privation, privation-with-plenty and plenty-with-privation. People born in the aeon of privation-with-plenty can attain liberation in the next aeon of privation, although if they were born in this latter aeon, they could not. However, abducted people, that is those who are carried out of their land of spiritual effort, can attain liberation in any aeon of the time cycles. The actual instant of liberation for a soul occurs at the border of the cosmos where there is no time in the sense that there are no vehicles of luminous gods to measure time (4.15).

3. Realms of birth: The life culminating in liberation must be in one of the fifteen lands of human habitation where spiritual effort is possible (SS 3.37). However, people who are abducted can achieve liberation in other lands as well, although the restriction that they be lands of human habitation applies to them also (SS 3.35). Abduction is only possible of people at the fifth and sixth stages of spiritual development (9.1). The realm of birth in the penultimate life can be in any of the four realms – heaven, hell, subhuman (micro-organisms, plants and animals) or human.

4. Gender and dress: A person freed of all sexual dispositions attains liberation. It is affirmed by the SB/SBT tradition that physical gender – female, male or hermaphroditic – and dress have no bearing on attaining liberation. Even a householder wearing their daily garb can be liberated. In the SS tradition also, liberation is said to take place in those freed of all sexual disposition. However, they must also be physically male and nude.

5. Ford: This refers to the way across to liberation. Founders of the ford

are the omniscient Jinas who proclaim religion and attain liberation. There are also souls who are enlightened in isolation, finding inspiration within themselves, independent of any discipline established by someone else. They are quasi-ford-founders. A third category of souls attain liberation as an ordinary person practising the discipline taught by the founder of the ford. In the SB/SBT tradition, these three categories also apply to women. The SS identifies two categories of liberated souls. The first category includes founders of the ford, and the second, ordinary people, both those who attained liberation in the presence of a ford-founder and those who attained liberation in the absence of a ford-founder.

6. Conduct: At the instant of liberation in the zone of liberation, the soul is no longer at the five stages of conduct (9.18) because the fifth and highest stage of conduct ends when the soul is disembodied.

7. Enlightenment and liberation through the self or others: Four classes of souls are identified. Of those who achieve enlightenment and liberation through their own initiative, there are those who acquire the qualities of a ford-founder and help others to liberation, and those who are enlightened and liberated in isolation. Of those who achieve enlightenment and liberation through instruction from others, there are also those who help others to liberation and those who remain satisfied with their own liberation.

8. Knowledge: A soul is liberated only after it has attained omniscience. Before becoming omniscient, however, a soul may possess two, three or four varieties of knowledge in combination (1.9): empirical and articulate knowledge; or empirical, articulate and clairvoyant knowledge; or empirical, articulate and mind-reading knowledge; or all four of these knowledges.

9. Height: Before liberation, the maximum height for Jinas is 500 bows (502–509 bows for the first Jina's mother and some others) and the minimum is two to nine fingers less than seven cubits, according to the SB tradition. The maximum is given by the SS as 525 bows and the minimum as a little less than 3.5 spans or two cubits. The maximum height applies to the earliest humans to attain liberation in a time cycle and the minimum to the latest to do so. When liberated, the soul's height is reduced by one-third. (For bow, finger, cubit and span, see appendix 3.)

10. Interval: Liberation of souls can take place continuously for two to eight time units. With intermittent liberation, two liberations may be one time unit apart and maximally may be separated by as much as six months.

11. Number: up to 108 souls may attain liberation during one time unit.

12. Relative numerical strength: the above eleven points are used as the gateways of investigation. So:

(1) Place: Abducted people, that is, those who are carried out of their lands of spiritual effort, and also those who migrate, are the smallest minority of liberated souls. There are many[1] more who obtain liberation in the region of birth.

(2) Time: Fewer people are liberated in the descending cycle than in the ascending cycle. Many more souls are liberated in the regions where time cycles do not occur.

(3) Realm of birth: There are four categories of souls considered here:

(3.1) Souls transmigrating from the animal (subhuman) realm to the human realm;

(3.2) Souls transmigrating within the human realm;

(3.3) Souls transmigrating from the infernal realm to the human realm;

(3.4) Souls transmigrating from the realm of gods to the human realm.

The first category accounts for the least number of liberated souls with many more in each successive category.

(4) Gender: According to the SB tradition, the number of hermaphrodites liberated is the least. Many more females are liberated and many more males than females.

(5) Ford: The ford-founders are the smallest minority of the liberated souls. There are many more who are liberated in isolation and who do not become ford-founders. There are many more than these who are hermaphrodites and are liberated during the rule of ford-founders. There are many more females than hermaphrodites who are liberated during the rule of ford-founders and many more males than females liberated thus.

(6) Conduct: The first three of the five stages of conduct (9.18) are optional for liberation. Only the last two are essential. The souls liberated with all five stages of conduct are the fewest. There are

[1] "Many" is used throughout this gateway as shorthand for the technically correct translation "numerably more". See appendix 1 for further details on Jaina concepts of numerable, innumerable and infinite.

many more souls with four stages of conduct. There are many more souls than these who are liberated with three stages of conduct.

(7) Mode of enlightenment: The number of people enlightened in isolation is the least. Hermaphrodites enlightened by ford-founders are many more, females enlightened by ford-founders are many more again and males enlightened by ford-founders are many more again.

(8) Knowledge: The people with two varieties of knowledge who achieve omniscience, the essential condition of liberation, are the fewest. The people with four varieties of knowledge who achieve omniscience are many more and the people with three varieties are many more again (because the fourth variety, mind-reading, is possible only for ascetics who undertake very difficult austerities).

(9) Height: Liberated souls with the minimum height of one cubit eight fingers are the fewest. There are many more with the maximum height of 333.3 fathoms.[2] However, in between these two extremes, there are many more liberated souls with a height of four cubits sixteen fingers and many more again with a height higher than four cubits sixteen fingers (but less than the maximum). The liberated souls with a height less than four cubits sixteen fingers (but more than the minimum) are somewhat greater in number again and the total number of other liberated souls is somewhat more than this.

(10) Interval: The souls liberated continuously for eight time units are the fewest of those liberated continuously. The souls liberated continuously for two time units are the next fewest, although they are many more. For every extra time unit of continuous liberation from three to seven time units, there are many more souls liberated. The souls liberated intermittently after a period of six months are the fewest of the souls liberated at intervals. Many more souls are liberated at intervals of one time unit. Many more than these are liberated at intervals exactly half the time between one time unit and six months. Many more are liberated in less than this half-period and somewhat more than these are liberated at intervals longer than this. The number of souls liberated at other

[2] Souls lose ⅓ of their height in liberation. Therefore, with two cubits as the minimum height before liberation, we get the 2 cubits – (2 cubits × ⅓) = 1⅓ cubit or one cubit eight fingers. Similarly with 500 fathoms as the maximum height before liberation, 500 fathoms – (500 × ⅓) = 333.3 fathoms.

times is somewhat more again.

(11) Number: The souls liberated simultaneously as one of 108 souls are the fewest. Infinitely more are liberated simultaneously in groups of between fifty and 107. Innumerably more than these are liberated simultaneously in groups of between twenty-five and forty-nine. Many more are liberated simultaneously in groups of two to twenty-five or just on their own.

The SB briefly describes the abode of the liberated souls as a slim wheel-shaped stretch of land, 45×10^5 yojanas in diameter, eight yojanas thick in the middle and gradually attenuating so that it is thinner than the thinnest wing of a butterfly at the periphery. Situated at the summit of the cosmic space, it is most pleasing, sweet-smelling, auspicious and bright – resembling the outer surface of a white parasol unfolded downward.

As regards the innate attributes of the liberated souls, the SB explains their essence as perfect knowledge and pure intuition, true world-view and total liberation. They are free of any activity because there is no cause of action, that is, karma, within them. Being free of activity themselves and because there is no medium of motion beyond, the liberated souls cannot pass into transcosmic space. They enjoy uninterrupted eternal bliss. Unlike sensuous pleasure, their bliss is unlimited. Unlike pleasure that is conditioned by the relief from pain, their bliss is unconditioned. Unlike pleasure that is due to the fruition of beneficial karma, their bliss is without cause. The bliss of liberated souls is the result of their absolute freedom from karma and from the passions that are the seeds of karma.

The SB here explains the essence of the entire treatise by explaining the path to liberation. In their beginningless wanderings, some souls happen to find an opening into truth spontaneously by pressure from within. Others find such an opening by the external pressure of guidance from enlightened teachers (1.3).

The opening signifies a lifting of the veil of delusion with which spiritual life begins. The veil of delusion is essentially a deluded world-view, a perverse set of values. With the lifting of the veil, the enlightened world-view arises as a state of emotional calm, dread and distaste for worldly life, compassion and faith in transmigration (1.2).

The enlightened world-view is followed by enlightened knowledge of the categories of truth (1.1–1.2) through linguistic analysis, the approved methods of knowledge, the gateways of investigation and the philosophical standpoints (1.5–1.8). The true knowledge of the five states of the soul

– the innate state and those due to the rise, suppression, partial suppression and partial elimination, and elimination of karma (2.1) – is then achieved. This is followed by the appreciation of the qualities and modes of the substances that are constantly subject to origination, cessation and continuity (5.17–5.22, 5.29–5.31).

By reducing passions and desires, guarding thought, word and deed (9.4), observing the five kinds of careful movement (9.5), and practising the ten virtues (9.6), the soul nourishes its dread and distaste for worldly life. It becomes devoted to the twenty-five supporting practices (7.3–SS 7.8) and gains stability of mind through the twelve reflections (9.7). It is consequently freed of attachment because of the inhibition of karmic inflows (6.1–6.4). By enduring hardships (9.9) and practising external and internal austerities, it stops accumulating and binding new karma (9.19–9.20).

The karma bound and accumulated in the past is worn off by the purity of the states beginning with the enlightened view without abstinence and ending in the state of the victor (9.47). Self-restraint in religious conduct begins with initiation into ascetic life and continues to the state of self-restraint with flickering greed (9.18). The soul then observes the self-restraint of the five kinds of unbound ascetics – "the husk" and so on (9.48–9.49) – until it reaches the final state of the unbound ascetics, "the successful".

The soul gradually rids itself of the types of mournful and wrathful meditation (9.31–9.36) and acquires the power of analytical meditation (9.37). It reaches the first two stages of white meditation (9.39) sometimes leading to the acquisition of supernatural powers such as:

1. healing by touch
2. healing by excreta
3. healing by bodily secretions
4. verbal curses and blessings
5. lordship of all creatures
6. subjugating all creatures
7. clairvoyance
8. a subtle (transformed protean) body which can enter into a minute pore of the filament of a lotus
9. a light (transformed protean) body which is lighter than air
10. a huge (transformed protean) body which is larger than Mount Meru
11. touching anything at any distance

12. walking at will on water or diving into land
13. flying with the help of rays, smoke, etc.
14. flying high and diving in the sky
15. unobstructed movement (by transforming the protean body)
16. invisibility (by transforming the protean body)
17. assuming many shapes at will (by transforming the protean body)
18. emission of hot and cold light (from red/fiery colouring, from the fiery body)
19. sensing touch, taste, smell, colour and sound at a distance
20. simultaneous, indiscriminate perception by all the senses
21. retention of knowledge
22. expansive knowledge
23. knowledge of the whole from the part
24. simple mind-reading
25. complex mind-reading
26. attaining the desired object
27. not attaining the undesired object
28. speech discharging milk
29. speech discharging honey
30. proficiency in debate
31. understanding all utterances
32. enlightening all beings
33. proficiency in occult sciences
34. words vomiting poison
35. slightly incomplete knowledge of the fourteen books of the early literature
36. complete knowledge of the fourteen books of the early literature.

The first twenty of these powers are physical, the next seven, mental and the last nine, verbal. However, the ascetic has no interest in any of them, but is set on the total elimination of the twenty-eight types of deluding karma (8.10). On the elimination of these types of karma, the soul attains the state of eliminated passions with a lingering veil of ignorance. Within an intra-hour (less than forty-eight minutes), the knowledge-covering, intuition-covering and obstructive karmas are simultaneously eliminated. Now the soul is freed from "seed bondage" (that is, causally active bondage, usually known as destructive karmas) and practises perfect conduct (9.18). It is now the victorious, the absolutely alone, the all-knowing, the all-intuiting, the perfectly pure, the enlightened one, the accomplisher of the mission and the successful.

Then, on the elimination of the non-destructive karmas – the sensation, body, status and lifespan karmas – the soul is freed of effect bondage. It has now burnt the karmic fuel accumulated in the past. It is like fire without fuel. It is absolutely tranquil because it is severed from its past worldly life and with no future worldly life because there is no cause to produce this. It is beyond all worldly pleasures and attains the bliss of liberation which is perfect, absolute, incomparable, eternal and unsurpassed by anything else.

APPENDIX ONE

Numbers

Numbers play an important role in the descriptions of Jaina cosmology, doctrine of karma, and lifespans of the different classes of living beings. A brief account of the Jaina classification of numbers is, therefore, given here for the reader.

Numbers are broadly divided into three classes: numerable, innumerable and infinite. The numerable numbers are further divided into three sub-classes: minimum, intermediate, and maximum. The innumerable numbers are also divided into three sub-classes: low-grade, self-raised, and innumerable-innumerable. Each of the three innumerable sub-classes is again divided into minimum, intermediate, and maximum. The infinite is also divided first into three sub-classes: low-grade, self-raised, and infinite-infinite and then the first two sub-classes are further divided as minimum, intermediate, and maximum while the third sub-class, infinite-infinite, is divided as minimum and intermediate only, there being no maximum in the case of the infinite-infinite. This classification of numbers is illustrated in figure 13 on p. 266.

To describe the process that leads to the definition of the various classes of numbers, it is necessary first to describe the rings of oceans and islands that encircle Jambū Island as these play a crucial part in our description. At the centre of the middle region of the cosmos is the island of Jambū which is circular in shape with a diameter of 100,000 yojanas (909,000 miles). Jambū is encircled by Lavaṇa Ocean which is twice as wide as Jambū, that is 200,000 yojanas (see figure 8, p. 76). Lavaṇa Ocean is encircled by the island of Dhātakī which is twice as wide as Lavaṇa Ocean, that is 400,000 yojanas. The island of Dhātakī is encircled by Kāloda Ocean which is twice as wide as Dhātakī Island, that is, 800,000 yojanas. In a similar way, Kāloda Ocean is encircled by Puṣkara Island which is twice as wide as

Classification of Numbers

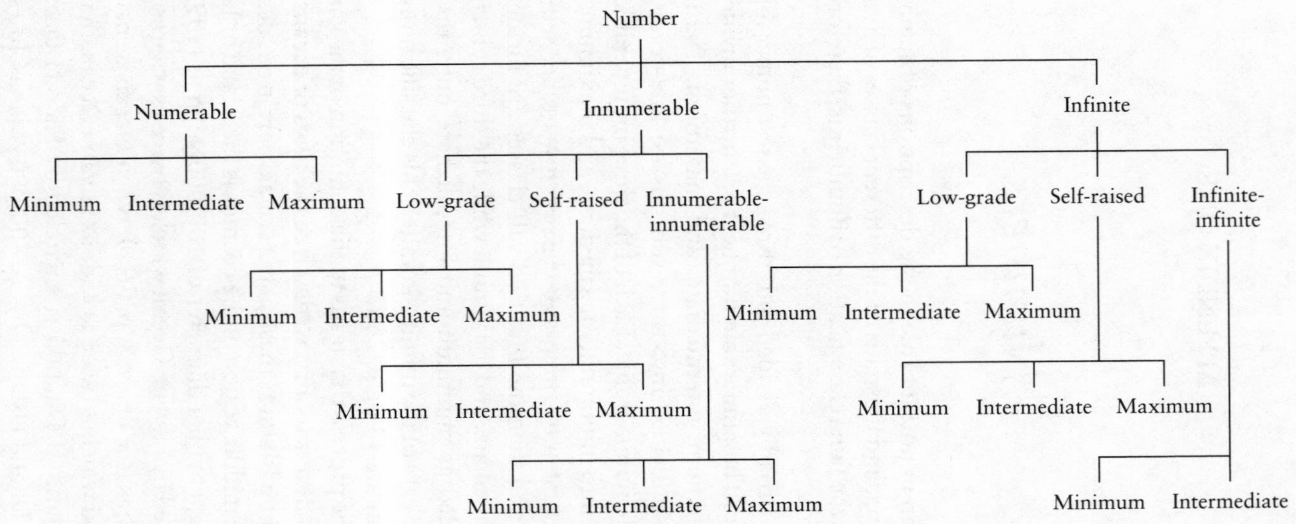

Figure 13

Kāloda Ocean, Puṣkara Island by an ocean which is twice as wide as Puṣkara, and so on. In brief, there are islands and oceans in succession, the succeeding one being twice as wide as the preceding one. The number of islands and oceans thus situated is innumerable. The last island and ocean are both called Svayambhūramaṇa.

With this in mind, let us now consider how the various classes of numbers are defined. Four circular stores, each with a diameter of 100,000 yojanas and a height of 1000 yojanas, are conceived. One of these four stores is made to vary in dimensions while the other three are kept constant and are named token store, counter-token store, and super-token store. The purpose of the four stores will be apparent in the following description.

The variable store, which initially has the same dimensions as the other three, is filled up with mustard seeds so that they form a cone which reaches 8.5 yojanas above the mouth of the store, there being only one mustard seed at the pinnacle of the cone. Now, out of this stock of mustard seeds, one mustard seed is dropped in each of the successive islands and oceans beginning from Jambū and reaching to the island or ocean where the last mustard seed is exhausted. Now, a new store is set up at the island or ocean where the last mustard seed was dropped. The new store is 1000 yojanas high and ring-shaped, having two circular walls, one wall on the inner and the other on the outer circumference of the island or ocean, as the case may be. This new store is also similarly filled with mustard seeds. Now, one mustard seed is deposited in the token store which is so called because a mustard seed is placed here as a token indicating the empty condition of the first variable store. Then the mustard seeds are dropped one by one on each successive island and ocean starting from the one that is adjacent to the new store, until the island or ocean where the last mustard seed is exhausted is reached. Another variable store is similarly set up at this last island or ocean and filled with mustard seeds, a single seed is again dropped in the token store and the rest are then dropped in the same way in the next successive islands and oceans, until the island or ocean where the last mustard seed is dropped is reached. The same process of setting up a new store and filling up and emptying it is repeated together with the process of depositing one mustard seed in the token store as each variable store is emptied. Eventually, the token store is completely filled to a pinnacle as a result of setting up and emptying the larger and larger stores.

The latest variable store is also now filled to a pinnacle and its mustard seeds dispersed on successive islands and oceans. Then, the mustard seeds in the token store are also dropped in the same way from where the last mustard seed of the variable store was dropped. When the contents of the token store have been emptied in this way, its first emptying is marked by depositing a mustard seed in a counter-token store. By repeating the process of filling up and emptying the variable stores, and depositing a seed each time in the token store until it is filled and can then be emptied with one mustard seed being deposited in a counter-token store, a situation is reached when the variable store, the token store, and the counter-token store will all be filled to a pinnacle. At this point, the super-token store is introduced to receive a mustard seed each time the counter-token store is emptied. By similar processes, the final situation will be arrived at when all the four stores – the variable, the token, the counter-token, and the super-token – will be filled with mustard seeds.

The total number of mustard seeds contained in these four stores together with the number of mustard seeds dropped in the islands and oceans make the number called **minimum low-grade innumerable.** This number is the base from which all the innumerable and infinite classes of number are calculated (see table below). The numerable classes of number are also worked out in relation to it; the **maximum numerable** number is the minimum low-grade innumerable minus one. The numbers between two and the maximum numerable are **intermediate numerables.** Two is the **minimal numerable** number as one does not lend itself to counting.

In the following table, the classes of number are arranged serially from lowest to highest and described both in words and algebraically. In the algebraic equations, U = the minimum low-grade innumerable, that is, the total number of mustard seeds that have passed through and are in the four stores as explained above.

TABLE OF NUMBERS*

Minimum numerable

2

Intermediate numerable

All numbers between minimum numerable and maximum numerable.

$3, 4, 5 \ldots (U - 1) - 1$

* *LP*, I. 129–81.

Maximum numerable
Minimum low-grade innumerable minus one.
$U - 1$

Minimum low-grade innumerable
The total number of mustard seeds that have passed through and are in the four stores as explained above.
U

Intermediate low-grade innumerable
All numbers between minimum low-grade innumerable and maximum low-grade innumerable.
$U + 1, U + 2, U + 3 \ldots (U^u - 1) - 1$

Maximum low-grade innumerable
Minimum self-raised innumerable minus one.
$U^u - 1$

Minimum self-raised innumerable
Minimum low-grade innumerable raised to itself.
U^u

Intermediate self-raised innumerable
All numbers between minimum self-raised innumerable and maximum self-raised innumerable.
[*Where* $U^u = V$] $V + 1, V + 2, V - 3 \ldots (V^v - 1) - 1$

Maximum self-raised innumerable
Minimum self-raised innumerable raised to itself minus one.
$V^v - 1$

Minimum innumerable-innumerable
Minimum self-raised innumerable raised to itself.
V^v

Intermediate innumerable-innumerable
All numbers between the minimum innumerable-innumerable and the maximum innumerable-innumerable.
[*Where* $V^v = W$) $W + 1, W + 2, W + 3 \ldots (W^w - 1) - 1$

Maximum innumerable-innumerable
Minimum innumerable-innumerable raised to itself minus one.
$W^w - 1$

Minimum low-grade infinite
Minimum innumerable-innumerable raised to itself.
W^w

Intermediate low-grade infinite
All numbers between minimum low-grade infinite and maximum low-grade infinite.
[*Where* $W^w = X$] $X + 1, X + 2, X + 3 \ldots (X^x - 1) - 1$

Maximum low-grade infinite
Minimum low-grade infinite raised to itself minus one.
$X^x - 1$

Minimum self-raised infinite
Minimum low-grade infinite raised to itself.
X^x

Intermediate self-raised infinite
All numbers between the minimum self-raised infinite and maximum self-raised infinite.
[*Where* $X^x = Y$] $Y + 1, Y + 2, Y + 3 \ldots (Y^y - 1) - 1$

Maximum self-raised infinite
Minimum self-raised infinite raised to itself minus one.
$Y^y - 1$

Minimum infinite-infinite
Minimum self-raised infinite raised to itself.
Y^y

Intermediate infinite-infinite
All numbers that follow the minimum infinite-infinite.
[*Where* $Y^y = Z$) $Z + 1, Z + 2, Z + 3 \ldots$

There are a numerable number of the intermediate numerables, an innumerable number of the intermediate innumerables, and an infinite number of the intermediate infinites. Whenever the number of infinite-infinite is mentioned in the texts, it always refers to the intermediate infinite-infinite numbers. This description of numbers is according to those versed in the scripture.†

† *LP*, I. 205.

APPENDIX TWO

Measurement of Time

A time unit is defined in 4.15 by the SB as that part of time which an atom, in its state of super-subtle minimum possible movement, takes to cross the space occupied by itself. The time unit is further described there as most incomprehensible and indeterminable; the omniscient lords alone can know it, but even they cannot express it because the time unit is too short-lived to be expressed in language which needs more than one time unit to draw and discharge the material particles of speech.

The SBT quotes a scriptural text in which time is identified with the modes of sentient and non-sentient entities (5.38). The implication is that a mode of an entity is equal to one time unit, in other words a mode changes in one time unit. The SBT quotes another scriptural text in which the time unit is counted among the six substances (5.38). Time is thus considered as a mode as well as a substance in the scripture.

Measurement of Time Units

Minimum self-raised innumerable (U^u) time units*	= 1 *āvalikā*
2^{24} āvalikās	= 48 minutes†
$2^{24}/48 = 2^{20}/3$ āvalikās	= 1 minute
$2^{20}/(3 \times 60) = 2^{18}/45 = 262{,}144/45$ āvalikās	= 1 second
i.e. 1 āvalikā	= $45/262{,}144$ second

* See appendix 1 for an explanation of "innumerable" numbers.

† One *muhūrta,* Indian hour, is forty-eight minutes of Western time measurement. One intra-hour can be anything up to forty-eight minutes.

APPENDIX TWO

The Derivation of the Figure 2^{24}

The shortest life-span of 2^8 āvalikās is that of the common-bodied vegetation (8.12) which springs up and dies 2^{16} times in one muhūrta (forty-eight minutes). In other words, 48 minutes = $2^{16} \times 2^8$ or 2^{24} āvalikās.‡ The initial measurement of time with the tiniest lifespan is significant, because a major end of such measurement is to determine the lifespans of sentient entities that go up to thirty-three ocean-measured periods in the case of the highest category of empyrean gods (4.38). The Jaina masters were enamoured of nature's amenability to accurate mathematical computation.

The Subtlety of the Time Unit

The subtlety of the time unit is explained in the scripture *Anuyogadvāra* , by the example of a strong young tailor tearing up a piece of cloth. Is the time taken to tear up the cloth equal to one indivisible time unit? No, because the piece of cloth has many threads which are not torn up simultaneously. The threads again are made up of fibres which in their turn consist of an infinite number of clusters of matter. Until the upper cluster is broken up, the lower one cannot be torn asunder. The upper cluster is broken at a moment which is different from the moment when the lower cluster is torn. A time unit, however, is subtler than the subtlest moment arrived at in this process.

The Numerable Periods of Time

Minimum self-raised innumerable (U^u) time units	= 1 āvalikā
$4446\ {}^{2458}/_{3773}$ āvalikās	= 1 pulse beat (inhalation-exhalation)
7 pulse beats	= 1 *stoka*
7 stokas	= 1 *lava*
38.5 lavas	= 1 *nālikā*
2 nālikās	= 1 *muhūrta*
1 muhūrta	= 48 minutes
30 muhūrtas	= 1 day and night
30.5 days and nights	= 1 month (solar)

‡ *LP*, XXVIII. 219–22.

12 months	=	1 year
8,400,000 years	=	1 *pūrvāṅga*
8,400,000 pūrvāṅgas	=	1 *pūrva*

The pūrva is followed by *truṭitāṅga, truṭita, aḍaḍāṅga, aḍaḍa, avavāṅga, avava, huhukāṅga, huhuka, utpalāṅga, utpala, padmāṅga, padma, nalināṅga, nalina, arthanipūrāṅga, arthanipūra, ayutāṅga, ayuta, nayutāṅga, nayuta, prayutāṅga, prayuta, cūlikāṅga, cūlikā, śīrṣaprahelikāṅga,* and *śīrṣaprahelikā.* Each successive period is 8,400,000 times longer than the preceding one.

Calculations Based on Similes

In 4.15, the SB states that the above sphere of arithmetical calculation is followed by calculations based on similes of pits. The SBT identifies three types of pits: transfer, time-based, and space-based, each of the three having a gross and subtle variety.

The similes of the gross and subtle transfer pits are explained as follows. A round pit, one yojana (9.09 miles) in diameter and one yojana deep, is tightly packed with sheep wool of one to seven days growth. Now, if one wool fibre is pulled out every time unit, the time taken to empty the pit completely is called one gross transfer pit-measured year. This period consists of a countable number of time units. If each of the fibres in the transfer pit is cut into innumerable pieces, and then one such piece is pulled out every time unit, the time taken to empty the pit is called one subtle transfer pit-measured year. This period consists of a numerable number of years multiplied by 10^7.

Now we come to the similes of the gross and subtle time-based pits. In the case of the gross time-based pit, a single wool fibre fragment in the subtle transfer pit is pulled out every one hundred years. The time required for emptying the pit in this manner is called one gross time-based pit-measured year. Now, if each wool fibre is further cut into innumerable pieces so that they become invisible, and then one piece is pulled out every one hundred years, the time needed to empty the pit is called one subtle time-based pit-measured year.

Lastly, we come to the similes of the gross and subtle space-based pits. In the simile of the gross space-based pit, the space units touched by all the wool fibres in the pit are pulled out one by one every time unit. The time required for emptying the pit in this manner is called one gross space-based pit-measured year. In the case of the simile of the subtle space-based pit, each wool fibre is cut into an innumerable number of pieces to fill up the pit. The space-units touched or not touched by the subtle wool fibres in the pit are now imagined to be pulled out one by one on each time unit. The time required for emptying the pit in this manner is called one subtle space-based pit-measured year. An innumerable number of ascending cycles in the cosmic cycle of time (see 3.27) is required to empty this pit. The total number of the single-sensed earth-bodied, fire-bodied, plant-bodied, water-bodied and air-bodied souls is determined by this simile.

Each of the pit similes is converted into an ocean simile by multiplying its number of years by 10^{15}. This creates two categories of similes, pit-measured periods and ocean-measured periods.

The Utility of the Measures through Similes

The similes of time-based pits and oceans are used to calculate the periods of ascending and descending cycles in cosmic time, the durations of knowledge-covering and other types of karmic bondage, and the lengths of repeated births in similar bodies or the same body of earth-bodied souls and the like, right up to infernals, humans, and gods. The total number of islands and oceans in the middle region is calculated as equal to 2.5 times the number of time units in the subtle transfer ocean-measured year.

APPENDIX THREE

Measurement of Space

The breadth of a human finger is the base unit for the measurement of space. The finger breadth is of three kinds: (1) an individual's finger-breadth (subjective measure), (2) a standard finger-breadth (objective measure) and (3) a super-standard finger-breadth. The following account of the finger-breadth is according to the scripture *Anuyogadvāra*.

The individual's finger-breadth is a variable measure, differing from aeon to aeon of the ascending and descending cosmic time cycles (see 3.27), and also from person to person. There is a constant ratio between the length of the face or body of a person and the breadth of his or her finger; the length of the face is normally twelve finger-breadths and the body is 108 finger-breadths. The individual finger-breadth (subjective measure) is used in measuring wells, ponds, parks, gardens, moats, ramparts, etc.

The standard finger-breadth (objective measure) is defined using the material atom, classified as practical and theoretical, as the base. The practical atom is said to be composed of an infinite number of theoretical atoms, yet is not amenable to fission even by the most sophisticated instrument. An infinite number of practical atoms make one *ussaṇhasaṇhiyā* which provides the initial unit for determining the nature of the standard finger-breadth (objective measure) according to the following equations:

8 ussaṇhasaṇhiyās	=	1 *saṇhasaṇhiyā*
8 saṇhasaṇhiyās	=	1 *uḍḍhareṇu*
8 uḍḍhareṇus	=	1 *tasareṇu*
8^{10} tasareṇus	=	1 standard finger-breadth (objective measure)

The standard finger-breadth is used in measuring the heights of infernals, animals, humans, and gods. The breadth of Lord Mahāvīra's finger is two standard finger-breadths (objective measure).

The super-standard finger-breadth is defined as 1000 × ½ finger-breadth of Lord Mahāvīra, that is 1000 × 1 standard finger-breadth. The super-standard finger-breadth is used as the measuring unit for the length, breadth, height, depth, and circumference of hells, heavens, continents, mountains, etc. It is also used to measure cosmic space.

The yojana is 9.09 miles long. The *Anuyogadvāra* gives the following equations, valid for all the three kinds of finger-breadth, to explain how the length of a yojana is calculated:

6 finger-breadths	=	1 *pāda*
2 pādas	=	1 *vihatthī* (Sanskrit: *vitasti*); span: the distance from the tip of the thumb to the tip of the little finger when the hand is fully extended, a unit of measure equal to about nine inches
2 vihatthīs	=	1 *rayaṇī;* cubit: a linear measure equal to the length of the forearm from the tip of the middle finger to the elbow, from 17 to 24 inches
2 rayaṇīs	=	1 *kucchī*
2 kucchīs	=	1 *daṇḍa* (Sanskrit: *dhanu*, bow); fathom = 6 feet
2000 daṇḍas	=	1 *gāuya*
4 gāuyas	=	1 yojana = 48,000 feet = 9.09 miles

The rajju is the largest measuring unit. It is given as (innumerable yojanas × 10^{14}) ÷ 7. It equals the distance between the eastern and western points of the Svayambhū-ramaṇa ocean, the last ring of the middle region of the cosmos. In other words, one rajju equals the diameter of the middle region. The equation for this is given as $(2^{n+1} - 3) \times 10^5$ yojanas, where the value of n is the total number of islands and oceans in the middle region (see 3.7–3.9)* In appendix 2, we calculated this as 2.5 times the number of time units in the subtle transfer ocean-measured

* *LP*, I. 64–5.

period, that is, 2.5×10^{15} times the time units in the subtle transfer pit-measured number of years.

Yojanas and rajjus are used in measuring cosmic space. If cosmic space is conceived as folded into a cube, the width of the cube is (innumerable yojanas $\times 10^{14}$) = 7 rajjus. The surface of one side of this cube is therefore $(7 \times 7) = 49$ square rajjus. The cubic measure of cosmic space is $(7 \times 7 \times 7) = 343$ cubic rajjus.

APPENDIX FOUR

The Doctrine of the Fourteen Stages of Spiritual Development

The stages of spiritual development are a recurrent theme in the *Tattvārtha Sūtra* (see 9.1, 9.10, 9.37–9.41, 9.47), although it appears in its ancient form. In the sutras, there is no mention of the first three stages or clear mention of the eighth and ninth stages. Nor does the commentary by the author (the SB) provide much elucidation. It is in the later SS and SBT commentaries that we find elaborate treatment of the classical doctrine of the fourteen stages of spiritual development (SS 1.8, 9.1, 10.1 and SBT 9.37–9.43). It occupies a central position in the *Ṣaṭkhaṇḍagāma* (extant scripture of the Digambara sect).

mithyādṛṣṭi

The First Stage

This is the soul's original and beginningless state of "deluded world-view" (see 9.1). At this first stage, the soul is in a spiritual slumber, unaware of its own bondage.

sāsvādana

The Second Stage

This stage has the unusual role of being a pit-stop for the soul on its way *down* from the fourth stage at which it had achieved its first taste of enlightened world-view (see below). It is therefore called the stage of "passing taste" or "lingering enlightened world-view"; the soul has lost the immediate experience of enlightenment but retains an "aftertaste" that lasts six *āvalikas* at most (see appendix 2 for measurements of time).

samyak-mithyātva

The Third Stage

The third stage is the transition on the soul's way up from the first stage of deluded world-view to that of enlightened world-view. It is a combination of deluded and enlightened world-view (see p. 282).

Moral and spiritual consciousness only dawn for the soul when it is sufficiently conscious of, and confronted with, the force that has eternally been keeping it ensnared. To facilitate this, the soul has an innate, beginningless "autonomous capacity" that is always struggling to relieve the soul of its karmic burden. This capacity is the will power which drives the soul towards liberation. In its beginningless spiritual journey, the push generated by this "autonomous capacity" sometimes brings the soul face to face with the concentrated pressure of deluded world-view and the tenacious passions. To proceed along its evolutionary path of spiritual progress, the soul must now subdue the pressure. At this juncture, souls that fail to resist the pressure have to draw back and continue at the beginningless first stage, that of deluded world-view.

But if the surge of autonomous capacity, which lasts an intra-hour (any time less than forty-eight minutes), is powerful enough, it enables the soul to come to grips with the pressure, the "Gordian knot", consisting of three view-deluding karmas and four conduct-deluding tenacious passions (8.10), and break it in the struggle that ensues. As a result the soul gets a vague vision of the goal of its spiritual endeavour.

In addition to the autonomous capacity, there are two more capacities which assist in this struggle: the capacity to generate a series of varied novel experiences and the capacity to generate progressively purer, homogenous experiences. During the operation of the capacity to generate varied novel experiences, which, like the first autonomous capacity, lasts only an intra-hour, the soul passes through states it has never experienced before. What the soul began automatically, without any moral or spiritual effort, it now does consciously with spiritual pressure.

During this surge of autonomous capacity and accompanying novel and varied experiences, the soul undergoes progressive purification through five processes: (1) destruction of the duration of karma, (2) destruction of the intensity of the karma, (3) construction of a complex series of karmic clusters (arranged in geometrical progression with an incalculable common ratio) which are transplanted from the mass of accumulated karmic matter and brought to premature fruition during this inspired intra-hour,

(4) an unprecedented type of bondage of very short-lived karmas, and (5) transformation of harmful karmic matter into other types of karma throughout the intra-hour. At the end of the operation, the knot is broken for ever, never to appear again. The purification that the soul undergoes has a colossal effect on the duration and intensity of the bondage of both new karmas and those already accumulated.

Now, the third capacity, mentioned above, that generates progressively purer experiences leads the soul to the verge of the first enlightenment (enlightened world-view) that comes like a flash due to the absolute suppression of the view-deluding karma. The soul undergoes the same five processes as occurred with the autonomous capacity. But here, there also occurs a new process called intercalation whereby the soul divides in two the clusters of view-deluding karma that would normally have risen after the operation of the third capacity. The first of the two parts of karmic matter is forced to rise during the last few time units when the third capacity is functioning, while the rise of the second part is postponed an intra-hour during which no view-deluding karmic matter is allowed to rise and produce its effect on the soul.

samyag-dṛṣṭi

The Fourth Stage

Thus, when the third capacity has finished functioning, the view-deluding karma has no effect on the soul for another intra-hour. This intra-hour period is the interval when the soul enjoys the first dawn of enlightenment, known as *samyag-darśana*, enlightened world-view. The soul realizes its own nature.

Although the vision is due to the suppression, rather than elimination, of the view-deluding karma and lasts only an intra-hour, it leaves an indelible impression on the soul. The soul attains insight it never had before. Like a person born blind who sees the world for the first time on the sudden acquisition of eyesight, so the soul now sees the truth. Even as a person suffering from a long-drawn-out disease experiences extreme delight on the sudden disappearance of the ailment, so does a soul eternally bound to the wheel of worldly existence feel spiritual joy and bliss on the sudden dawn of enlightenment. Such enlightenment is attained on more than one occasion during the spiritual career leading to final liberation.

At this fourth stage the soul is prone to fall down to the third or second stage as it faces the rising of the view-deluding karma which was postponed for an intra-hour. These karmic clusters were divided into three heaps in the last time unit when the third capacity was functioning, the time unit immediately preceding the dawn of enlightenment. Of these three heaps, one is pure and, as such, will not obscure enlightened world-view, the second is semi-pure and so will partially obscure the view, and the third, being impure, will obscure the view completely. Any one of these three heaps can come into effect at the end of the period of enlightenment. If the pure heap comes into effect on account of the persistent purity of the soul, then the soul sticks to the fourth stage of spiritual development and retains enlightened world-view. But if the semi-pure heap comes into effect, the soul feels rebuff and slips to the third stage, a combination of enlightened and deluded world-view. From this stage, the soul either goes up to the fourth or down to the first stage again. If the impure heap comes into effect and a tenacious passion arises, the soul slides to the second stage, lingering enlightened world-view, and gradually falls back to the first stage, deluded world-view.

The fourth stage is pivotal; it is the beginning of spirituality. To the soul that has reached this stage, liberation is assured. Perfection of morality, however, is achieved in the stages that follow.

deśa-virata, sarva-virata, apramatta-virata

The Fifth, Sixth and Seventh Stages

The soul must now actively cultivate morality to reach the higher stages. The capacity for self-restraint begins to grow at the fifth stage, "enlightened world-view with partial self-restraint". This is the stage at which a layperson takes one or more of the five small vows (see 7.1–7.2, 7.13–7.34).

The sixth stage of "complete self-restraint" is the stage at which a person takes the great vows of an ascetic (7.1–7.14). There are now only occasional lapses in morality.

Still higher self-restraint is achieved at the seventh stage, which is absolutely free from all sorts of laxity, and at which deep meditation becomes possible.

We have explained the dawn of enlightened world-view through the operation of the three capacities. The same three capacities can function again to partly suppress and partly eliminate the seven deluding karmas: the three varieties of view-deluding karma and the four tenacious passions (conduct-deluding karmas, see 8.10) so that the soul attains the enlightened world-view once more. This enlightened world-view can last for a longer period and is called "felt as such". Anyone stationed at the fourth, fifth, sixth or seventh stage who has regained the enlightened world-view by partially suppressing and partially eliminating these karmas or by completely eliminating them can then enter the eighth stage.

apūrva-karaṇa, anivṛtti-karaṇa, sūkṣma-sāmparāya, upaśānta-kaṣāya

The Eighth, Ninth, Tenth and Eleventh Stages

During these stages, the soul is on one of the two ladders: the ladder of suppression, or the ladder of elimination, of the gross and subtle flickering passions (conduct-deluding karmas). The ladder it is on will depend on whether it has partially suppressed and partially eliminated the seven deluding karmas in the earlier stages or totally eliminated them.

The eighth stage, "gross passions with novel experiences" (9.1), is the first "rung" of these ladders (*SKHĀ*, I. 180). However, no karma is actually suppressed or eliminated at this stage; harmful karma is merely diminished in nature, duration and intensity and beneficial karma is augmented through new and positive motivation (*TV*, X.1).

The ascetic then climbs to the ninth stage with progressively purer and purer experiences. On the ladder of suppression, the following sub-types of the conduct-deluding karma (see 8.10) are gradually suppressed: (1) hermaphroditic disposition, (2) female disposition, (3–8) the six quasi-passions: laughter, relish, ennui, grief, fear, abhorrence, (9) male disposition, (10–13) the four passions of non-abstinence, (14–17) the four passions of partial abstinence and (18–19) flickering anger and pride.

Thereafter (20) flickering deceit is suppressed and (21) the flickering greed is attenuated, but not yet suppressed at the first time unit of the tenth stage of spiritual development called "complete self-restraint with flickering greed".

In the first time unit of the eleventh stage – "complete self-restraint with suppressed passions" – the soul suppresses (21) flickering greed. It has now suppressed twenty-one karmas while climbing the ladder of suppression as well as the seven deluding karmas suppressed in advance of this climb (before the eighth stage), making a total of twenty-eight deluding karmas that it has suppressed. Because this eleventh stage is attained through suppression rather than elimination of the karmas, a fall is inevitable. The soul may be at this eleventh stage for only one time unit or up to a full intra-hour (just short of forty-eight minutes) before falling down to the sixth, fifth, or fourth, or to the second stage. If the soul dies at this stage, it is born as a god in the highest celestial regions, falling down to the third stage of spiritual development (*DOK*, p. 73).

However, if the soul has completely eliminated the three varieties of the view-deluding karma and the four tenacious passions during stages four to seven, instead of climbing the "ladder of suppression of passions" as explained above, the soul can climb the "ladder of elimination of passions". Endowed with great karmic purity, the soul draws upon the three innate capacities for reaching the eighth stage, and at the ninth stage eliminates the following karmas: the eight passions (four non-abstinence, and four partial-abstinence), the hermaphroditic disposition and the female disposition. The ascetic then eliminates the six quasi-passions (laughter, relish, ennui, grief, fear, abhorrence) by merging them into the male disposition, and then similarly merges the male disposition in flickering anger, flickering anger in flickering pride, flickering pride in flickering deceit, and flickering deceit in flickering greed. Then the soul attenuates flickering greed at the tenth stage.

kṣīṇa-moha

The Twelfth Stage

The soul which has climbed the "ladder of elimination" and attenuated flickering greed in the tenth stage, moves directly to the twelfth stage called "complete self-restraint with eliminated passions", radically eliminating the entire mass of deluding karma. In the last time unit of the twelfth stage, the soul eliminates the five knowledge-covering, four intuition-covering, and the five obstructive karmas, thereby attaining the thirteenth stage.

sayoga-kevalī

The Thirteenth Stage

This is the stage of "omniscience with physical activity". The soul remains in this stage for at least an intra-hour and for as much as just short of $8{,}400{,}000^2 \times 10^7$ years (SS 3.31).

It should be noted here that the lifespan of someone who is bound to attain omniscience and liberation in that very life cannot be reduced or prolonged (2.52). Yet usually the sensation karma of an omniscient has a longer duration than his lifespan karma and it is a cosmic law that the soul must experience in full the fruits of all karmas (2.52). If the soul possesses such non-obstructive karmas (2.1) which will take longer to ripen and fall away than the lifespan karma (that is, they would normally ripen in the next life), the soul reduces the duration of these karmas to that of the lifespan karma. This equalization is possible by the process called "expansion of the soul units of the soul".

The process of expanding the soul units lasts for eight time units only, and is an indispensable means to prematurely ripen and exhaust the karma of longer duration. The soul undertakes this process in the thirteenth stage just an intra-hour before its final liberation. In the first time unit of the process, the soul stretches itself vertically both ways and touches the zenith as well as the nadir of the cosmos, the thickness of this vertical column being the same as that of the body. In the second time unit, the soul expands itself at front and back to the edges of the cosmos. In the third time unit the soul expands on both sides to the edges of the cosmos. The soul has now divided the cosmos into four parts. In the fourth time unit, the soul expands in the remaining gaps and thus fills up the whole cosmos. Then in the next four time units, the soul retraces the steps and returns to its original shape in the eighth time unit. Now the soul has equalized the length of the other karmas with that of the lifespan karma.

Before entering into the last and final stage, the fourteenth stage, called "omniscience with no activity", the soul prepares to stop all activity, gross and subtle. It begins by using one activity to stop another. The gross activities of the body are used to stop the gross activities of speech and the mind. Then it uses the subtle activity of the body to stop the gross activity of the body as well as the subtle activities of speech and mind. The soul then enters the third stage of white meditation which is accompanied with subtle activities, and has no fall (9.42). It now has to stop the subtle bodily activity by means of the activity itself, for there is none other than this. By means of this meditation, the soul contracts and fills the cavities created in the embodied state. It is now reduced in dimension by one-third of the previous height. Then it enters the fourth stage of white meditation which stops even the residual subtle activity and has no reversion (9.43).

ayoga-kevalī

The Fourteenth Stage

The soul is now as motionless as a mountain rock. All the remaining karmas are eliminated. This state of absolute motionlessness is the fourteenth and the last stage of spiritual development in the instant before death. The soul then frees itself of the sensation, body, lifespan and status karmas and attains disembodied eternal liberation.

APPENDIX FIVE

The Eight Classes of Material Clusters

The formation of material clusters is explained in 5.32–5.36. In Jainism, an infinite number of classes of material clusters are postulated to explain physical phenomena and the interaction between the soul and matter. The classes are determined by the number of atoms in the cluster. Atoms can exist in isolation, and such single atoms form one class. Similarly the two- and three-atom clusters also form separate classes. In this way, we can conceive of material clusters that consist of a numberable, innumerable and infinite number of atoms (for the Jaina conception of "numerable", "innumerable" and "infinite", see appendix 1). Because there are as many classes of material clusters as there are different numbers of atoms in the clusters, there are numerable classes of material clusters of numerable atoms, innumerable classes of material clusters of innumerable atoms, and infinite classes of material clusters of infinite atoms.

Out of the various classes of material clusters, only eight will be described here, because it is only these that are necessary to explain problems discussed in the *Tattvārtha Sūtra* (see 2.37). The eight classes of clusters consist of progressively higher and higher infinite numbers of atoms and each class is suitable for constituting a specific aspect of the soul's bodily existence. A single atom less or more disqualifies the cluster from forming that bodily aspect. The eight classes, from those with the lowest to those with the highest number of infinite atoms, are suitable to constitute respectively: (1) the gross body, (2) the protean body, (3) the conveyance body, (4) the fiery body, (5) speech, (6) respiration, (7) the mind, and (8) the karmic body (which is the finest body). The difference between these eight higher classes is obtained by multiplying the number of atoms in the preceding class by another infinite number. It should be noted here that with the increase of the mass of clusters, their volumes do not increase but become more and more condensed. In other words, the succeeding bodies are progressively finer and finer, or subtler and subtler.

For various types of "infinites", see figure 13 in appendix 1.

APPENDIX SIX

The Books of the Jaina Scripture

Tattvārtha Sūtra is based on the Jaina scriptures which are said to embody the sermons of Lord Mahāvīra transmitted through his immediate disciples and also through the distinguished successors of those disciples who flourished in the millenium that followed. However, the scriptures gradually fell into oblivion and the remnant that was available was a very meagre part of the grand legacy. Furthermore, while the Śvetāmbaras accept the authenticity of the surviving scriptural texts, the Digambaras view most of these texts as unauthentic (for discussion of the Jaina sects, see pp. xxxiii–xxxiv).

The entire Jaina sacred literature is divided into the Outer Corpus consisting of many texts, and the Inner Corpus consisting of only twelve texts called the *Aṅgas* or limbs (see 1.20). The SS commentary says that the Inner Corpus and the *Pūrvas* (early literature) were composed by the *gaṇadharas* (heads of monastic groups) who were Lord Mahāvīra's immediate disciples and the books of the Outer Corpus were compiled by later *ācāryas* (spiritual masters). The essence of all the books was delivered by the Omniscient Himself.

History of the Scriptural Corpus

The scriptural corpus of the Jainas is said to have been organized in the first council held at Pāṭaliputra about 150 years after Mahāvīra's nirvāṇa, in the early fourth century BCE (c. 390–380 BCE). Bhadrabāhu and Sthūlabhadra, who belonged to the sixth generation following Mahāvīra, played an important role at this council. Bhadrabāhu is credited with knowledge of the entire scripture including the *Dṛṣṭivāda,* the twelfth book of the Inner Corpus, said to have included fourteen *Pūrvas,* early, perhaps pre-Mahāvīran texts.

About seven centuries after this first council, two other councils were held – one at Mathurā and the other at Valabhi (modern Saurāṣṭra), presided over by Skandila (300–343 CE) and Nāgārjuna respectively. A fourth council was held at Valabhi, in 453 or 466 CE, at which Devardhigaṇi Kṣmāśramaṇa established the definitive Śvetāmbara scriptural corpus, giving Nāgārjuna's readings a secondary place. Devardhi is reported to have distributed copies of the scriptures to all the centres of scriptural studies which were flourishing in those days.

Inner Corpus

In his *Tattvārthavārtika*, Akalaṅka briefly describes the subjects of each of the twelve *Aṅgas* (limbs) of the Inner Corpus:

1. *Ācāra:* the five varieties of correct movement and three kinds of guarding (see 9.2–9.5).
2. *Sūtrakṛta:* knowledge, humility and reverence, the acceptable and unacceptable objects, monastic initiation, ordination, etc.
3. *Sthāna:* numerical description of scriptural topics.
4. *Samavāya:* the totality of every entity with respect to its substance, space, time and modes.
5. *Vyākhyāprajñapti:* sixty thousand questions and answers about the existence or non-existence of the soul.
6. *Jñātṛdharmakathā:* a large collection of narratives and didactic tales.
7. *Upāsakādhyayana:* the householder's discipline.
8. *Antakṛddaśā:* biographies of ten ascetics who were in the order of Lord Mahāvīra and attained liberation: Nami, Mataṅga, Somila, Rāmaputra, Sudarśana, Yamalīka, Valīka, Kiṣkambala, Pāla and Ambaṣṭhaputra. Biographies of groups of ten ascetics, who were in the orders of other Jinas and attained liberation, are also included.
9. *Anuttaraupapādikadaśā:* biographies of ten ascetics who flourished in the order of Lord Mahāvīra and were subsequently born in the highest celestial regions: Ṛṣidāsa, Vānya, Sunakṣatra, Kārtika, Nanda, Nandana, Śālibhadra, Abhaya, Vāriṣeṇa and Cilātaputra. Biographies of groups of ten ascetics, who were in the orders of other Jinas and attained rebirth in the highest celestial realms, are also included.
10. *Praśnavyākaraṇa:* arguments and counter-arguments on questions related to the popular and Vedic topics.

11. *Vipākasūtra:* the karmic ripening of beneficial and harmful deeds.
12. *Dṛṣṭivāda:* reputed heretical teachers and their doctrines.

The description by the *Nandi*, an Outer Corpus scripture, of these twelve Aṅgas is slightly different from that followed by Akalaṅka. However, neither description tallies with the extant versions of the Aṅgas.

Similarly, these extant texts are no longer of the length described in the past. In his *Dhavalā* commentary on the Digambara scripture *Ṣaṭkhaṇḍāgama,* Vīrasena describes the twelve books of the Inner Corpus, specifying that the *Ācāra* contained 18,000 verses of thirty-two syllables each, *Sūtrakṛta* 36,000 verses, *Sthāna* 42,000, *Samavāya* 164,000 and so on up to *Vipākasūtra* with 18,400,000.

The extant version of the *Sthāna,* the third Aṅga, gives the names of the ten householders described in the seventh Aṅga, *Upāsakādhyayana* (or *Upāsakadaśā*). These names tally with those in the extant *Upāsakādhyayana.* However, the *Sthāna* list of the ten ascetics named for the eighth Aṅga, *Antakṛddaśā,* differs from that in the extant version of this book. Similarly, there is some difference between the *Sthāna* list of the ten ascetics for the ninth Aṅga, *Anuttaraupapādikadaśā,* and those in the extant version. Akalaṅka's descriptions of the eighth and ninth Aṅgas also differ. Thus, there is no agreement between the compilers of these texts, perhaps due to loss of a considerable part of the scripture in the process of handing it down orally from generation to generation.

The twelfth book of the Aṅgas, *Dṛṣṭivāda,* was lost long ago, although the Digambara tradition retains a remnant of it in its extant corpus. The SS commentary (Digambara tradition) names the five sections of the *Dṛṣṭivāda* as *Parikarma, Sūtra, Prathamānuyoga, Pūrvagata* (early literature) and *Cūlikā* (appendices). The *Pūrvagata,* which may pre-date Mahāvīra, is divided into fourteen sections. The subjects of study of the first thirteen sections are inferred from inadequate evidence as: the origin of substances and modes; measurements; potentialities of animate and inanimate objects; existence and non-existence from the standpoints of substance, space, time and modes; the five kinds of knowledge; truth; the soul; doctrine of karma; forfending future faults; occult sciences; merit; the ten vital powers; and self-restraint. No information can be guessed on the fourteenth section.

The relationship between the *Pūrvagata* and the rest of the Inner Corpus has been a controversial issue. The SBT commentary of 1.20 says that the fourteen Pūrvas were composed before the eleven Aṅgas. This is confirmed by the *Cuṇṇi* on *Āvaśyaka-Niryukti, 735*, where it is said that

Gautamasasvāmī, a principal disciple of Lord Mahāvīra, composed the fourteen pūrvas in three sittings. The other four sections of the *Dṛṣṭivāda* were probably composed at the same time.

Among modern scholars, L. Alsdorf's opinion on the *Dṛṣṭivāda* deserves careful consideration.

> I must confess that I do not believe in the legendary and biographical contents of the fourth part of the *Dṛṣṭivāda* but regard the Jaina tradition on this point as unfounded. I agree with Schubring (*Lehre der Jainas, 38*) who has made it at least very probable that the real contents of the *Dṛṣṭivāda* consisted of an exposition and refutation of heretical doctrines and that this was the reason for its loss; it was thought undesirable to preserve these old discussions because their study could lead to a revival of heretical views and actions. . . . It is certain that, though the traditional subdivision of the *Dṛṣṭivāda* is probably genuine, the detailed tables of contents given in the *Nandi* and in the fourth Aṅga (*Samavāya*) are entirely fantastic because at the time when they were composed, the text was already lost and its contents no longer known.*

Outer Corpus

Different books of the Outer Corpus categorized the books of the scripture in different ways. Thus, for instance, in the *Anuyogadvāra* scripture, the Outer Corpus is divided into the *Kālika* and *Utkālika,* respectively texts that are studied at a particular time and texts that are studied at any time. The Utkālikas (studied at any time) are further divided into the *Āvaśyakas* (books of compulsory duties) and others. Alternatively, in the *Nandi* scripture, the categories are arranged so that the Kālika and Utkālika are categories of the non-Āvaśyaka (non-compulsory duties) group. Such diversities in classification of the scripture are indicative of a transitional period when the scriptural corpus was in the making.

The twenty-nine titles, listed by the *Nandi* as the Utkālika, and the thirty-one it lists as Kālika, cover almost all the titles in the groupings now used for the Outer Corpus (see below). However, there are some titles in the *Nandi* which are no longer known.

* *A New Version of the Agaḍadatta Story* (New Indian Antiquary, vol. I, no. 5, 1938, p. 287).

In the SB commentary of the *Tattvārtha Sūtra*, the Āvaśyakas (books of compulsory duties) are listed as:

1. *Sāmāyika* (observance of equanimity)
2. *Caturviṃśati-stava* (praise of the twenty-four Jinas)
3. *Vandana* (obeisance)
4. *Pratikramaṇa* (recoiling from past bad deeds)
5. *Kāyavyutsarga* (abandonment of the body)
6. *Pratyākhyāna* (forfending of future faults)

The Extant Scriptural Corpus: Śvetāmbara

The extant scriptural corpus, now accepted as authentic by the Śvetāmbara sect, consists of forty-five books, although at one time there was a tradition that accepted more books. The exact date when the forty-five book corpus, arranged into six groups, was finalized is not definitely known. Some scholars have deduced that it was done earlier than the thirteenth century CE, as it is found in the *Vicārasāra* by Pradyumnasūri who flourished in that century. The books are:

INNER CORPUS

Eleven Aṅgas: *Ācāra, Sūtrakṛta, Sthāna, Samavāya, Bhagavatī, Jñātṛdharmakathā, Upāsakadaśā, Antakṛddaśā, Anuttaraupapādikadaśā, Praśnavyākaraṇa, Vipāka.*

OUTER CORPUS

Twelve Upāṅgas: *Aupapātika, Rājapraśnīya, Jīvâjīvâbhigama, Prajñāpanā, Sūryaprajñapti, Jambūdvīpaprajñapti, Candraprajñapti, Nirayāvalikā, Kalpāvataṃsikā, Puṣpikā, Puṣpacūlikā, Vṛṣṇidaśā.*

Six Chedasūtras: *Niśītha, Mahāniśītha, Vyavahāra, Daśāśruta, Bṛhatkalpa, Jītakalpa.*

Four Mūlas: *Uttarādhyayana, Daśavaikālika, Āvaśyaka, Piṇḍaniryukti.*

Ten Prakīrṇakas: *Catuḥśaraṅa, Āturapratyākhyāna, Bhaktaparijñā, Saṃstāraka, Taṇḍulavaicārika, Candraveddyaka, Devendrastava, Gaṇividyā, Mahāpratyākhyāna, Vīrastava.*

Two Cūlikāsūtras: *Nandi, Anuyogadvāra.*

There are only eleven Aṅgas because all Śvetāmbara sects agree that the twelfth is lost. However, the two Śvetāmbara reform sects, the Sthānakavāsī and Terāpantha, recognize as authoritative only thirty-two of the forty-five books listed above. These are grouped somewhat differently:

Eleven Aṅgas: as above.
Twelve Upāṅgas: as above.
Four Mūlas: *Daśavaikālika, Uttarādhyayana, Nandi* and *Anuyogadvāra*.
Four Chedas: *Niśītha, Vyavahāra, Bṛhatkalpa* and *Daśāśrutaskandha*.
One Āvaśyaka.

While accepting these thirty-two as authoritative, the Terāpantha considers only the eleven Aṅgas to be absolutely valid, the other scriptures being subject to scrutiny in the light of the Aṅgas.

Generally the books of the scripture are not ascribed to authors, but there are a few exceptions. For instance, Ārya Śyāmasūri is said to be the author of *Prajñāpanā,* the fourth Upāṅga (outer limb), and Sayyambhavasūri, the author of *Daśavaikālika,* the second Mūlasūtra. Bhadrabāhusvāmī is credited with *Vavahāra* and *Kappa,* which are the third and fifth Chedasūtras, with the eighth chapter of *Daśāśrutaskandha,* which is the fourth Chedasūtra, with *Piṇḍaniryukti,* the fourth Mūlasūtra, and with *Oghaniryukti,* one of the books in the scriptural canon of more than forty-five books (see p. 293). Devardhigaṇi Kṣamāśramaṇa is the author of the *Nandi*, the first Cūlikāsūtra, and Āryarakṣita of the *Anuyogadvāra*, the second Cūlikāsūtra.

The Extant Scriptural Corpus: Digambara

According to Digambara tradition, the teachings of Lord Mahāvīra were arranged into twelve Aṅgas by his pupil Indrabhūti Gautama, and were handed down from teacher to pupil orally until they gradually fell into oblivion. Only fractions of them were known to Dharasena who practised penances at Girinagar in the country of Saurāṣṭra sometime in the second or third century of the common era (650–800 years after Mahāvīra's nirvāṇa). Dharasena felt the necessity of preserving the knowledge and so called two sages, who afterwards became famous as Puṣpadanta and Bhūtabali, and taught them portions of the fifth and twelfth Aṅgas, *Viāhapaṇṇatti* and *Diṭṭhivāda.* These were subsequently written down in sutras by the two eminent pupils. Puṣpadanta composed the first 177 sutras and his colleague Bhūtabali wrote the other 5,823 which made up the 6000 sutras of the *Ṣaṭkhaṇḍāgama,* regarded by Digambaras as the only authentic extant remnant of the scriptures.

Earlier Translations of Tattvārtha Sūtra

The following are the earlier translations in non-Indian languages:

German Translation

Jacobi, Hermann. 1906. "Eine Jaina-Dogmatik: Umāsvāti's Tattvārthādhigama-Sūtra". *Zeitschrift der Deutschen Morganlandischen Gesellschaft* (Leipzig), vol. 60; 287ff, 512.

English Translations

Jaini, J. L. 1956. *Tattvārthasūtram*. Delhi.

Jain, S. A. 1960. *Reality*. Trans. of *Sarvārthasiddhi* of Pūjyapāda. Calcutta.

Dixit, K. K. 1974. *Tattvārthasūtra*. Trans. of Sukhlalji's commentary in Hindi. L. D. Institute of Indology, Ahmedabad.

Participating Jaina Organisations

INSTITUTE OF JAINOLOGY

International

The Institute of Jainology works to educate Jainas about their great heritage and to raise awareness of Jainism in the world community. The Institute encourages Jainas to work together in a spirit of unity on the basis of an enlightened understanding of their faith. The principle activities of the Institute are the production of books, magazines, periodicals and video and audio tapes on Jaina subjects, and the organization of, and participation in, workshops and seminars.

Particular attention is also given to encouraging and facilitating projects for the protection of the environment, based on the fundamental Jaina principle of non-violence to all life. In 1990, the Institute co-ordinated the entry of the Jaina community into the Network for Conservation and Religion of the World Wide Fund for Nature. An international delegation of Jainas presented the *Jain Declaration on Nature* to WWF president HRH Prince Philip. The *Declaration* is the inspiration for on-going Jaina environmental programmes.

Trustees: Shri R. P. Chandaria, UK; Shri Nirmal Sethia, UK; Shri Rati Shah, UK; Shri Vinod Udani, UK; Shri Vijay Shah, Belgium; Professor Padmanabh S. Jaini, USA; Shri Nagindas Doshi, Singapore; Shri Manu Chandaria, Kenya.

Administrative Office: Unit 18, 26–28 Wadsworth Rd, Greenford, Middlesex UB6 7JZ, United Kingdom.

Registered Office: 31 Lancaster Gate, London W2 3LP, United Kingdom.

OSHWAL ASSOCIATION and NAVNAT VANIK ASSOCIATION

United Kingdom

The Oshwal and Navnat Vanik Associations represent 95 per cent of the British Jaina population. They are primarily social organisations but with a strong commitment to the education of their members. They are represented on the board of the Institute of Jainology.

BHAGWAN MAHAVIRA MEMORIAL SAMITI
New Delhi, India

The Bhagwan Mahavira Memorial Samiti was founded in 1973 to commemorate the 2500th anniversary of Lord Mahāvīra's passing into nirvāṇa. The trust board represents all four Jaina sects: Śvetāmbara, Digambara, Sthānakvāsi and Terāpantha. It works to promote education and practice of Jaina teachings and principles.

JAIN VISHVA BHARATI
Ladnun, India

The Jain Vishva Bharati is accorded Deemed University status by the Government of India. It is the first university of Jainology and ahiṃsā (non-violence) in the world and is the creation of His Holiness Acharyashri Tulsi, ninth pontiff of the Terāpantha order of Śvetāmbara Jainas. The translator, Dr Nathmal Tatia, is director of the research centre there.

Glossary

The glossary entries are largely from the commentaries to the sutras, the figures and the appendices. Words from the actual sutras have not been included as the text includes both the original Sankrit sutra and its English translation.

Numbers refer to sutras unless otherwise stated.

abandoning (external articles and internal passions; unfit articles)	*vyutsarga*	9.20, 9.22
absence of delusion	*amūḍhadṛṣṭitā*	6.23
absence of doubt	*vicikitsāvirahatā*	6.23
absence of misguided tendencies	*niḥkāṅkṣitā*	6.23
absence of suspicion	*niśśaṅkitatva*	6.23
absolute non-existence	*atyantābhāva*	5.29
absolutely alone (the)	*kevalī*	10.1
absolutist deluded view	*ekānta-mithyā-darśana*	8.1
abstinence	*virati*	6.23
accomplisher of the mission	*kṛtakṛtya*	10.7
action, activity	*yoga, karma yoga*	6.1, 6.9, 6.13, 8.1
actuality	*bhāva*	1.5
actuality view	*evaṃbhūta naya*	1.35
adorable one	*arhat*	9.9
aftertaste (second stage of spiritual development)	*sāsvādana*	9.1
agent	*kāraka*	1.35
aggression	*ārambha*	6.16, 6.18
agnostic deluded view	*ajñānika-mithyādarśana*	8.1
agnosticism	*ajñānavāda*	7.18, 8.1
alimental food	*kavala-āhāra*	2.31
air-bodied	*vāyu*	2.14
all-encompassing	*sarvabhāva-jñāpaka*	1.30
all-intuiting	*sarvadarśī*	10.1
all-knowing	*sarvajña*	10.1
analogy, knowledge through	*upamāna*	1.6, fig. 1
analytic meditation	*dharmadhyāna*	9.29, 9.37
anger	*krodha*	8.10
animals, animal birth (including vegetation, microscopic life, air-bodied etc.), *see also* subhuman	*tairyag-yoni*	6.17, 8.11, 4.28
apprehension	*abhinibodha*	1.13, fig. 1
approved means of knowledge	*pramāṇa*	1.6, 1.10, 10.7
approving of an evil act	*nisarga-kriyā*	6.6
arbitrary interpretation of scriptural teachings	*ānayana-kriyā*	6.6

articulate	*ākārātmaka*	5.24
articulate comprehension	*avāya, apāya*	1.15
articulate knowledge	*śruta-jñāna*	1.11, 1.20, fig. 1
ascending cycle (of six aeons)	*utsarpiṇī*	SS 3.27
assuming many shapes at will	*kāmarūpitva*	10.7
atom	*aṇu*	5.11, 5.25, 5.27, app. 3
attachment	*rāga*	SS 7.8
attaining the desired object	*abhilaṣitārthaprāpti*	10.7
attention	*praṇidhāna*	2.11, 2.19
attenuated aggression	*alpārambha*	6.18
attenuated possessiveness	*alpaparigrahatva*	6.18
auspicious, *see also* beneficial	*śubha*	3.7, 8.12
austerity	*tapas*	9.3, 9.6
autonomous	*kevala*	1.30
autonomous capacity	*yathāpravṛttakaraṇa*	app. 4
banishment	*apeta*	1.15
becoming	*vartanā*	5.22
before and after	*paratvāparatva*	5.22
belief in greatness of the doctrine	*prabhāvanā*	6.23
belief in transmigration of the soul	*āstikya*	1.2
bellicosity	*parāghāta*	8.12
beneficence	*dāna*	2.4, 2.5, 8.14
beneficial, *see also* auspicious	*śubha, puṇya*	2.49, 5.21, 6.3, 6.22
body, five types of	*kāya, śarīra*	2.37, 5.19, 6.1, 7.7, 8.12
body-making karma, body karma	*nāma-karma*	8.5
bondage, karmic	*bandha*	1.4, 8.1–26
effect bondage, causally inactive	*phalabandhana*	10.7
seed bondage, causally active	*bījabandhana*	10.7
calmness (of the passions)	*praśama*	1.2
capable of voluntary movement	*labdhi-trasa*	2.13
capacity to generate progressively purer, homogenous experiences	*anivṛttikaraṇa*	app. 4
capacity to generate series of varied novel experiences	*apūrvakaraṇa*	app. 4
category of truth	*tattvārtha*	1.2, 1.8
cessation	*vyaya*	5.29, 5.30
change	*parivartana*	2.10
of material clusters	*dravya-parivartana*	2.10
of realms of birth	*bhava-parivartana*	2.10
of space units	*kṣetra-parivartana*	2.10
of states of the soul	*bhāva-parivartana*	2.10

of time units	*kāla-parivartana*	2.10
change (as function of time)	*pariṇāma*	5.22, 5.41
charity	*dāna*	6.13, 7.33
circular	*vṛtta*	5.24
clairvoyance	*avadhi-jñāna*	1.9–10, 1.12, 1.21–23, 1.26, 1.28, 1.32, 10.7, fig. 1
classes of material clusters	*vargaṇā*	app. 5
clusters (of matter)	*skandha*	5.25
combined (state)	*sannipātika*	2.1
common body	*sādhāraṇa-śarīra*	5.15, 8.12
common person's view	*naigama naya*	1.34
compassion	*anukampā, kāruṇya*	1.2, 6.13, 7.6
complete knowledge of the fourteen books of the early literature	*abhinnākṣara-caturdaśapūrva-dharatva*	10.7
complete self-restraint free of laxity	*apramattasaṃyata*	9.1
complete self-restraint with gross passions attended by various novel experiences	*apūrvakaraṇa nirvtti-bādara-samparāya*	9.1
complete self-restraint with gross passions and similar but progressively purer experiences	*anivṛtti-bādara-samparāya*	9.1
complete self-restraint with subtle flickering greed	*sūkṣmasamparāya*	9.1, 9.18
complete self-restraint with eliminated passions but rise of knowledge-covering karma	*kṣiṇakaṣāya-vītarāga-chadmastha*	9.1
complete self-restraint with suppressed passions but rise of knowledge-covering karma	*upaśāntakaṣāya-vītarāga-chadmastha*	9.1
conduct-deluding (karma)	*cāritra-mohanīya*	6.15, 8.10, 9.15
concentration	*dhyāna*	9.27
of thought on a single object	*ekāgra-cintā-nirodha*	9.27
on the scriptural commandments	*ājñāvicaya*	9.37
contemplation	*vitarka*	9.45
continued cognition	*prattipatti*	1.15
continued identity and transformation of the soul; *also* continuity of one's own nature through change	*tadbhāva*	2.19, 5.41
conveyance body	*āhāraka-śarīra*	2.37, 2.49
conviction backed by reason	*pratvavāvadhāraṇa*	1.2
cosmic space	*lokākāśa*	1.8, 5.9, 5.12, 5.13

counter-token	*pratiśalākā*	app. 1
craving for reward	*nidānakaraṇa*	7.32
cubit	*aratni, ratni*	10.7
cultivation of knowledge	*jñānopayoga*	5.23
cycle of birth and death	*saṃsāra*	9.7
damage to the environment such as digging earth, tearing leaves etc.	*ārambha-kriyā*	6.6
deceitful actions	*māyā-kriyā*	6.6
deluded articulate knowledge	*śrutājñāna*	1.32, 2.9
deluded clairvoyance	*vibhaṅga*	1.32, 2.9
deluded conduct	*cāritramoha*	1.8
deluded empirical knowledge	*matyajñāna*	1.32, 2.9
deluded knowledge	*viparyaya (jñāna)*	1.32
deluded world-view	*mithyādarśana*	1.7
descending cycle	*avasarpiṇī*	SS 3.27
descent (birth by)	*upapāta*	2.32, 2.35, 9.49
destruction of the duration of karma	*sthitighāta*	app. 4
destruction of the intensity of karma	*rasaghāta*	app. 4
destructive karma	*ghāti-karma*	9.48, 10.1
determination	*niścaya*	1.15
determiner	*sākāra*	2.9
determining	*avadhāraṇa*	1.15
discipline of enquiry, fourteen-membered	*caturdaśa mārgaṇāsthāna*	1.8
disrespect for scriptural teachings	*anavakāṅkṣā-kriyā*	6.6
divine saint	*devarṣi*	4.26
divulging the sins of others	*vidāraṇa-kriyā*	6.6
doctrine of non-absolutism	*anekānta-vāda*	5.31
dread of worldly existence, *see also* fear of worldly existence	*saṃvega*	6.23
duration of the same body	*bhavasthiti*	3.39
earlier literature	*pūrva*	2.49
effect bondage	*phalabandhana*	10.7
egalitarianism (deluded), *see also* equal validity of all doctrines	*vainayika-mithyādarśana*	7.18, 8.1
elimination	*apanoda*	1.15
emission of hot and cold light	*tejonisarga*	10.7
empirical knowledge	*matijñāna*	1.9, 1.13–14, 1.20, 1.27, 1.32, 8.7
endeavour	*ūha*	1.15
enlightened conduct	*samyak cāritra*	1.1
enlightened in isolation	*pratyekabuddha*	10.7
enlightened knowledge	*samyak jñāna*	1.1

enlightened one (the)	*buddha*	10.1
enlightened world-view	*samyak darśana*	1.1
enlightenment through self and others	*pratyekabuddha-bodhita*	10.7
entirely asymmetrical body	*huṇḍa (saṃsthāna)*	8.12
equal validity of all doctrines, *see also* egalitarianism	*vainayika-mithyādarśana*	8.1
evacuating bowels or vomiting at gatherings of men and women	*samantānupāte-kriyā*	6.6
evil urges of body, speech and mind	*prayoga-kriyā*	6.6
examination	*parīkṣā*	1.15
exceptional intellectual and creative power	*vijñāna*	9.6
excessive use of consumer goods	*upabhogādhikatva*	7.27
exclusion	*apāya*	1.15
existence	*sat*	1.8, 5.29
expansion of the units of the soul by the omniscient to coincide with the space units of cosmic space	*kevali-samudghāta*	2.10, 5.15–16, app. 4
expansive knowledge	*bījabuddhitva*	10.7
expert in teaching the heart of the scripture	*āmnāyārtha-vācaka*	9.6
expulsion	*apagama*	1.15
extended entity	*kāya*	5.1
extraordinary state of knowledge (the)	*jñānātiśaya*	9.9
extreme possessiveness	*bahu-parigraha*	6.16
extreme privation	*duṣamā-duṣamā*	3.27
faulty donation	*udgama-doṣa*	9.5
faulty donor	*utpādana-doṣa*	9.5
faulty method of seeking alms	*eṣaṇādosa*	9.5
fear of worldly existence, *see also* dread of worldly existence	*saṃvega*	7.7, 10.7
felt as such (enlightened world-view)	*vedaka*	app. 4
female disposition	*strīveda*	8.10
female founder of the ford	*tīrthakarī*	10.7
female gender	*strīliṅga*	2.6, 10.7, 2.51
finder	*upalambhaka*	1.35
fitness for reordination	*parāñcika*	9.22
flickering passions	*saṃjvalana kaṣāya*	8.10
flying high and diving in the sky	*pradīna, avadīna*	10.7
flying in the sky with the help of rays, smoke, etc.	*jaṅghācaraṇatva*	10.7
ford-founder's rule; ford	*tīrtha*	6.23, 8.12
for others	*parātha*	1.6
for self	*svārtha*	1.6
fortune	*aiśvarya*	10.6
founder of religion (ford-founder)	*tīrthaṅkara*	8.12

fourteen stages of spiritual development	*caturdaśa guṇasthāna*	app. 4
freedom from passion	*kleśavimokṣa*	10.7
gateway of investigation	*anuyogadvāra*	1.5, 1.8, 10.7
generic view	*saṃgraha naya*	1.34
grasping	*grahaṇa*	1.15
gross passion	*bādara kaṣāya*	app. 4
guide	*naya*	1.35
half the time it takes all karmic particles to undergo their complete course of binding and falling from the soul	*ardhapudgalaparivartana*	1.8, 2.3
harbouring passions and possessiveness	*apratyākhyāna-kriyā*	6.6
harmful karma	*pāpa*	1.4, 6.4, SS 8.26
healing by bodily secretions	*sarvauṣadhitva*	10.7
healing by excreta	*vipruḍauṣadhitva*	10.7
healing by touch	*āmarśauṣadhitva*	10.7
heavy body	*garimā*	2.37
hermaphrodite	*paṇḍaka*	1.8, SS 7.7
hermaphroditic disposition	*napuṃsaka-veda*	2.51, 8.10, 6.15
hermaphroditic gender	*napuṃsaka-liṅga*	2.6, 2.51
huge body	*mahimā*	2.37, 10.7
hunch-backed body	*kubja (saṃsthāna)*	8.12
ignorance	*ajñāna*	2.6
immediate knowledge, *see also* innate knowledge	*pratyakṣa*	1.6, 1.10, 1.12, fig. 1
immobile being	*sthāvara*	2.12–13
implication	*arthāpatti*	fig. 1
inactivism	*akiriya*	7.18, 8.1
inarticulate sensation	*avagraha*	1.15, 1.18
inarticulate sound	*anakṣarātmaka*	5.24
in a straight line along rows of space units	*anuśreṇi*	2.27
inclination of the ascetic to abstain	*samādāna-kriyā*	6.6
incomparable	*asādhāraṇa, nirupama*	1.30, 10.7
Indian hour	*muhūrta*	app. 2
indicator	*vyañjaka*	1.35
individual body	*pratyeka-śarīra*	8.12
individual's finger-breadth	*ātmāṅgula*	app. 3
inference	*anumāna*	1.6, 1.10, 1.13
infinite	*ananta*	2.40, 5.9, 5.39, 8.25, app. 1
infinite-infinite	*ananta-ananta*	app. 1

inflow, karmic	*āsrava*	1.4, 6.2, 9.1, 9.7
infralinguistic knowledge	*asaṃjñi-śruta*	1.31, fig. 1
inhibition	*saṃvara*	9.1
initiator (who confers initiation)	*pravrājaka*	9.6
initiatory admission	*sāmāyika*	9.18
innate knowledge, *see also* immediate knowledge	*pratyakṣa*	fig. 1
Inner Corpus	*aṅga-praviṣṭa*	1.20
innumerable, countless	*asaṃkhyeya, asaṃkhyāta*	2.39, 5.7, 5.15, 9.47, app. 1
innumerable-innumerable	*asaṃkhyāta-asaṃkhyāta*	app. 1
inquisitiveness	*jijñāsā*	1.15
instantaneous bondage	*īryāpatha-bandha*	6.5, 10.2
instinctive knowledge	*ogha-jñāna*	1.14
instinct of possessiveness	*parigraha-saṃjñā*	2.25
intellectual illusion	*mativipluti*	7.23
intelligence as thoughtful knowledge	*sampradhāraṇasaṃjñā*	2.25
intelligence as subconsciously motivated behaviour	*saṃjñā*	2.25
intelligent (rational) beings	*saṃjñī*	2.25
intense anxiety for fulfilment of desires	*nidāna*	9.34
intercalation	*antarakaraṇa*	app. 4
interlocking of bones on both sides	*nārāca*	3.38, 8.12
interlocking of bones on both sides, strengthened with pin and plate	*vajrarṣabhanārāca*	8.12
interlocking of bones on one side with half-pin and half-plate	*ardhavajrarṣabhanārāca*	8.12
interlocking of bones on one side and pin on the other	*ardhanārāca*	8.12
intermediate	*madhyama*	1.8, app. 1
intra-hour (any time between two time units and forty-eight minutes less one time unit)	*antarmuhūrta*	app. 2
inventing and manufacturing lethal weapons	*pratyaya-kriyā*	6.6
invisibility	*antardhāna*	10.7
involuntary purging of karma	*akāmanirjarā*	6.20
invulnerable	*nirupakrama*	2.52
junior instructor of the scripture	*śrutoddeṣṭā*	9.6
knowledge	*jñāna*	1.1, 1.13, 2.4, 2.5, 10.7
knowledge of the whole from the part	*padānusāritva*	10.7

ladder of elimination	*kṣapakaśreṇi*	10.1, app. 4
ladder of suppression	*upaśamaśreni*	app. 4
land of spiritual effort	*karmabhūmi*	3.37
laughter	*hāsya*	8.10, 8.26
light body	*laghimā*	2.37, 10.7
limitation	*apavyādha*	1.15
limited view	*vikalādeśa*	1.6
linear view	*ṛjusūtra naya*	1.34
lingering enlightened world-view resembling aftertaste	*sāsvādana-samyagdṛṣṭi*	9.1, app. 4
linguistic	*bhāṣālakṣaṇa*	5.24
linguistic analysis	*nikṣepa*	10.7
linguistic (knowledge)	*saṃjñi-śrutā*	fig. 1
linguistic symbol	*vyañjana*	9.46
lordship of all creatures	*īśitva*	2.37, 10.7
lotus position	*kamalāsana*	9.19
low-grade	*parīta*	app. 1
made by effort	*prāyogika*	5.24
maintaining equanimity for a set period of time	*sāmāyika*	6.23
male disposition	*puṃveda*	8.10, 6.15, 2.51
male gender	*puṃliṅga*	2.6, 2.51
malicious activity	*prādoṣikī*	6.6
massive elimination of karma	*mahadvyaya*	10.2
matter	*pudgala*	5.1, 5.4, 5.10, 5.14, 5.19, 5.23, 8.2
matter-atom	*dravyāṇu*	5.28
maturation	*paryāpti*	8.12
maximum	*utkṛṣṭa*	app. 1
meaningful	*arthaniyata*	9.5
measured	*mita*	9.5
mediate knowledge	*parokṣa jñāna*	1.6, 1.10–11, fig. 1
memory	*avadhāraṇa, smṛti*	1.15, fig. 1
milking position	*godohāsana*	9.19
mind	*anindriya, manas*	1.14, 2.11
mind-potential	*mano-labdhi*	6.2
mind-reading	*manaḥparyāya (manaḥparyaya)*	1.9, fig. 1, 1.24–26, 1.29
minimum	*jaghanya guṇa*	app. 1, 1.8, 5.33
mobile beings	*trasa*	2.12, 2.14, 8.12
mobile beings only figuratively	*gati-trasa*	2.13
moisture	*upakleda*	8.12
morality	*dharma*	9.6

mores	*śīla*	6.23, 7.16, 7.19
mortification of the body	*kāyakleśa*	9.19
mournful meditation	*ārtadhyāna*	9.29, 9.35
movement	*vicāra*	9.46
multiple contemplation	*pṛthaktva-vitarka*	9.42
murderous activity	*prāṇātipāta kriyā*	6.6
mutual non-existence	*itaretarābhāva*	5.29
natural	*vaisrasika*	5.24
natural deluded view	*naisargika*	8.1
near-perfect enlightened world-view	*samyaktva-vedanīya*	2.3, 8.10, 8.26
negation, *see also* non-existence	*abhāva*	fig. 1
non-absolutism, doctrine of	*anekānta vāda*	5.31
non-abstinence, non-abstinent	*avrata, avirati, avirata*	6.6, 8.1, 9.35
non-abstinent passions	*apratyākhyānāyaraṇīya kaṣāya*	8.10
non-destructive karma	*aghāti-karma*	2.1, 10.2
non-existence, *see also* negation	*abhāva*	5.29
non-possession	*parigraha-virati (aparigraha)*	7.1
non-speculative (uncommitted) deluded world-view	*anabhigṛhīta mithyādarśana*	8.1
non-sentient entity	*ajīva*	1.4, 5.1, 6.8, app. 2
non-violence	*hiṃsā-virati (ahiṃsā)*	7.1
not attaining the undesired object	*aniṣṭānāvāpti*	10.7
nourishment	*āhāra*	2.31
nun administrator	*pravartinī*	9.24
obstructive karma	*antarāya-karma*	8.5, 8.14
occupying uninspected and unswept places and leaving things there	*anābhoga-kriyā*	6.6
ocean-measured period	*sāgaropama*	4.15, app. 2
omniscience; omniscient knowledge	*kevala-jñāna*	1.9, 1.13, 1.30, 10.4, fig. 1
oscillation of the mind between the substance and the mode	*vicāra*	9.46
Outer Corpus	*aṅga-bāhya*	1.20
oviparous	*aṇḍaja*	2.34
partially abstinent passions	*pratyākhyānāvaraṇīya*	8.10
passions	*kaṣāya*	6.5, 6.6, 6.15, 8.1, 8.2, app. 4
perfect	*paripūrṇa, uttama*	1.30, 10.6, 10.7

perfectly pure, the	*śuddha*	10.1
philosophical standpoints	*naya*	1.6, 1.34–35, 10.7
physical enthusiasm	*kāya-kriyā*	6.6
physical mind	*dravya-manas*	2.11
physical sex	*dravya-liṅga*	2.51
physical speech	*dravya-vāk*	5.19
pillar of bones (non-abstinent pride is like a)	*asthi-stambha*	8.10
pillar of rock (tenacious pride is like a)	*śaila-stambha*	8.10
pillar of straw (flickering pride is like a)	*tṛṇa-stambha*	8.10
pillar of wood (partially abstinent pride is like a)	*dāru-stambha*	8.10
pin	*vajra*	8.12, 9.27
pin between two bones	*kīlikā*	8.12
pit-measured period	*palyopama*	4.15, app. 2
plant-bodied soul	*vanaspati*	2.13
plate	*ṛṣabha*	8.12
plenty	*suṣamā*	SS 3.27
plenty-with-privation	*suṣamā-duṣamā*	SS 3.27
possessive clinging	*parigraha-kriyā*	6.6
post-non-existence	*pradhvaṃsābhāva*	5.29
potential	*labdhi*	2.5, 2.18, 2.48
power of thought	*manobala, saṃjñā*	2.11
practical atom	*vyāvahārika aṇu*	app. 3
practical view	*vyavahāra naya*	1.34
practice of the Jina's discipline	*jina-kalpa*	9.6
pre-non-existence	*prāgabhāva*	5.29
presentable	*ādeya*	8.12
privation	*duṣamā*	SS 3.27
privation-with-plenty	*duṣamā-suṣamā*	SS 3.27
probability	*sambhava*	fig. 1
produced by formal instruction or instigation of others (deluded views)	*paropadeśapūrvaka*	8.1
proficiency in debate	*vāditva*	10.7
proficiency in occult sciences	*vidyādharatva*	10.7
promotion of deluded views	*mithyādarśana-kriyā*	6.6
proof	*sādhaka*	1.35
psychic colouring	*bhāva-leśyā*	3.3
psychic mind	*bhāva-manas*	5.19
psychic speech	*bhāva-vāk*	5.19
quadrangular	*caturasra*	5.24
quality (of substance)	*guṇa*	5.37, 5.40

quality-atom	*bhāvāṇu*	5.28
quasi-ford-founder	*no-tīrthaṅkara*	10.7
quasi-linguistic knowledge (language has no specific role)	*śruta-niśrita*	fig. 1
quasi-passion	*no-kaṣāya*	6.15, 8.10
rationality, *see also* recognition	*saṃjñā*	1.8
reasoning	*cintā, tarka*	fig. 1, 1.15
recognition, *see also* rationality	*saṃjñā*	fig. 1
related to modes, philosophical standpoints	*paryāyārthika naya*	1.6
related to substance, philosophical standpoints	*dravyārthika naya*	1.6
reprobate	*abhavya*	1.8
retention	*avasthāna*	1.15
retention of knowledge	*koṣṭhabuddhitva*	10.7
revealer	*nirbhāṣaka*	1.35
rift in earth (non-abstinence-producing anger is like a)	*bhūmi-rāji*	8.10
rift in rock (tenacious anger is like a)	*parvata-rāji*	8.10
rift in sand (partial abstinence-covering anger is like a)	*vālukā-rāji*	8.10
rift in water (flickering anger is like a)	*udaka-rāji*	8.10
ringed	*parimaṇḍala*	5.24
rivals of lords	*prativāsudeva*	2.52
rope (measure of astrophysical distance)	*rajju*	3.1, app. 3
sanctuaries dedicated to Jina	*arhadāyatana*	9.9
sap drawn from parents	*oja-āhāra*	2.31
sceptical deluded view	*mithyādarśana*	8.1
scriptural knowledge	*āgama*	fig. 1
scriptural matrices, eight	*pravacana-mātaraḥ*	9.49
seed bondage (causally inactive bondage)	*bījabandhana*	10.7
seeking shelter only after due permission and careful consideration	*anuvīcyavagrahayācana*	SS 7.6
self-raised	*yukta*	app. 1
semi-supreme lords	*ardhacakravartī, vāsudeva*	2.52
senior instructor of the scripture	*śrutasamuddeṣṭā*	9.6
sensation-producing karma, *also* sensation karma	*vedanīya*	2.1, 8.5, 8.19, 9.16
sense as cognitive capacity of the physical organ	*upakaraṇendriya*	2.17
sense as a cluster of matter	*dravyendriya*	2.16
sense as a mode of the soul	*bhāvendriya*	2.16

sense as a physical organ	*nirvṛttīndriya*	2.17
senses (the five)	*indriya*	2.20
sensing	*ālocana*	1.15
sensing of touch, taste, smell, colour and sound at a distance	*dūrād sparśanādikaraṇa*	10.7
sensory perception	*indriya-pratyakṣa*	fig. 1
sentience	*upayoga*	2.8, 5.44
sentient application	*upayoga*	2.18–19
sentient instrument	*jīvādhikaraṇa*	6.8
sentient entity	*jīva*	1.4
sentient potential	*labdhi*	2.18
sevenfold predication	*saptabhaṅgīnaya*	5.31
sexual disposition	*veda*	2.6, 2.51
sexual gender, *see also* physical sex	*liṅga*	2.51
simultaneous indiscriminate perception by the senses	*sambhinnajñanatva*	10.7
sitting by pressing calf muscles under the thighs	*vīrāsana*	9.19
sitting on the toes keeping the heels erect	*uthatuhāsana*	9.19
slightly incomplete knowledge of the early literature	*bhinnākṣara-caturdaśa-pūrvadharatva*	10.7
space-based pit	*kṣetra-palya*	app. 2
space unit	*pradeśa*	app. 2
space units and units of the media of motion and of rest penetrate each other without resistance	*anyonya-pradeśa-praveśa-vyāghā-tābhava*	5.13
specific enquiry, *see also* speculation	*īhā*	1.15
specific mental activity	*āyoga*	2.19
specific view of reality	*deśaparikṣepī naya*	1.35
speculation, *see also* specific enquiry	*īhā*	1.15
speculative (committed) deluded world-view	*abhigṛhīta mithyādarśana*	8.1
speech discharging honey	*madhvāsravitva*	10.7
speech discharging milk	*kṣīrāsrāvitva*	10.7
stages of spiritual development	*guṇasthāna*	1.8, 9.10
stain made by dirty grease, like the	*khañjana-rāga*	8.10
stain made by lac, like the	*lākṣā-rāga*	8.10
stain made by mud, like the	*kardama-rāga*	8.10
stain made by turmeric, like the	*haridrā-rāga*	8.10
standard finger-breadth (objective measure)	*utsedhāṅgula*	app. 3
standard pit	*vyavahāra-palya*	3.39
standing position	*sthāna*	9.19
state that distinguishes the soul	*bhāva*	2.1
store	*palya*	app. 1
strata	*prastāra*	3.2

strong conviction	*upabrmhaṇa*	6.23
subhuman, *see also* animals	*tairyag-yoni*	1.3, 4.28, 10.7
subjugating all creatures	*vaśitva*	2.37, 10.7
subsidiary vows	*guṇavrata*	7.21
substance	*dravya*	1.27, 1.30, 5.2, 5.5, 5.37, 5.40
subtle	*sūkṣma*	app. 2
subtle body	*aṇimā*	2.37, 10.7
subtle flickering passions	*sūkṣma sāmparāya*	app. 4
successful, the	*snātaka*	9.48, 10.7
supernatural powers	*ṛddhiviśeṣa*	10.7
super-standard finger-breadth	*pramāṇāṅgula*	app. 3
super-token	*mahāśalākā*	app. 1
supporting cause	*upagraha, nimitta*	5.17
supporting practice	*bhāvanā*	7.3, 10.7
supreme lords	*cakravartī*	2.52
supreme plenty	*suṣamā-suṣamā*	SS 3.27
symmetrical body	*samacaturasra (saṃsthāna)*	8.12
symmetrical above the navel	*nyagrodhaparimaṇḍala (saṃsthāna)*	8.12
symmetrical below the navel	*sāci, svāti (saṃsthāna)*	8.12
teacher of animate, inanimate and mixed objects	*digācārya*	9.6
tenacious passions	*anantānubandhī-kaṣāya*	8.10, 9.47
theoretical (atom)	*sūkṣma*	app. 3
thing barely contacted	*vyañjana*	1.18
thing perceived	*artha*	1.17
thought	*vicāraṇa*	1.15
time	*kāla*	5.22, 5.38
time-based ocean-measured period	*addhā-sāgaropama*	app. 2
time-based pit-measured period	*addhā-sāgaropama*	app. 2
time spent in the same body	*kāya-sthiti*	3.18
time spent in the same species	*bhava-sthiti*	3.18
time unit	*kālāṇu-samaya, addhū -samaya*	app. 2
token	*śalākā*	app. 1
too short-lived	*parama-niruddha*	app. 2
tortuous activity	*paritāpikā-kriyā*	6.6
touchless moving	*aspṛśadgati*	10.5
touching anything at any distance	*prāpti*	10.7
trainee's vows	*śikṣāvrata*	7.16
tranquil (because it has no future lives)	*śānta*	10.7
transcendental bliss	*sātābhyadhika*	10.2
transcosmic space	*alokākāśa*	1.8, 2.29

transference of beneficial and harmful karmic matter	*guṇasaṃkrama*	app. 4
transfer pit	*uddhāra-palya*	app. 2
transformation	*pariṇāma*	2.19, 5.41
triangular	*tryasra*	5.24
turn	*vigraha*	2.28–29
two bones bound by skin, sinews and flesh	*sṛpaṭikā*	8.12
unbound, the (ascetic)	*nirgrantha*	9.48
unbound, the, may keep the bonds	*sagrantho nirgranthaḥ*	8.1
understanding all utterances	*sarvarutajñatva*	10.7
undertaking others' duties out of anger or conceit	*avahasta-kriyā*	6.6
undetermined	*anākāra*	2.9
unfit for reordination	*anavasthāpya*	9.22
ungrasped	*anarpita*	5.31
unitary contemplation	*ekatva-vitarka*	9.42
unlimited character	*sakalādeśa*	1.6
unprecedented (type of bondage)	*apūrva*	app. 4
unwholesome thought	*akuśala saṅkalpa*	9.4
urge	*kriyā*	6.6
urges for tactile gratification	*sparśana-kriyā*	6.6
urges for visual gratification	*darśana-kriyā*	6.6
urges that lead to a deluded world-view	*mithyātva-kriyā*	6.6
urges that lead to an enlightened world-view	*samyaktva-kriyā*	6.6
urges that produce instantaneous inflow	*īryāpatha-kriyā*	6.6
usher	*prāpaka*	1.35
using instruments of destruction	*adhikaraṇa-kriyā*	6.6
variable store	*anavasthita palya*	app. 1
verbal curses and blessings	*abhivyāhārasiddhi*	10.7
vertebrates born with placenta	*jarāyuja*	2.34
vertebrates without placenta	*potaja*	2.34
view-deluding karma	*darśanamoha, darśanamohanīya*	8.10
view of the immediately present (philosophical standpoint)	*sāmprata naya*	1.35
visible	*cākṣuṣa*	5.28
vitality, ten vitalities	*prāṇa*	2.14
viviparous	*jurāyuja*	2.34
vitality	*bala*	7.22
vow	*vrata*	7.1
vulnerable	*sopakrama*	2.52

walking at will	*prakāmya*	2.37, 10.7
wanton destruction of the environment	*anarthadaṇḍa*	7.16
white (pure) meditation	*śukla-dhyāna*	9.29, 10.7
wholesome thought	*kuśala*	9.4
willpower	*adhyavasāya*	app. 4
words vomiting poison	*āsiviṣatva*	10.7
worthy of liberation	*bhavya*	2.7, 10.4
wrathful meditation	*raudra-dhyāna*	9.29, 9.36, 10.7

Index